Children
—— THE ——
CHALLENGE

RUDOLF DREIKURS, M.D.
WITH
VICKI SOLTZ, R.N.

A PLUME BOOK

PLUME
Published by the Penguin Group
Penguin Books USA Inc., 375 Hudson Street,
New York, New York 10014, U.S.A.
Penguin Books Ltd, 27 Wrights Lane,
London W8 5TZ, England
Penguin Books Australia Ltd, Ringwood,
Victoria, Australia
Penguin Books Canada Ltd, 10 Alcorn Avenue,
Toronto, Ontario, Canada, M4V 3B2
Penguin Books (N.Z.) Ltd, 182–190 Wairau Road,
Auckland 10, New Zealand

Penguin Books Ltd, Registered Offices:
Harmondsworth, Middlesex, England

Published by Plume, an imprint of New American Library, a division of
Penguin Books USA Inc. This edition of *Children: The Challenge*
reissued in 1987 by E. P. Dutton.

First Plume Printing, December, 1990

10 9 8 7 6 5 4 3 2

 REGISTERED TRADEMARK—MARCA REGISTRADA

Library of Congress Cataloging-in-Publication Data

Dreikurs, Rudolf, 1897-1972.
    Children : the challenge / Rudolf Dreikurs, with Vicki Soltz.
      p.   cm.
    "A Plume Book."
    Originally published: New York : Hawthorn Books, 1964.
    Includes index.
    ISBN 0-452-26655-6
    1. Child rearing.   2. Child psychology.   I. Soltz, Vicki.
  II. Title.
HQ769.D653   1992
649'.1—dc20   91-44068
                                              CIP

Printed in the United States of America

WIN THE CHALLENGE...

"The problems that our children present are increasing in frequency and intensity, and many parents do not know how to cope with them. They realize that children cannot be treated as they were in the past; but they do not know what else to do.... The variety of conflicting suggestions thrown at parents provides more confusion than direction....

"We do not suggest that parents be either permissive or punitive. What parents have to learn is how to become a match for their children, wise to their ways and capable of guiding them without letting them run wild or stifling them."

Dr. Rudolf Dreikurs has created an extraordinary guide designed to meet the needs of *all* parents—helping them to develop a consistent approach to raising children in a warm and nurturing environment.

RUDOLF DREIKURS, M.D., was an eminent child psychiatrist who practiced in Chicago. Along with this book, he was the author and co-author of many other child-rearing and family guides, including *Logical Consequences, Discipline Without Tears, The Challenge of Marriage,* and *The Challenge of Parenthood.*

ALSO BY RUDOLF DREIKURS

Logical Consequences (with Loren Grey)
A Parents' Guide to Child Discipline
  (with Loren Grey)
Discipline Without Tears (with Pearl Cassel)
The Challenge of Marriage

To my daughter, Bonnie, who for twenty years has been the source of so much rich experience.

V.S.

CONTENTS

PREFACE

THE PROBLEMS that our children present are increasing in frequency and intensity, and many parents do not know how to cope with them. They somehow realize that children cannot be treated as they were in the past; but they do not know what else to do. They may not even know that new methods of dealing with children exist and have been tested. The variety of conflicting suggestions thrown at parents negate the validity of any specific approach and merely provide more confusion than direction. Why, then, should anyone trust our approach?

While working with parents and children for forty years, it became evident to me that the methods we suggest for the solution of family conflicts are indeed effective. They have been tested in the laboratory of our family counseling centers. Many parents somehow have discovered for themselves a way to reach their children and to win their co-operation. However, they do not know why they act as they do, nor why they succeed. Our recommendations are based on a specific philosophy of life and a distinctive concept of man as it has been presented by Alfred Adler and his co-workers. The general trend in psychology seems to be moving in our direction. We do not suggest that parents be either permissive or punitive. What parents have to learn is how to become a match for their children, wise to their ways and capable of guiding them without letting them run wild or stifling them.

In previous papers and books I have outlined some of the basic principles for dealing with children. Parents and children themselves have contributed many new ideas, providing examples of effective approaches which we, the professionals, had not visualized. We are still learning from each other as we work on the common problems which children present to our whole adult society.

I have asked Mrs. Vicki Soltz to undertake the task of stating in her own way the principles on which we operate. She has been a leader of several of our study groups, which have acquainted mothers with principles rather than giving them concrete answers and advice. While all points have been carefully discussed between us, she has presented them in her own language as a mother. After all, we are not teaching parents psychology, but rather we are attempting to present to them practical steps in a new direction.

I trust that our common endeavor will fulfill this task that we have set ourselves—to help. Even the greatest skill will not eliminate difficulties and mistakes. All we can hope for is that parents will be more secure in the knowledge of what to do, although they may not always feel like doing it. Problems will still arise and continue to exist.

We fully appreciate and sympathize with parents who wish to fulfill their responsibility but often are faced with a task for which they are not prepared. As the child needs training, so do parents. A training in new responses to the child's provocation may lead to new attitudes and open new avenues for harmonious relationships.

R. D.

CHILDREN: THE CHALLENGE

CHAPTER 1

OUR PRESENT DILEMMA

Mrs. Price poured coffee for her neighbor, Mrs. Albany, and sat down to chat. Seven-year-old Mark dashed into the kitchen, followed by brother Tom, five. Mark climbed up onto the counter with practiced skill and opened a top cupboard door. Tom followed Mark onto the counter top with equal skill.

Mother shouted, "Get down from there. I mean it! Get down."

"We want some marshmallows," Mark screamed back at her.

"You can't have marshmallows now. It's too close to lunch. Now get down this minute."

Mark grabbed the sack of marshmallows and jumped down from the counter, followed by Tom. Tom snatched the sack from Mark and the two boys dashed out of the kitchen while Mrs. Price called, "Come back here. I said you couldn't have them."

The screen door slammed on her last words.

Mrs. Price sighed and said to her guest, "Oh! Those kids! I simply don't know what to do with them. They are just wild Indians all the time. Never a moment's peace."

W E often *don't* know what to do with our children. On every side and in every gathering, children make themselves obtrusive and obnoxious. At amusement parks, where families go to have fun, few appear to be having a good time. Overexcited and overtired children scream for more and more rides. Distraught parents crossly say, "No more," and then yield to the screaming. Harassed fathers dig into their pockets and spend more than they had intended. Spankings are administered in public. Finally, mothers impatiently drag resisting children by the arms and they all arrive home wondering why they went.

In restaurants, children often display deplorable manners. They may disturb other diners with their petulance, their loud demands for attention, their restless running around. Many refuse to eat unless coaxed.

In supermarkets, children often misuse the turnstiles and guard rails. Many run up and down the aisles, demand special treats, and cry or have temper tantrums when refused.

In all such public places we hear angry, demanding storming, screaming children answered by weary, resentful, desperate parents.

At home, our children show a deplorable lack of co-operation. Many refuse to accept any responsibility for helping with home tasks. They are noisy, inconsiderate, boisterous, and unmannerly. They sometimes show a colossal lack of respect for their parents or any other adult. They frequently insult us and we take it.

Our children are defiant and we stand helpless. We beg, plead, wheedle, punish, and bribe in an attempt to get the children to conform to some sort of order. One grandmother stated in despair, "Children just don't mind any more!" This unruly, defiant behavior has become so common that it is accepted as normal. "Children are like that."

At school, many children refuse to accept their responsibility for learning. Teachers ask parents to see to it that the students do their homework, but they are unable to say how this can be done without fight and struggle.

Far too frequently, headlines give accounts of children in trouble. Potentially delinquent behavior appears at earlier and earlier ages. Judges demand that parents get their children off the streets at night but fail to point out how to do it. Nationwide research in juvenile delinquency brings forth volumes of papers but few indications for possible solutions.

Many parents are becoming increasingly upset and bewildered. They had hoped to raise happy, well-behaved children who felt sure of their proper place. Instead they see their children becoming dissatisfied, bored, unhappy, contemptuous, and defiant. Over the nation pediatricians and psychiatrists report an alarming increase in severly disturbed children.

In an attempt to do something about this situation, parents enroll in child study courses, join in group discussions, attend P.T.A. lectures, and read innumerable books, pamphlets, and newspaper articles. The true significance of this vast program of parent education is recognized by very few. Parental ability to raise children seems to have become lost. Past generations did not need instruction for raising their young. What has happened? In former times there were traditions for child-raising which were upheld by society as a whole. Every family followed a common scheme. Only in our times has it become necessary to develop an extensive program of parent education. Why?

We are frequently told that our present predicament is the result of adult insecurity, emotional instability, or immaturity; of poor examples, of lack of morals or proper social values, or of a lack of religion. We do witness changes in our moral values; but our moral standards may be even higher than in earlier times, as is attested by our increasing concern with "social evils." As for security, each generation has found cause for insecurity in the stress and strain of its time, whether it blamed the First World War, the depression, or the Second World War, or now the atom and hydrogen bombs.

We hear a great deal about the lack of maturity, applied both to young parents and to their children. "Maturity" is an evasive term, used for the most part to indicate an "unchildlike" state. Used in this manner, it implies that there is a sort of inferiority in the state of childhood. In the name of "good manners" and "social adjustment" we seem to prefer the sophisticated cover-up of real feelings. Actually, maturity means full growth and development—the full realization of potential. This happy state is realized by very few individuals. Completeness of growth and development takes a lifetime. Why ask for it during youth and young adulthood?

Adults have never given children a good example. In former times a child simply wasn't allowed to do what the adults did. "Do as I say, not as I do!" As far as religion is concerned, ministers and deeply religious parents have the same difficulties with their children as do their less devout neighbors. Sunday schools are often a madhouse of uncontrollable children. Every Sunday school superintendent can vouch for the behavior problems in general and tough cases in particular among his pupils. There is something deeper that is wrong. Underneath it all is the fact that *we don't know what to do with our children,* because the traditional methods of child-raising no longer work and we have not learned new methods which can take their place.

Every culture and civilization develops a definite pattern for raising children. Comparative studies of primitive societies offer an excellent opportunity to understand the significance of tradition. Each tribe had its own tradition and raised its children in a different way. Consequently, each tribe developed distinctive behavior patterns, characters, and personalities. Each culture had its own procedures with which to meet life problems and situations. But every man and woman and every child knew exactly what was expected. All behavior was established by tradition.

Our western culture has been more complex than primitive societies, but nonetheless it has had its traditional patterns for child-raising. There were principles such as "children are to be seen and not heard" that were followed in every home. Standards of behavior for children were the same throughout. However, our growing perception of the meaning of democracy and its effects upon interpersonal relationships has profoundly changed this same western culture. From the time of the kings and serfs up through the signing of the Magna Carta, the French and American revolutions, and the Civil War to the present time, mankind has gradually come to realize that man is created equal, not just before the law, but equal in the sight of his fellow man. The implication of this growth is that democracy is not just a political ideal, but *a way of life.* Rapid changes take place, but few are aware of the nature of this change. It is largely the impact of democracy that has transformed our social atmosphere and made the traditional methods of child-raising obsolete. We no longer have rulers such as prevailed in the autocratic society from which we are emerging. In a society of equals we can't rule *over* another. Equality means that each decides for himself. In an autocratic society, the ruler was superior to and had power over the submissive. Regardless of his station in the world, the father of each family ruled over the members, including his wife. Today this is no longer true. Women proclaimed their equality with men; and as the husband lost his power over his wife, both parents lost their power over their children. This was the beginning of a general social upheaval that has been widely felt but little understood. Other areas in our social fabric have been likewise affected. Management and labor are moving toward a closer relationship of equals. The desegregation of the Negro is an urgent social problem spurred by an ever widening understanding of the meaning of democracy. Such major changes in our social structure are more readily perceived than the subtle change wrought by the fact that women and children claim their share in equality.

Adults are usually deeply disturbed at the notion that children are their social equals. They indignantly deny such a possibility. "Don't be ridiculous. I know more than my child does. He can't possibly be my equal." No. Of course not. Not in knowledge or experience or skill. But these things don't indicate equality—even among adults. Equality doesn't mean uniformity! Equality means that people, despite all their individual differences and abilities, have equal claims to dignity and respect. Our conviction that we are superior to our children stems from our cultural heritage: that people are inferior or superior according to their birth, their money, their sex or color, or their age and wisdom. No individual ability or trait can guarantee superiority or the right to dominate.

There is another factor that may play a part in our feeling that we must be superior to our children. We may have a hidden doubt of our own worth, a deep sense of not measuring up to our own ideals. Then a child, in his helplessness, makes a delightful object of comparison by which we can feel grand! But this is a false illusion. In fact, our children are often much more capable than we are and tend to outsmart us on many occasions. This concept of equality has been growing within our culture, although we have not been aware of it and are not quite ready to understand it.

Children are particularly sensitive to a social climate. They have been quick to catch on to the idea that they share in the equal rights of everyone. They sense their equality with adults and no longer tolerate an autocratic dominant-submissive relationship. Parents, too, vaguely realize that their children have become their equals and have lessened the pressures of the you-do-as-I-say form of child-raising. At the same time, they lack new methods based on democratic principles with which to guide and educate their children into democratic social living. Thus, we are faced with our present dilemma.

This change in our social atmosphere from the autocratic relationship of the superior-inferior, of dominance and submission, to the democratic relationship of equals has been recognized by our educators. They sincerely want to be democratic. However, there is a widespread confusion about the application of democratic principles. As a result, we have frequently mistaken license for freedom and anarchy for democracy. To so many, democracy means freedom to do as one pleases. Our children have reached the point where they defy restrictions because they assume their right to do as they please. This is license, not freedom. If each member of the family insists on doing as he pleases, we have a houseful of tyrants with resulting anarchy. When everyone does as he pleases, the result is constant friction. Friction disturbs interpersonal relationships, which in turn intensifies the conflict. In an atmosphere of such constant conflict, stress and strain produce tension, anger, nervousness, and irritability; and all the negative aspects of social living flourish. Freedom *is* part of democracy; but the subtle point that we cannot have freedom unless we respect the freedom of others is seldom recognized. No one can enjoy freedom unless his neighbor has it too. In order for everyone to have freedom, we must have order. And order bears with it certain restrictions and obligations.

Freedom also implies responsibility. I am free to drive a car. But if I also feel free to drive it north in a southbound lane, my freedom will end very soon. The freedom to drive my car implies that I accept the restrictions in accordance with the rules of safety for everyone. We can be free only if *order* is observed. This order is not imposed by an autocratic authority for *his* benefit, but is maintained by each for the benefit of all.

The popular practice of letting children have unrestricted freedom has made tyrants of children and slaves of the parents. These children enjoy all the freedom while their parents assume all the responsibilities! This is hardly democracy. Parents have taken the disastrous consequences of the excess freedom assumed by their children; they have covered up for them, taken the brunt of punishment for them, borne their insults, endured their multiple demands, and thereby lost their influence over their children. The children, without knowing what bothers them, sense the loss of order because there are no restrictions to guide them. They become more concerned with getting their own way than with learning the principles and restrictions necessary for group living. As a result, the ever present capacity for social interest, or interest in one's fellow man, remains stunted and underdeveloped. This has resulted in a sense of confusion and has increased the maladjustment of children. Well-defined restrictions give a sense of security and a certainty of function within the social structure. Without this, a child feels at a total loss. His ever renewed efforts to "find himself" take the destructive course we see manifest in our many unhappy, defiant children. Freedom implies order. Without order, there can be no freedom.

To help our children, then, we must turn from the obsolete autocratic method of demanding submission to a new order based on the principles of freedom and responsibility. Our children no longer can be forced into compliance; they must be stimulated and encouraged into voluntarily taking their part in the maintenance of order. We need new principles of child-raising to replace the obsolete traditions.

In the following chapters we will present the principles that we have evolved through the years in our work with parents and children. Our Child Guidance Centers are laboratories of human relationships where we can test the efficacy of our approaches. It will be necessary, first, to clarify fundamental requirements for living as equals within the family. It will take time and sustained effort for the basic principle to become entrenched into tradition.* But without them, the present confusion and ineffectiveness of the adult population in dealing with its young will have no chance of being corrected.

* It is interesting to note that as soon as the democratic development affects any country anywhere in the world where people have lived under autonomous cultural conditions and where children have behaved according to the cultural pattern of their own environment, the children are now beginning to misbehave in a similar manner, causing the same distress to their parents and teachers as we find in the United States.

CHAPTER 2

UNDERSTANDING THE CHILD

Six-year-old Bobby sat at the table coloring with his crayons while Mother was planning the week's menus. He began to tap his foot against the floor. "Cut it out, Bobby," Mother said crossly. Bobby stopped with a little shrug. But he soon started again. "Bobby, I said to stop that noise," Mother again reprimanded. Bobby stopped again. But after another short while, he was again tapping his foot. Mother slammed down her pen, reached over and slapped Bobby, yelling, "I said stop that! Why do you keep doing something that annoys me? Why can't you sit still and be quiet?"

Bobby doesn't know why he keeps tapping his foot. He can't possibly answer Mother. But there *is* a reason. And there is a way to handle the situation without Mother and Bobby winding up in a conflict that is distressing to both of them.

However, in order to know how to stimulate children to function in a useful and co-operative way, we must know something of the psychological mechanisms involved.

As we see it, all human behavior has a purpose and is a movement toward a goal. Sometimes we know what the purpose of an act is—sometimes we don't. All of us have had the experience of saying to ourselves, "Now what in the world made me do that?" Our puzzlement is justified. We were acting for a reason that lies hidden from our conscious awareness. The same is true for our children. If we want to help a child change his direction, we must understand what makes him move. Unless we are aware of what is in back of his behavior, we have little chance to change it. We can only induce him to behave differently by changing his motivation. Sometimes we can discover the purpose of a child's behavior by examining the results he obtains. In the above example, Mother became annoyed. Bobby wanted to annoy Mother—not consciously, of course. He has a hidden reason for wanting to. Yelling at Bobby, and slapping him, scored a victory for *him,* since he had gotten Mother's full attention. Why should he stop? Look at the magnificent results! He can keep his big mother occupied with him. Here is the clue to Bobby's secret and hidden goal. Bobby has no idea that he feels this way; but he acts according to this goal hundreds of times a day. When Mother responds as she did, she fortifies Bobby's hidden purpose by yielding to his demands. If he knew that he no longer would get results—if tapping ceased to annoy Mother, what would be the sense in doing it? He would soon give it up. And if his quiet moments of constructive play brought a warm smile, a pleased hug and a word of praise, he would be less inclined to get Mother's attention through disturbing behavior. If Mother gives Bobby the satisfaction of annoying her, or tries to get him to stop and shows him her defeat by slapping him, she only adds to his incentive to annoy or to defeat her. Bobby's foot is expressing his feelings for him—"Look at me! Say something to me, instead of burying your nose in your notes!" If Mother can see this, then she knows what his motive is. He seeks to find a place by means of getting her attention. With this knowledge, Mother has a better chance to handle the situation. It is a grave mistake to keep after him; he only continues to annoy her. We will discover later many ways in which Mother can resist Bobby's demands.

The Desire to Belong

Since the child is a social being, his strongest motivation is the desire to belong. His security or lack of it depends upon his *feeling of belonging* within the group. This is his basic requirement. Everything he does is aimed at finding his place. From infancy on, he is very busy exploring methods of being a part of his family group. From his observations and his successes, he draws conclusions—not formed in words, but definite nonetheless—"Ah! *This* is how I can belong. This is how I can have significance." He has chosen the method through which he hopes to gain his basic goal. The method becomes the immediate goal and forms the basis for his behavior, or, in other words, his motive. The desire to belong is his basic goal while the method he devises for attaining his basic goal becomes his immediate goal. Therefore, we can say that his *behavior is goal-directed*. A child is never aware of the motive behind his behavior. When asked why he tapped his foot, Bobby would be honest in saying that he doesn't know. His whole approach to solving the problem of finding his place is one of sensing his way. He doesn't reason it out consciously. He acts from an inner motivation. He learns by trial and error. He will repeat the behavior that gives him a sense of having a place and abandon that which makes him feel left out. And here we have the basis for guiding and directing our children. However, there are many pitfalls unless we understand *in what way* the child thinks he can belong.

Before discussing the various methods, or the mistaken goals, children have for gaining the all-important feeling of belonging, we need to understand something of the total child; his observations, his environment, and his position in the family.

The Child's Observations

Children are expert observers but make many mistakes in interpreting what they observe. They often draw wrong conclusions and choose mistaken ways in which to find their place.

Three-year-old Beth was a happy, delightful child who had progressed so rapidly in her development that she was a joy to her parents. She walked before she was a year old and was completely toilet trained at eighteen months. At two she was speaking clearly and distinctly in well-formed sentences. She was very adept at winning adult approval with her cute ways and her ability to do things. All of a sudden she began to whimper and whine for what she wanted, and consistently soiled and wet herself. Two months prior to this seemingly regressive behavior a baby brother had arrived. For the first three weeks, Beth had been highly interested in the baby. She watched intently as Mother bathed, changed, and fed him. Whenever Beth offered to help, Mother firmly but kindly refused. Then Beth seemed to gradually lose interest, and she no longer came to the nursery. Shortly thereafter she started her disturbing behavior.

Beth had seen all the attention her baby brother received. She suddenly realized that this much anticipated brother took Mother away from her. Mother now gave a lot of her attention to the baby instead of her. Beth's observations are correct. Mother devotes much time to the helpless baby. But Beth made a mistake when she interpreted this to mean that she had lost her place and that soiled pants and helplessness could make a person important. She imagined that she could regain her lost position by being a baby herself. She failed to recognize the many advantages she had over the baby.*

* We discuss the solution to Beth's problem later on.

Five-year-old Jerry and his mother fought constantly. Jerry argued about everything his mother told him to do. No matter what she wanted done, Jerry refused. He had violent temper tantrums in which he frequently broke toys, dishes, or furniture. He was skillful in avoiding his chores, which his mother assigned, and had to be forced and punished. His mother was puzzled, because she set a good example of discharging duties before pleasure. Jerry had been quick to discover that whatever his mother said was law to his Daddy, who gave in to Mother's angry pressure in order to have peace. Of all things, Daddy hated a ruckus. On the few occasions when Mother wanted to be firm with Jerry, his father tried to plead for him.

Jerry observed and admired his mother's power. His impression was that one has a prominent place if one has power; therefore, he sought to gain a similar prominence. He imitated his mother by using anger as a means of gaining power. His mother actually had no control over him. He sensed it, although she didn't. She assumed that when she punished him, she had the upper hand, never realizing that his next display of outrageous behavior was retaliation and a further round in the power contest between them. Jerry actually was ahead in the struggle. Since his methods of gaining significance through a display of power were so successful, where is his mistake? Can Jerry be considered a happy child? Is Jerry learning how to function in a group with its mandatory give and take? Is Jerry going to be able to handle *all* life situations with a display of temper? Can he be top man on all occasions? What will be his relationships with girls, and eventually with his wife? How does he see a man's position in the world?

The Child's Environment

A child watches all that goes on around him. He draws his own conclusions from what he sees, and he searches for guiding lines for his behavior. During early childhood he must make adjustments to and learn how to handle both his inner and his outer environment. The child's *hereditary endowment* is his "inner" environment. He spends most of his first year experimenting with and learning how to handle his body. He learns how to move his arms and legs in co-ordination so that he can change position and grasp what he wants. He learns how to make his body function as he desires. He learns to see and to interpret what he sees; to hear, feel, smell, taste, and digest. As time goes on, he learns how to use his intelligence and to accomplish the tasks confronting him. In all these accomplishments he learns how to handle his inner environment. He discovers his abilities and his deficiencies. If he meets with difficulties or is faced with a handicap, the child will either give up or compensate. Sometimes the child will even create a special skill when he is confronted with a weakness (a process called overcompensation).

Edith was born without her right arm while Elaine, her twin, was normal. Undaunted by this severe handicap, Edith accomplished everything with her one arm and hand which her sister did with two. During the crawling phase, she kept up with her sister by tugging with her heels and scooting along on her bottom. She learned to dress herself, fasten buttons, tie her shoes, arrange her hair and take her bath—all with her left hand. She became adept at housework and could even sew. Now she is married and a highly effective homemaker. Occasions when she needs help are very rare.

Allen had polio when he was five. It left him with weakened muscles in his right leg. His mother helped and encouraged him with his exercises. Swimming was highly recommended, and Allen found great pleasure in it. By the time he was sixteen he had completely overcome the weakness and was the star on the high-school swimming team.

Four-year-old Mitzie was the youngest of four children and was born with a severe visual handicap. She was not totally blind, however. At four, she was completely helpless. She was dressed and fed and could do little more than walk if her hand was held. Everyone in the family waited on her and tried to keep her amused. Faced with this handicap, Mitzie had given up and let others do everything for her.

At this point the reader may object that we oversimplify. We have said nothing about the influence which others had upon these handicapped children. This is deliberately done. We have illustrated that each child had made a decision as to how he would handle a handicap. And each child had much more influence on those around him than was recognized. Edith's early determination to keep up with her sister won Mother's admiration and made it easy for Mother to encourage her. Allen's willingness to help himself out of his difficulty aided Mother in her efforts to provide swimming. Mitzie's total resignation into helplessness won the pity and service of all around her. Had the original decision of each child been different, the story of each might have ended differently.

At the same time that the child is learning to cope with his inner environment, he is making contact with his outer environment. A baby's first smile is his first outward movement towards social contact. He responds to the encouragement of those around him and finds pleasure in returning a smile with a smile of his own. The first dynamic interpersonal relationship is established. He senses the pleasure he can create by smiling. His contact with his outer environment grows along with his development in handling his inner environment. Here, too, if he meets with obstacles, he will either give up or compensate.

There are three factors in the child's outer environment which affect the development of his personality. The first is the *family atmosphere*. In his relationship with his parents the child experiences society at large. The parents establish a definite family atmosphere; through them the child experiences the economic, racial, religious, and social influences in his environment. He absorbs the family values, mores, and conventions, and tries to fit within the pattern, or the standards, set by the parents. His concept of material advantages reflects the economic orientation of the family. He develops his attitudes toward different races in line with those of his parents. If tolerance is a family pattern, the children may accept tolerance as a value that they wish to support. If parents look down upon people who are different, children may possibly capitalize on this and seek superiority in racial and social relationships. The significance of early religious training is well recognized, although the child's reaction to it may vary greatly. Children are also quick to observe how the parents treat each other.

The relationship between the parents sets the pattern for all the relationships within the family. If the parents are warm, friendly, and co-operative, the same relationship may possibly develop between children and parents and between the children themselves. Co-operation can become a family standard. If the parents are hostile and compete with each other for dominance, the same pattern usually develops among the children. If the father is dominant and firm while the mother is meek and lenient, the "masculine ideal" may become a principal pattern, particularly for the boys. However, today, with the high degree of equality between the sexes, girls may also decide to follow the "masculine" line. The relationship between the parents gives the children a guideline from which they may choose to develop their own individual roles. If the mother is the dominant figure, the children may try to gain similar prominence by imitating her. Keen competition between parents can make competition the family standard. Whatever trait all children of a family have in common is an expression of the family atmosphere established by the parents. However, all children of one family are not alike, but are usually quite different. Why?

The Child's Position in the Family

The second factor in the outer environment is the *family constellation*. This term indicates the characteristic relationship of each member of the family to each other, just as one star in its relationship to other stars forms the constellation of the Big Dipper. Each family has its own distinctive configuration. In the interchange of responses and influences with each other, different personalities emerge. The position of the individual within the constellation—the role he plays— will have, to some extent, an influence upon the patterns of the whole family and the personality of each other sibling.

A family starts out with Mother, Father, and Baby. The role of Mother is different from that of a wife. The role of Father is different from that of a husband. The very presence of the baby presents new dimensions to the relationship between husband and wife. Baby is their only child, but his position looks slightly different from his viewpoint. He is on the receiving end of their attention. Mother and Daddy, as parents of an only child, are on the giving end of the attention, with Mother providing the most because of her function as Mother. Among these three a definite pattern of give and take develops—a pattern of interactions. It is even possible that one parent may be on the side of the child against the other parent. Such alliances are usually provoked by the baby and imposed upon his parents by his behavior.

When the second baby arrives, the positions of each of the original three members of the group change. "King Baby" is suddenly dethroned. He must now take a stand in regard to the change in his position, in regard to the usurper, and in regard to Mother and Daddy, who somehow permitted this occurrence. New elements enter into all interrelationships as a result of the change in the constellation. The newcomer is now the baby, and the first child finds it necessary to re-establish himself in a new position—that of the older of two children. Meanwhile, the baby discovers his position as "baby" of the family. But this position has a different meaning to the second child than it did to the first one, because of the presence of an older sibling.

When the third child arrives, there is again a change in the meaning of each one's position within the whole constellation. Mother and Daddy are now parents of three children. The eldest has been dethroned before and the second is now dethroned in his turn. He finds himself in the middle —between the elder and the baby. With each succeeding birth, the family constellation takes on a new configuration with new interactions and new meanings. This is why we find that children in one family are not all alike in spite of the areas of a united front. We are much more likely to find similarities between the oldest children of two different families than between the first and the second child of the same family.

As the constellation evolves, each child finds his place in his own way. And usually, like the grass on the other side of the fence, the other fellow's position looks better. The second child presents a threat to the first. Here, as in his adjustments to his inner environment, the first child will either give up or compensate by trying to stay ahead, at least in certain areas. The same is true for the second child in his relationship to the first. He usually resents the advancement of the first child and will either seek to surpass him or give up. The significance of the numerical position depends entirely upon what the individual child makes of it—how he interprets it. All first-born children do not automatically race to stay ahead. Each family constellation will be unique according to the interpretations within it. These early deductions lead to lifelong lasting impressions. Since most families are highly competitive, the competition between the first and second child is usually very intense, stimulating each to move in an opposite direction. It is even further accentuated if the parents pit one child against the other in the mistaken idea that they stimulate each child to greater effort. They achieve the opposite: each child cedes the field to the more successful sibling and in his discouragement, takes an opposite tack. In whatever way the first child has succeeded, the second considers this field as conquered and will seek a totally different approach.

Let us illustrate the highlights of the effects of an evolving constellation.

Mr. and Mrs. A. are both college educated, active, alert, and dynamic, with very high standards of scholarship and achievement. When Patty was born, they were totally delighted, and quite naturally expected "great things" from her. Each stage of her development was much admired and encouraged. Mrs. A's pride was boundless when Patty took her first step at ten-and-a-half months. Toilet training was well established by the time she was little more than a year old. Both parents were thrilled with their very bright baby. Patty sensed the approval she had and increased her efforts to keep it. When she was fourteen months old, Skipper was born. From the beginning, he seemed to be more frail than Patty. He didn't gain weight properly, and he cut his teeth much later than Patty had. Father had visions of a robust, "manly" son. He worried and fretted over Skipper. Meanwhile, Patty studied the situation. As Skipper grew, she, too, noticed that she could do more. But Skipper presented a threat—a sort of obstacle. How could she keep her place with Mother and Daddy? Naturally, Patty didn't reason or think things out. She sensed the situation and responded on the level of unconscious perception. She sensed Daddy's disappointment in this frail son and capitalized on it by increasing her vigorous activities. But every time Skipper gained a new achievement, Patty felt alarm. Now she must accomplish something new in order to stay ahead—in order to maintain that first place. As time passed, Patty became more and more absorbed in trying to meet the achievement standards of her parents and in trying to stay well ahead of Skipper. She gradually developed the mistaken conviction that she *had* to be first and best. She also discovered ways of hindering and discouraging Skipper, and she belittled what he could do.

Meanwhile, Skipper's awareness of his inner and outer environment increased. He began to sense that in some way he didn't measure up to what Daddy and Mother expected. He also sensed and resented his sister's cleverness and efficiency. He tried many things, expecting that he might not succeed. Very early he became discouraged and more or less gave up. He gradually developed the mistaken conviction that he just didn't have much of a chance. When Mother or Daddy would say, "Patty could do it when she was your age! Why can't you?" he felt a surge of despair and something akin to hatred of Patty. Instead of feeling challenged to try harder, he accepted these comments as further proof of his conviction that he didn't have a chance.

At this point in the development of the interrelationships of this family, one can see that Skipper no longer presented a threat to Patty; she had solved the problem by redoubling her efforts toward achievement. Skipper's outer environment upon his arrival was different from that of Patty's; for while he had the same parents with the same achievement standards, he also had an older sister who already had lived up to them. Handicapped with less physical robustness, Skipper evaluated his situation, sensed his way, met obstacles which seemed to him to be insurmountable, became discouraged, and arrived at the conviction that he hadn't much chance to compete through achievement. How could he find a place? Well, Mother and Daddy *did* show a lot of concern over his lack of ability—they did keep busy with him: pushing, coercing, admonishing. His response to his parents' impatience with his fumbling efforts was to cry a lot. Mother and Daddy felt sorry for him, and he got lots of attention. So—let it rest there.

When Patty was three years and three months old, Kathy was born. Patty became aware of the fact that she now had another girl to compete with. Her knowledge of life had greatly increased, and with conscious awareness, she saw how helpless this infant was. She developed remarkable efficiency in helping Mother with this helpless creature. But as Kathy grew and developed skills, Patty became alarmed. Now the constellation had changed. Patty had two siblings to stay ahead of. Any achievement on the part of either one of the others posed a threat to her position as the one who could accomplish things. She began to feel resentment toward the younger ones when they succeeded in winning approval. However, expression of this "jealousy" brought rebukes upon her head. In order to overcome this obstacle, she began to develop the art of dissembling.

Skipper saw Kathy as another clever girl who added a little more to the hopelessness of his position. His distinction as a boy didn't help much, because somehow he wasn't much of a boy. Skipper was now the middle child—and, worse luck, an oddball to boot. He was neither a clever girl nor a masculine boy. He cried easily at every defeat and discouragement. Everyone rebuked him for being a sissy. He withdrew further, made only half-hearted attempts to deal with life. He played more with Patty than with Kathy, but took the subservient role and let Patty "boss" him.

Kathy was cute and charming and the center of attention throughout her babyhood. She had four people in her service. As her awareness of her environment grew, she sensed the standard of achievement of her parents, realized that Patty had a real head start and that Skipper somehow didn't make the grade. But above all, she saw that both Patty and Skipper got scolded a lot—Patty for being cross and flighty (thereby getting even with her parents for paying too much attention to the others); Skipper for being careless and for always crying about something. By the time Kathy was two, she had discovered that she could be the happy, contented, "good" one in the family. And so she found her place.

When Patty was six and a half, and filled with the self-importance of going to school and of being Mother's big helper, Arlene was born. While Arlene presented another threat to Patty, she didn't feel it so greatly because she was now pretty well established. Nonetheless, her safest bet was to do everything to keep this one a baby. As the years passed and Mother asked Patty to "help Arlene" with this or that, Patty was more than glad to do things for helpless Arlene. But when Mother asked Patty to teach Arlene how to tie her shoes, Patty balked. And while making a great show of teaching, she managed to point out to Arlene how dumb she was. Skipper more or less ignored Arlene. Another girl!—more of the same. Mother so frequently said that Skipper seemed half asleep all the time. Kathy played by herself, showed great inventiveness, and seldom got into trouble or provoked a scolding. She didn't excel in anything, but neither did she bother anyone. Arlene remained the "baby," demanding and receiving a great deal of attention from everyone in the family.

And so by the time Arlene was three, the family constellation showed dynamic parents with high achievement standards; Patty, nine and a half, a clever, efficient child, a bright scholar, with a conviction that she had significance only if she were first—only if she excelled; Skipper, eight and a half, weak, ineffective, discouraged, convinced that he had significance only in being the "cry-baby" and making others feel sorry for him; Kathy, six, in the middle, claimed by neither the older nor the younger sibling, but happy, content, "good" morally—the one who pleased through good conduct, unconcerned with achievement; and Arlene, three, the cute but dumb "baby." Each person had a distinct place, a distinct role, a definite feeling about how he could make his way in life.

Needless to say, not all families of four children develop in the same way. Our illustration merely shows what *one* family did. It is perfectly possible for the first child to become discouraged and for the second child to succeed in surpassing him. For instance, the first child might be a girl who is quite plain while the second is very lovely and succeeds in capturing so much attention that she outshines her older sister. What develops in the family constellation depends upon the *interpretation* each child gives to the situation and his chances, and upon the decisions which he makes for coping with it. Our illustration family could have presented a totally different picture. If Patty had felt that the achievement standards of her parents were too much for her, if she had felt that her brother was too great a threat, she might have chosen to limit her field of achievement or have given up. Then Skipper might have felt that the field of scholarship was open to him, and he might have excelled in school as a compensation for the lack of robust health. Kathy could just as well have decided to become the robust "tomboy," full of mischief—the "little devil" of the family. This might have led Arlene to become the "good" one of the family.

Each person within the family constellation behaves according to the way he sees his position in the family. At the same time, his behavior has a subtle influence on the behavior of each other child. Each one's action presents a problem to each other child, who in turn faces this problem and makes a decision as to how he intends to manage it. His decision is influenced by his interpretation of his own position and of the meaning of the other fellow's action. If the interpretation is faulty—and it is, so frequently—one can easily see how a mistaken direction develops. If the parents are aware of these mistaken concepts (and unfortunately, most parents are as little aware of the significance of the child's behavior as he is), they can better guide the child into more correct evaluations. The manner in which this can be done will be revealed in the balance of this book.

During the summer, George, ten, and David, eight, shared the care of the lawn. Mother refused to allow them to go swimming until the mowing done the night before had been raked up. David had the front, while George had the back. At noon, David came in and announced, "Mother, I've been a good boy and have my work done. George is playing up the street and hasn't even touched his part." "Yes, honey, you are always good," Mother responded. "Please go get George and tell him I want him." David found George and said, "Mother wants you and you're in for it. I've got my part of the yard done and you haven't." Whereupon, George turned on David and punched him. A battle ensued. When they got home, David was crying and burst forth to Mother about the drubbing which George had given him— "all for nothing." Mother turned to her eldest. "Oh, George, why do you have to be such a bad boy? Why don't you do your work? Why are you so mean to your little brother? You should love each other instead of fighting."

This distressing relationship between the boys had started shortly after the birth of David, when two-year-old George became completely unmanageable. He was impudent, defiant, destructive, and always in trouble. Mother was constantly "after" him. David was an exceptionally happy baby. He responded quickly to Mother's expression of love and affection. Time and again, Mother remarked about how good he was. She vaguely understood that George was jealous of the baby, but couldn't see why, since she still devoted much time to him. However, as George saw it, baby David had usurped his place with Mother and since she was so impressed with the baby's "goodness," George gave up entirely in this field (instead of compensating and developing skills with which to impress Mother), and turned to being "bad" in order to get Mother's attention. And while David *is* good, he manages subtly to get George to fight with him so that he can put George into further bad light, thus being sure to maintain his "good" position. George is willing to fight David in order to get even with him for having dethroned him. Both keep their parents busy with them, each in a different way. Each acts according to his interpretation of his position and co-operates with the other to maintain the equilibrium. Naturally, neither child has any conscious awareness of his mistaken interpretation, nor of the part he plays in maintaining the competitive strife.

In a family of three children, the second child, who once had the distinction of being the baby, has been dethroned and is now the middle child. His position is extremely difficult. The first and third child are often in an alliance against their common enemy, and the second is in the middle of a squeeze play. He suddenly discovers that he still doesn't have the advantage of being older, nor does he any longer have the privilege of being the baby. As a result, he tends to feel slighted and abused. He has the impression that life and people are unfair, and he may be provocative in order to feel even more justified in his assumptions. Unless he finds a means of changing his opinions, he is likely to carry the conviction through life that people are unfair and that he has no chance in life. However, if the middle child should happen to be more successful than his siblings, he might capitalize on being more concerned with justice. In a family where the mother sets high standards, her daughter, if a middle child between two boys, might imitate her and be equally perfectionistic. She may use her femininity to gain such distinction, first in her family, then later in life. But if robust masculinity is highly valued in the family, the middle girl might compete with her brothers and become a "tomboy" and be more of a "man" than either of them. Equally, if the parents feel disappointed because they have no son, one girl might possibly try to find favor through boyish behavior. A boy between girls might reverse the picture. If he can outshine the girls by being a "real" boy, he has a distinct advantage, even though he is in the middle. However, if Mother is the dominant figure and the middle boy senses her contempt for an ineffective father, he might find himself in an extremely difficult situation. He may retreat, figuring that men don't count for much. On the other hand, he may either form an alliance with Mother against Daddy and become more of a man, or he may form an alliance with Daddy to subtly defeat Mother and her power. His development will depend upon his interpretation of his situation and his unconscious decisions.

In a family of four, the second and fourth children frequently form an alliance. We can recognize the alliance when we see that two children display similar interests, behavior, and personality traits. Competition between children is expressed by their fundamental differences in interest and personality. There is no general rule as to where alliances and competition will develop among the children. However, they are of extreme importance in the over-all picture of the family. Whatever similarity exists between all children expresses the general family atmosphere; their individual differences are the result of their role in the family constellation.

An only boy among girls, regardless of his position, would find his sex either an advantage or a disadvantage, depending upon the family value placed upon the male role and his own estimate of his ability to live up to it. The same would be true of an only girl among boys. A weak or sickly child among healthy, robust children might discover the role of an invalid advantageous if the family pities him. But if robust health is of high family value and weakness is scorned, he would find himself faced with an obstacle. He would have the choice of giving up and living in self-pity—of feeling that he had no place and that life had abused him—or of striving to overcome the illness and matching the activities of the healthy ones, even, perhaps, outdoing them. In a vigorous family, either choice will present difficulties. If, for instance, he has a congenital heart condition, no amount of striving can win him a place among the healthy. If he gives up, he will be scorned. He may seek status through an entirely different kind of endeavor and become a scholar among athletes.

If a child has been born after the death of the first child, he has a double hazard to face. He is in reality a second child living with a ghost ahead of him. At the same time he now has the position of a first child. In addition, the chances are that his mother, having experienced the loss of her firstborn, will be overprotective and try to wrap him in cotton batting. He may choose to bask in this stifling atmosphere or may rebel and strive for independence.

The baby of the family has a unique place. He soon discovers that because he starts out quite helpless, he has many servants. Unless parents are alert, it becomes very easy for the baby to maintain his privileged position and to keep the other members of the family busy waiting upon him. The role of the "helpless little thing" who finds receiving more appealing than doing is easy but dangerous.

An only child encounters a particularly difficult situation. He is a child in an adult world—a dwarf surrounded by giants. He has no siblings among whom to establish relationships close to his own age level. His goal may become one of pleasing and manipulating adults. He either develops adult viewpoints, is precocious in understanding and always on tiptoe, hoping to reach the adult level; or he is hopelessly an eternal baby, always inferior to others. His relationship to other children is often strained and uncertain. He fails to understand them, and they find him a "sissy." He does not develop a feeling of belonging to children unless he is exposed early to group experiences with them.

There is no "ideal" size family. No matter how many children there are, there are always specific problems. They vary according to the number within the family and according to the interpretation each makes of his place within it. No matter what the size of the family, there is a constant flow of influences and pressures among its members. No one factor alone influences the growth of any one child. All children influence each other and their parents as well. Each is active in determining how he and the others develop, as is shown in the case of George and David (pages 27–28). As George saw the situation, baby David was a usurper who took over the whole field of Mother's love and attention. Being a "good" boy was therefore futile. But if he misbehaved, Mother at least paid attention to him! He preferred being scolded to being ignored, as he saw it. Paradoxical as it may sound, George now desires to be "bad" because this serves his purpose to establish a place for himself within the family. "I am the 'bad' one. They can't do anything with me. Herein lies *my* significance." Naturally, George doesn't actually think these words. But this is what he believes. George turned to misbehavior to win back Mother's attention. He is not happy. Having met an obstacle that he considered insurmountable, he became discouraged and sought an answer to his problem in the negative possibilities. George saw no other way to overcome the obstacle that David presented. He failed to see that he had advantages in being able to do more than the helpless baby. When Mother constantly responded to his bad behavior, she thereby *encouraged* it. When Daddy added his scolding and said, "Why can't you be like your brother?" George had further proof that he could win attention by being "bad" and further evidence that the baby was "good." David, as he grew older and "gooder," put pressures on George that incited him to further disobey the mandate to love his brother, whom he already considered an enemy who had pushed him down. David kept his place by staying "good" and provoking George to be "bad." Mother and Daddy helped in the relationship by scolding the "bad" one and championing the "good" one, pitting the children against each other. And so the relationship was intertwined and continuous.

From the foregoing it can be seen that there is an infinite variety of responses that a child can make toward the various aspects in his outer environment. There is no rule of thumb by which a parent can determine what will happen. But the parent who is aware of the family constellation has information by which he can interpret much that formerly seemed mysterious. Sensitive observation may yield surprising understanding. When we perceive a situation we are in a much better position to cope with it.

The Child's Response

There has been a great deal written and said about "molding a child's character"—as if a child were a bit of clay and we had the job of shaping him into a socially acceptable human being. This is a gravely mistaken concept. As we have shown, quite the opposite is true. Earlier than we realize, children shape and mold themselves, their parents, and their environment. A child is an active and dynamic entity. He shares equally in establishing the relationships between himself and each other person in his environment. Each relationship is unique unto itself, depending entirely upon what each partner contributes to it. Each relationship evolves through the action and reaction—or the interaction— between two people, be they adult and adult, child and child, or adult and child. The ingredients of this interpersonal transaction can be changed by either party, thereby changing the whole relationship. Children develop their relationships to others through the use of their own creative powers and their ingenuity in trying to find their place. A child will try something: if it works and if it fits in with his goal, he retains it as a method of finding his personal identity. Sometimes the child may discover that this same technique fails to work with all people. Now he has two courses open to him. He can either retreat and refuse to co-operate with such a person, or he can use a new technique and develop an entirely different relationship.

Nine-year-old Keith was an only child. He was pleasant and agreeable at home. He helped his mother with the housework, and did everything he could to please both parents. He was quiet, polite, obedient, kept his room in order, and always put his toys away. However, he had trouble at school. His teacher said he was "withdrawn." He never disturbed, but he sat daydreaming instead of doing his work. He needed constant prompting from the teacher. Keith had no friends among his classmates, refused to join in ball games or to contribute in any way to the activities of the classroom.

At home, Keith had the distinction of being an only child in an adult world, and he found his place by pleasing the adults around him. At school, he was surrounded by children who teased him because he ignored them and kept distant from them. His first attempts to please through his work had failed to make a big impression. The teacher did not consider him exceptional, nor did she give him a special place among all the other children. He had no idea how to meet the competition in games among his classmates. He couldn't pitch a ball to perfection, nor could he impress his classmates with his good manners. He beat a hasty retreat into daydreams and avoided any attempt to form new relationships.

Children can develop entirely different relationships with each parent.

Five-year-old Margo and seven-year-old Jimmy kept Mother hopping all day and were into constant mischief. What one didn't think up, the other did. Whenever they wanted something they first asked in a whining voice and then cried and finally stormed until they got what they wanted. However, when Daddy was around, they behaved perfectly. One look from him and they did as they should. Daddy couldn't understand the tales Mother told him when he came home. "They always mind for me," he bragged.

The children knew that Mother would yield to their demands and merely scold them for their misbehavior, but Daddy meant what he said. He conveyed firmness together with kindness, and the children knew the limits. There were no limits with Mother.

Whatever difficult or distressing situation arises from the various personalities in the family, it can be improved if the family is working together to establish harmonious living. There is no perfect relationship. The most we can hope for is to work toward improvement. If a parent understands that a middle child feels pushed aside, he has a clue for helping him to find a place through useful contributions. Knowledge that a first child is discouraged by the rapid advancement of the second child permits the parents to give added encouragement to him so that he gains confidence in his own abilities. When the parents know that the baby of the family may possibly develop great skill in keeping the family serving him, they are in a position to help the child to realize that he, too, can achieve—and doesn't have to find significance in having things done for him.

The interpretation a child makes about his position within the family constellation and his subsequent response can be as infinite as human creativity permits. The sensitive and alert parent can study the situation and ask himself, "Just what does my child think and believe about his situation?"

Too often, we adults are prone to superimpose upon the child what we ourselves would conclude under similar circumstances instead of recognizing his "private logic," which alone accounts for what he is doing.

The third factor in the child's outer environment is the prevalent methods of training. As we proceed in our discussion of effective and adequate training methods, the importance of the various factors so far mentioned will become more clear. For the moment, however, it is apparent that we need to detach ourselves, step back, and take a good look at our children. How has the child dealt with his inner environment? What compensations, or even overcompensations, has he developed? What impressions has he gathered from his observations? What is his place in the family constellation and what does it mean to *him?* Further clues as to how to determine the answers to these questions will be found as we move further into the discussion of training methods.

CHAPTER 3

ENCOURAGEMENT

ENCOURAGEMENT is more important than any other aspect of child-raising. It is so important that the lack of it can be considered the basic cause for misbehavior. *A misbehaving child is a discouraged child.* Each child needs continuous encouragement just as a plant needs water. He cannot grow and develop and gain a sense of belonging without encouragement. However, the techniques of child-raising that we use today present a series of discouraging experiences. To the young child, adults seem excessively large, extraordinarily efficient, and magically capable. The child's original courage alone keeps him from giving up entirely in the face of these impressions. What a wonderful thing a child's courage is! Were we to be placed in a similar situation of living among giants to whom nothing was impossible, could we acquit ourselves as well as our children do? Children respond to their various predicaments with a tremendous desire to gain skills and to overcome the deep sense of their own smallness and inadequacy. They so dearly want to be an integrated part of the family. However, in their attempts to gain recognition and to find a place, they meet with constant discouragement. The prevalent methods of teaching them so often contribute even further to their discouragement.

Penny, four, was on her knees at the kitchen table watching Mother put groceries away. Mother had put the egg container from the refrigerator on the table and had taken the egg carton from the grocery sack. Penny reached for the carton, wanting to put the eggs into the container. "No, Penny!" cried Mother. "You will break them. I'd better do it, dear. Wait until you are bigger."

Mother had unintentionally lowered the boom of discouragement onto Penny. How heavily she has impressed upon Penny that she is too small! What has this done to Penny's self-concept? But do you know that even a two-year-old can handle eggs carefully? We saw one reverently placing egg after egg in the hollow in the container. And what a glow of pride he exhibited when the job was finished! And how happy Mother was with his accomplishment!

Three-year-old Paul was putting on his snow suit so that he could go to the store with Mother. "Come here, Paul. Let me finish for you. You are too slow."

Paul is made to feel inefficient in the face of Mother's magic ability to do things quickly. Discouraged, he gives up and lets Mother dress him.

In a thousand subtle ways, by tone of voice and by action, we indicate to the child that we consider him inept, unskilled, and generally inferior. In the face of all this he still tries to find his place and make his mark!

Instead of allowing our children to test their strength in a hundred different ways, we confront them constantly with our prejudice—our doubt in their ability—and then justify this by setting up standards for various age levels by which children may be trusted to do things. When a two-year-old wants to help clear the table, we quickly grab the plate from him, saying, "No, honey. You'll break it." To save a plate we break a child's confidence in his own budding ability. (Do you suppose plastic dishes were invented by someone with small eager hands around?) We thwart a child's attempts to discover his own strength and ability. We stand over him—big, clever, efficient, and competent. The baby puts on his shoe. "No. You have it on the wrong foot!" In his first attempts to feed himself he makes a mess of his face, his high chair, his bib, and his clothes. "What a mess you make!" we cry, and take the spoon from him and feed him ourselves. We show him how inept he is and how clever we are. On top of this we become cross with him when he retaliates by refusing to open his mouth! Little by little we tear down the child's attempts to find his place through usefulness.

Without realizing what we are doing we discourage our children. In the first place, we reject them as being weak and inferior—an attitude which in itself produces an atmosphere of discouragement. We lack faith in the child's ability to function *now*. We assume that when he is "older" he will be able to do things; but since he is so small at the moment, he is incomplete and incapable.

When a child makes a mistake or fails to accomplish a certain goal, we must avoid any word or action which indicates that we consider *him* a failure. "Too bad that it didn't work." "I'm sorry it didn't work out for you." *We need to separate the deed from the doer.* We must have it clear in our own minds that each "failure" indicates only a lack of skill and in no way affects the *value* of the person. Courage is found in one who can make a mistake and fail without feeling lowered in his self-esteem. This "courage to be imperfect" is equally needed by children and adults. Without it, discouragement is inevitable.

Half of the job of encouraging a child lies in avoiding discouragement either by humiliation or by overprotection. Anything we do that supports a child's lack of faith in himself is discouraging. The other half lies in knowing how to encourage. Whenever we act to support the child in a courageous and confident self-concept, we offer encouragement. There is no pat answer to the problem. It involves careful study and thought on the part of the parents. We must observe the *result* of our training program and repeatedly ask ourselves, "What is this method doing to my child's self-concept?"

The child's behavior gives the clue to his self-estimate. The child who doubts his own ability and his own value will demonstrate it through his deficiencies. He no longer seeks to belong through usefulness, participation, and contributions. In his discouragement he turns to useless and provocative behavior. Convinced that he is inadequate and cannot contribute, he determines that at least he will be noticed, one way or another. To be spanked is better than to be ignored. And there is some distinction in being known as "the bad boy." Such a child has become convinced that there is no hope of gaining a place through co-operative behavior.

Encouragement, then, is a continuous process aimed at giving the child a sense of self-respect and a sense of accomplishment. From earliest infancy he needs help in finding his place through achievement.

Barbara, seven months, had a temper tantrum whenever she was placed in her playpen and left alone. Her mother was amazed that so young a baby could have such a temper. She arched her back, kicked furiously, and screamed so hard that she turned purple. The youngest of five, Barbara had been held a great deal from birth on. She was on Mother's lap at the table and usually under her eye in her playpen. When Mother had to be out of the room, one of the older children would be asked to keep Barbara amused. At nap- or bedtime, she wasn't put to bed until she was quite sleepy. She cried only a short time before falling asleep. Mother listened for her to awaken and would be at her side as soon as she stirred. Barbara greeted her happily. Mother thought of her as a happy baby.

At the tender age of seven months, Barbara is showing signs of discouragement. She sees herself as having a place only if others are engaged in amusing her, and she is lost if no one pays attention to her. She is unable to participate in the function of the home unless she is the center of attention.

One may ask, "But how can an infant participate?" The first demand made upon any human being is to become self-sufficient. A child needs to learn how to take care of himself, and this learning process starts at birth. Barbara needs to learn how to amuse herself and be independent of constant attention. Mother loved Barbara very much and wanted her to be a happy baby. But she became overprotective. Barbara quickly perceived that crying brought results. Mother made every effort to prevent her from crying and being unhappy. In her honest effort to encourage Barbara in being a happy child, Mother has unknowingly discouraged her being self-sufficient. Mother can stop falling for Barbara's temper tantrums, let her cry if she wishes, provide toys for her to play with, and leave Barbara to her own resources. This would be encouragement. A definite time each day should be set aside during which Barbara is left to take care of herself. Perhaps the best time to initiate this new training program might be the middle of the morning when the older children are in school and Mother is occupied with household tasks. However, it is very difficult to ignore a crying baby. Barbara's mother can reinforce her own courage by realizing that love for her child means advancing Barbara's best interests. It is not necessary for a "good mother" to give in to all the demands of her child. A baby who is happy only when she is the center of attention is not a truly happy baby. Genuine happiness is not dependent upon the attention of others but arises from within oneself as a result of self-sufficiency. The baby of the family needs this knowledge more than the others because she *is* the baby and has so many ahead of her who already can do so much.

Three-year-old Betty wanted to help Mother set the table for dinner. She picked up the bottle of milk, intending to fill the glasses. Mother grabbed the bottle and said very kindly, "No, darling. You aren't big enough. I'll pour the milk. You can put the napkins on." Betty looked crushed, turned, and left the room.

Children have immense native courage and eagerly try to do the things they see others doing. Suppose Betty does spill some milk. The loss of the milk is less important than the loss of confidence. Betty had the courage to undertake a new challenge. Mother could offer encouragement by having faith in Betty. If milk had been spilled, Betty would be faced with failure and would need instant encouragement. Mother should acknowledge the courage of the attempt, wipe up the spilled milk, and quietly say, "Try again, Betty. You can do it."

Five-year-old Stan was playing rather listlessly in the sandbox at the playground two blocks from his home. Quiet, thin, and solemn-faced, he slowly poured the sand from one hand to the other. His mother sat on a nearby bench. Presently Stan asked, "Can I swing now?" "If you like," Mother replied. "Give me your hand so you won't get hurt." Stan arose from the sandbox and took his mother's hand. "We have to be careful and stay way back so we won't get hit," Mother explained as they approached the swings. Stan sat in the swing. "Do you want me to push you?" "Can I pump?" Stan asked. "You might fall out," Mother answered. "Here, I'll push you. Now hang on good and tight." Stan sat quietly, firmly holding on, while Mother pushed him. Soon he tired of swinging and slipped from the seat. "Be careful, dear,"

Mother said as she took his hand again. "You don't want to get hit by the other swings." They passed the turning bars. Stan stood watching several other children as they swung, turned, and hung by their knees. "Can I do that, Mother?" "No, Stan, it's too dangerous. Come over to the slide. Be very careful going up. You don't want to fall. I'll catch you at the bottom." Stan slowly and cautiously climbed the steps of the slide. He sat down and inched his way down the slide while holding securely to the sides. A tiny smile played around his lips. "Wait, now, till the other children finish. They might bump you. Now you can go up again." After a few more times down the slide, Stan said that he wanted to go home. He was tired. He took Mother's hand, and they left. At no time had he shouted, laughed, run, or bounced. He didn't have a very good time.

Stan's mother discourages by extreme overprotection. Her fear that Stan might get hurt has hampered the boy so that he is afraid to move in any direction. He is unable to join the activities of other children his age. He makes no move for himself, always asking first if he can do something. When he is allowed to, he does so half-heartedly, with no spirit and no fun. His listlessness and solemnity are signs of deep discouragement. Life has its bumps and bangs. Children need to learn how to take pain in their stride. *A bruised knee will mend: bruised courage may last a lifetime.* Stan's mother needs to realize that her efforts to protect her son from getting hurt actually point out to him how incapable he is and increase his fear of danger. A five-year-old boy is quite capable of taking care of himself at the playground, although one should not leave him there alone. But he certainly can exercise vigorously on the equipment and thereby gain confidence in his ability to dodge the danger of a moving swing and to handle himself on the turning bars. Why shouldn't he experience the thrill of a fast zoom down the slide?

Children need room in which to grow and test their ability

to cope with dangerous situations. We do not have to become careless; we can stand by if the task is too big.

Eight-year-old Susan and ten-year-old Edith arrived home with their report cards. Susan went quietly to her room while Edith ran to Mother. "Look, I got all A's." Mother looked the report card over and expressed her delight with the good grades. "Where is Susan?" she asked. "I want to see her card." Edith shrugged her shoulders. "She doesn't get good grades like I do," Edith commented. "She's dumb." Susan was on her way out to play when Mother saw her and called her back. "Where is your report card, Susan?" "In my room," she answered slowly. "What did you get?" Susan wouldn't answer, but stood looking at the floor. "I suppose you got all bad grades again, didn't you? Get your card and let me see it." Susan had three D's and two C's. "I'm ashamed of you, Susan," Mother exploded. "There isn't any excuse for this. Edith always has good grades. Why can't you be like your sister? You're just lazy and won't pay attention. This is a disgrace to the family. You can't go outside to play. Go to your room."

Susan's bad grades are the result of discouragement. She is a second child who feels she hasn't a chance to meet the standards set by Mother and the accomplishment of her "smart" older sister. Mother heaps further discouragement upon Susan. First, without seeing the card, Mother indicates that she expects bad grades. Since Mother has no confidence in her, Susan gives up and considers herself a failure. Then Mother says that she is ashamed of her. Susan sees herself as unworthy. Next, Mother praises Edith's good grades, and by implication again gives Susan justification for her self-doubt. Mother says that Susan should be like Edith and holds up an impossible goal. Susan is already impressed with the impossibility of being like Edith. Edith, being two years older, is always ahead of her, and Susan sees no reason even to try to catch up. Mother criticizes Susan by calling her lazy, giving her additional proof that she is unworthy. Further discouragement is added when she points out that Susan is a disgrace to the whole family. Susan is aware that Edith considers her dumb. Edith wants to keep her place as the smart one and adds to her sister's discouragement by pushing her further down. On top of all this, Mother punishes Susan by denying her the right to go out and play.

Contrary to popular opinion, stimulating competition between the two girls does not encourage. Instead, it emphasizes the hopelessness of the situation to the discouraged child and creates apprehension in the successful one that she may not be able to stay ahead. She is overambitious and sets up impossible goals for herself. Unless she is always ahead, she may consider herself a failure, too.

In order to encourage Susan, Mother must stop holding Edith up as an example. All comparisons are harmful; Susan can only function in her own right—not as a copy of Edith. Unless Mother has faith in Susan and expresses it, she cannot help her. Under the circumstances, Susan is doing exactly what everybody expects from her. Her abilities will increase only if her confidence is restored. Avoiding her tendency to criticize, Mother can point out and acknowledge any accomplishment, no matter how small it may be in the beginning.

Let us repeat the same incident and show how one can provide encouragement to an already deeply discouraged child:

Susan and Edith arrived home with their report cards. Susan went quietly to her room while Edith ran to Mother with her card. "Look, Mother. I got all A's." Mother looked over the report card, signed it and said, "Fine. I'm glad you enjoy learning." (In this remark, Mother put the emphasis on the learning, not on the grades. She modified her exuberant praise to an acknowledgment of a job well done.) Realizing that Susan was avoiding the issue, Mother waited until she was alone with her. "Do you want me to sign your report card, honey?" Susan reluctantly brought it to her. Mother examined it, signed it, and then said, "I'm so happy to see that you enjoy reading [one of the C subjects]. It's fun, isn't it?" She gave Susan a hug and suggested, "Would you like to help me set the table?" As they worked, Susan seemed disturbed. Finally, she said, "Edith got all A's and I got mostly D's." "It is not so important that you get the same grades as Edith. You, too, may come to the point where you will enjoy learning, and you may find out how much more capable you are than you have thought till now."

It is difficult for us to visualize what would happen to Susan if Mother suddenly changed her tune. At first, Susan will not believe her; Mother has stopped the hidden agreement which has existed until now by which Edith alone has been capable of getting good grades. Susan is convinced that she has little chance in the field of scholarship. From her viewpoint, any effort she makes is hopeless. In spite of this, she has exerted herself to the point of getting a C in reading. This indicates her strength. When Mother acknowledged this valiant effort, she gave Susan a chance to re-evaluate her position and reduced the overwhelming competition. In this manner she provided inspiration for further effort. Susan now has a chance to see that her grade of C does have some merit. She is in a position to feel, "If this much is good (instead of hopeless) maybe I can do more." This very small glimmer of hope becomes the encouragement which inspires Susan to try some more.

Ten-year-old George was a restless boy both at home and at school. He started many projects but never finished anything. His grades in school were barely average. He was the oldest of three boys, the next younger being eight and the youngest, three. George enjoyed playing with the baby but fought constantly with his brother Jim. Jim got good grades in school and finished things he started, although his interests were not as widespread as

George's. One day George had nearly completed a pair of book ends he was making. Since his mother was concerned about his not finishing things he started, she thought to encourage him. "These are lovely, George. You are doing beautiful work." To her utter surprise, George burst into tears, flung the book ends on the floor and screamed, "They aren't lovely. They're horrible." And he dashed from the workshop to his room.

George's mother had done the obvious in trying to encourage him. She praised him. However, George's reaction showed her that praise didn't encourage him, but did the exact opposite—added to his discouragement. Why? Praising accomplishments should encourage, should it not?

Here is an example of the fact that there is no pat answer nor any definite rule for encouraging children. It all depends upon the child's response. George has become overambitious: he holds up impossible goals for himself. When Mother praised him he became angry, because he didn't believe that he ever could do anything well enough. He felt her praise to be a mockery. George wanted the finished article to be of ultimate perfection. His efforts fell far short of his ideal due to his lack of skill, which can come only from practice. Wishing to achieve perfection instantly, he is dissatisfied with anything less. When his mother praised what he felt was so far short of what he expected from himself, he felt, "Even she doesn't understand. No one understands what a failure I am." And so his anger.

George needs encouragement very badly. He sees himself as an absolute failure in everything that he does. In starting one project after another, he gives the appearance of being busy and active. By not finishing anything, he avoids facing the failure of his imperfection. His younger, successful brother adds to his self-degradation. His overambition is the result of his feeling outstripped by Jim. Unless he can "stay ahead" of Jim, he is nothing. The conviction that he must stay ahead of his younger brother is itself a false goal. The task becomes even more impossible when George sees what it takes to stay ahead. He feels he can only be a failure. No amount of praise for what he is doing will give George encouragement. It would be useless for Mother to tell him that he doesn't have to be perfect—this would only add to his conviction that no one understands. He feels that he *must* be perfect. He identifies *what he does* with *what he is*. Even if he should succeed in something, he would consider it merely an accident. Any action which supports his over-ambition or his self-estimate of failure will increase his discouragement. George needs to have his attention diverted from perfection of accomplishment to the satisfaction of contributing. However, George feels that unless the contribution is perfect, he is a failure.

George needs more essential help toward a re-evaluation of himself and his place in the family. The parents are probably personally involved; George's perfectionism does not come from nowhere. Either Father or Mother—or both—probably have too high standards of accomplishment. They may tell George that he does not have to be perfect; but by their own example, they contradict their words. This family needs open discussion with all the children about how good one has to be before one is "good enough." Instead of praising George, it would be more effective to tell him, "I'm glad to see you enjoyed working on the book ends."

Ethel, five, was happily struggling to make her bed. Pulling the covers this way and that, she finally got them up where she wanted them. Mother came into the room, saw the imperfectly made bed, and said, "I'll make the bed, honey. Those covers are too heavy for you."

Mother not only implied that Ethel was inferior because she was small, but set about proving her own superiority by deftly smoothing the covers while Ethel stood disgraced. Her pleasure of accomplishment in the difficult matter of pulling up the covers vanished in the face of Mother's perfectionism. Ethel will soon feel, "What's the use? Mother does it so much better."

If Mother had shown delight in Ethel's desire to make the bed with a remark such as "How nice that you can pull the covers up," or "Look at my big girl making her own bed!" Ethel would have felt a glow of accomplishment and a desire to continue. No matter how many wrinkles she has in her finished work, Mother should resist the temptation to show her daughter how much better she can do it, remaking the bed later when the girl is not looking. At no time should Ethel's attention be directed toward the wrinkles she leaves. After she has made her bed several times alone, Mother could add encouragement by deftly placed suggestions, such as, "What would happen if you rolled all the covers back and pulled them up one at a time?" or "What would happen if you pulled here?" When it comes time for a change of linen, Mother might suggest that they could make the bed together and begin a talking game—always avoiding criticism, always presenting supportive suggestions. "Now we both pick up a corner of the mattress and hide a piece of the sheet under it. Now we pull together so that the top of the sheet meets the headboard. How do you do, Mr. Headboard." And so on. Thus, learning is made a pleasant game; there is no suggestion that Ethel doesn't know how to do it, and Mother and daughter are having fun doing something together.

Wally, four, accompanied his mother on a visit to the neighbor's, whose daughter, Patty, eighteen months, was playing with her toys on the living room floor. "Run play with Patty, Wally," Mother suggested. "Now be a good boy and don't tease her." Wally shrugged out of his jacket and dashed into the living room while the two mothers sat down to coffee. It wasn't long until Patty let out a scream. Both mothers rushed to the living room. Wally stood with a smug expression on his face, Patty's doll clutched against his chest. Patty was crying loudly and a small red mark was becoming visible on her forehead. Patty's mother ran to her, picked her up, hugged and kissed her. Wally's mother grabbed him. "Oh, you naughty boy! What did you do to her? You took her doll away from her and you hit her, didn't you? How can you be so mean? Now I'm going to spank you." She whacked him twice and he burst into tears. "Honestly, I don't know what to do with him," she said to her friend, who had Patty quieted by now. "He just will be mean to younger children." Wally sullenly watched Mother as she tried to get Patty to smile again. Patty turned her head away and buried it in the curve of her mother's neck. "Let's finish our coffee," said Patty's mother. "She's all right. I'll just hold her." Wally's mother turned on him again. "You're such a naughty boy! Shame on you for hurting someone smaller than you are. You sit on this chair now and behave yourself or I'll spank you again."

There is a great deal of movement in this incident; but for the purpose of this chapter we will speak only of the discouragement. The first thing that happened to reinforce Wally's poor self-concept was his mother's implied expectation that he would be bad. Whenever we admonish a child to "be a good boy" we imply that we expect him to consider being bad and that we lack faith in his desire to be good. Then Mother indicated in what manner she expected him to misbehave by telling him not to tease. Further, Mother makes no distinction between Wally's *behavior* and Wally *himself*. She identifies Wally as a naughty boy, as a mean boy. Thus Wally's self-concept is reinforced by Mother's expectations, her lack of faith, and her words. Wally *behaves* in an unfriendly way because he lacks confidence in his ability to get positive attention from his mother. He doubts his place except in cases where he makes a nuisance of himself. A bully is always a child who, as a result of initial discouragement, has assumed that one is big only when he can show his power. He is discouraged; not naughty and mean. We must distinguish between the doer and the deed. We must recognize misbehavior as a mistaken approach brought about through discouragement. Mother adds insult to injury by seeming to care more for the cute baby's smile.

The helpful approach to this situation would be to avoid all the discouraging remarks. They don't "teach" anything. To present Wally with faith in his ability to play with Patty can be accomplished more through an attitude than through words. "Let's go next door, and you can play with Patty if you wish." The presentation of such a happy expectancy is all that is needed. When they arrive, Mother could again leave the decision to the boy as to whether he wants to play with Patty or sit next to his mother. Once the rumpus occurred, Mother could quietly enter the room, take Wally by the hand and say, "I'm sorry you feel so cross today, son. Since you don't feel like playing, we will go home." Of course, this makes it necessary for the mothers to sacrifice their visit. But such procedure can "teach" Wally that he may come with Mother again if he is willing to behave himself. Otherwise, she may leave him with a relative or another neighbor once—and he may then reconsider his behavior.

If Wally's mother were to avoid all the discouraging acts pointed out, she would have accomplished more than half the battle against discouragement. If she can accept Wally as dear, even though his behavior is unfriendly, she offers encouragement without condoning his misdeeds. When she grants him the right to do wrong she places upon him the responsibility for his behavior and indicates that he has to bear the consequences. When she suggests that they will come again when he is ready, she expresses her faith that he will reconsider and will feel better and will want to play.

There are other ways of handling this incident which will be discussed in the chapter on fighting.

Both mothers act in a discouraging way toward Patty by being overconcerned with her mishap. The small bump on her head didn't hurt Patty so much as to warrant Mother's instant reaction of excitement, of picking her up and making a big fuss over the hurt. Patty learns from such experiences that she can't stand a little pain and that she must have immediate consolation. Her dependence on her mother becomes reinforced, and her courage and self-sufficiency are undermined. She may easily develop a concept of herself as the readily hurt baby who must depend on others for protection. Our adult lives are filled with pain and discomfort. They are part of life. Unless children learn to tolerate pain, bumps, bangs, and discomforts, they will live with a serious handicap. *We cannot protect our children from life.* Therefore, it is essential to prepare them for it. Feeling sorry for children is one of the most seriously damaging attitudes we can have. It so greatly demonstrates to them and to ourselves that we lack faith in them and their ability to cope with adversities.

A more casual attitude on the part of Patty's mother would help Patty to learn how to accept pain. This doesn't mean that we must never offer comfort for pain and distress. That would be heartless! It is the manner in which we offer it which makes the difference. "I'm sorry you got a bump, but it will soon be better and you can bear it that long." Instead of immediately picking Patty up, her mother could observe that the injury was minor. She could reassure Patty, "You're all right, darling. It's just a little bump." And let it go at that. Patty isn't in any mood to be diverted at the moment. Efforts in this direction provide stimulation for further suffering since it keeps Mother busy with her. After the comfort has been offered, Mother can quietly help Patty to arrange the toys and then withdraw her attention in order to allow Patty room for dealing with her problem. Patty is the one who is hurt and the one who must overcome not only the pain, but also the loss of a friendly atmosphere and a feeling of inadequacy. If Mother gives her a chance and has faith in her, she will quickly recover and discover her courage and her ability to put up with discomfort.

Rachel was learning to embroider. She had been working in happy concentration. With satisfaction and pride she held the guest towel up to admire her work. Then she took it to Mother to find out how to do a stitch about which she felt uncertain. "That's the lazy daisy stitch, Rachel. But, really, dear. Look at your back stitches. You can do better than that! They are all too long. It makes it look messy. Why don't you take it out and do it over again? Then it will be real nice." Rachel's face had changed from beaming interest to extreme distress. She sighed and the corners of her mouth twitched. "I don't think I want to do any more now," she said. "I think I'll go outside."

In view of Rachel's satisfaction and pride in her work, Mother's comments were crushing. "You can do better than that," is *never* encouragement. It implies that what has been done isn't good enough—doesn't measure up to standard. What Rachel had thought looked lovely looks "messy" to her mother. So again Rachel meets discouragement. To suggest that she take it out and do it over again was more than Rachel could bear. She dropped the whole matter and turned to something else. Rachel's mother could easily have observed the effect of her words had she watched her child's face.

A more helpful approach would be for Mother to show her again how to do the lazy daisy stitch and to enter into Rachel's enthusiasm for her work. "It's so pretty, dear. And what lovely stitches you have here—" pointing out the few nice ones Rachel has accomplished. "When you have it finished we surely will have to use it in the bathroom." Thus Mother enjoys with Rachel the enthusiasm of accomplishment and accepts the work as having usefulness. When Mother points out the places where Rachel has the correct small stitches, she encourages Rachel to continue working toward greater skill. We can build only on strength, not on weakness. The good stitches are a strength. Rachel's attention should be called to the good points of her work.

It sometimes takes a lot of courage on the part of the parent to let a child go ahead with a new experience.

Peter, seven, had just been given his allowance and wanted to buy a model airplane he had seen at the hobby shop in the busy shopping center. "I can't take you to the store right now, Peter," Mother said. "We'll go tomorrow." "I can go up on my bike, Mother," Peter suggested. "You've never been uptown on your bike, Peter, and you know how much traffic there is," Mother replied. "I can take care of myself, Mother. Lots of kids go up there on their bikes." Mother thought it over for a minute. She pictured the line of bikes she had frequently stumbled over outside the hobby shop. She also pictured the traffic hazards. Then she considered that Peter rode his bike to school every day and handled himself very well. "All right, honey. Go ahead. Get your model." Peter dashed joyously out of the house. Mother quieted her uneasy feelings. He's so little, she thought. But he won't learn any younger. Nearly an hour later Peter dashed into the house with his package. "See, Mother. I got it!" "I'm so pleased, Peter," Mother beamed. "Now you can do your own shopping. Isn't that wonderful?"

As uneasy as Peter's mother had felt, she realized his need to become self-sufficient. She had conquered her fears and displayed faith in his ability to handle his bike. The boy responded to her confidence. Mother followed through with an acknowledgment of his accomplishment. Finally, she granted him independence by promising him further opportunities to do his own shopping.

Six-year-old Benny invariably buttoned his sweater wrong. The buttons didn't come out even. Mother let the matter go for a while. Then one day she said, "Benny, I have an idea. Why don't you see what would happen if you started with the bottom button, which you can see easily." Delighted with a new approach, Benny followed the suggestion and beamed happily when he came out even on top. Taking her cue from the success of this method, Mother tried it again on another problem. Benny hung his pajamas up on the clothes rack, but since he thrust the bottom part onto the peg in a wad it usually fell down before long. Mother suggested, "What do you suppose would happen if you were to take the bottoms by the elastic and give them a shake before you put them on the peg?" Benny thoughtfully reached for the fallen garment, took hold of it by the elastic at the top, shook it, and hung it on the peg. It stayed up! He smiled and then grinned. "Say, that does it!"

Benny's mother found a means of encouraging Benny without in the least suggesting that the way he already did these two things was wrong. She relied on his spirit of adventure and his desire to try new ways. Benny could see the results. Mother didn't have to point them out to him. Her smile and the twinkle in her eye told him that she shared the pleasure of his ability.

These illustrations begin to show the importance of encouragement and to point up some of the pitfalls into which we unknowingly fall. Encouragement is so important that it will be mentioned time and again throughout the rest of the book. Naturally, we cannot expect any lasting effects from one act of encouragement. It has to be continuous in order to prompt abiding changes in the mistaken self-concept of a discouraged child.

Praise, as a means of encouragement, must be used very cautiously. It can be dangerous, as we saw in the case of George. If the child sees praise as a reward, then lack of it becomes scorn. If he is not praised for everything he does, the child feels that he has failed. Such a child does things in the hope of winning a reward rather than doing them for the satisfaction of contribution. Therefore, praise could easily lead to discouragement since it would fortify the child's mistaken concept that unless he is praised he has no value. It is better to use simple comments such as, "I'm glad you can do it!" "How nice!" "I appreciate what you have done." "See, you can do it."

Parental love is best demonstrated through constant encouragement toward independence. We need to start this at birth and to maintain it all through childhood. It is made manifest by our faith and confidence in the child as he is at each moment. It is an attitude which guides us through all the daily problems and situations of childhood. Our children need courage. Let us help them to develop and keep it.

In closing this chapter, we would like to give a word of encouragement to parents. As you read this book, you will discover many areas in which we present techniques which make sense: at the same time we point out the mistakes which you, like most parents, have made. Unless we discover our errors we may be unable to make progress. In pointing out the mistakes in child-raising practices that are customary today, we in no way infer criticism nor condemnation of today's parents. They are victims of circumstances beyond their control. We try to offer help and to show the way out of the present difficulties. We certainly do not want to heap further discouragement onto the heads of bewildered and discouraged parents.

The importance of courage in parents cannot be over-emphasized. Whenever you feel dismayed or find yourselves thinking, "My gosh, I did it all wrong," be quick to recognize this symptom of your own discouragement; turn your attention to an academic and impersonal consideration of what can be done to make matters better. When you try a new technique and it works, be glad. When you fall back into old habits, don't reproach yourself. You need to constantly reinforce your own courage, and to do so, you need the "courage to be imperfect." Recall to your mind the times that you have succeeded, and try again. Dwelling on your mistakes saps your courage. Remember, one cannot build on weakness—only on strength. Admit humbly that you are bound to make mistakes and acknowledge them without a sense of loss in your personal value. This will do much to keep your own courage up. Above all, remember that we are not working for *perfection*, but only for *improvement*. Watch for the little improvements, and when you find them, relax and have faith in your ability to improve further. The application of the principles put forth in this book will take time. You can't do it all at once. Each small improvement is a step forward. Each step forward is the source of further encouragement.

CHAPTER 4

THE CHILD'S MISTAKEN GOALS

Mother was writing a letter. Joyce, three, playing with her toys on the floor nearby, suddenly jumped up, ran to Mother, and asked for a hug. Mother responded and then said, "Why don't you put your doll in the wagon and take her for a ride?" "I want you to play with me!" "After while, Joyce. I have to finish this letter now." The child slowly went back to her play. After a few minutes, she asked, "Can you play now, Mommie?" "Not yet, dear," Mother answered absently. Silence for a few minutes. "Mother, I have to go to the bathroom." "All right, Joyce, go ahead." "But I can't get my coveralls down." "Yes, you can," Mother answered, looking up. "You are a big girl now, you know." Joyce made a few half-hearted attempts. "All right, honey. Come here. I'll help you this time." Joyce left the room and Mother resumed her writing. Presently the girl was back again needing help to pull her coveralls up. Mother again assisted and then returned to the letter. All was quiet for a few minutes until Joyce again asked, "Can you play now?" "In a few minutes, darling." Soon Joyce again came to Mother, hugged her knees, and said, "I love you, Mommie." "I love you, too," Mother answered, giving her daughter another hug. Joyce returned to her toys. Mother finished the letter and started playing with Joyce.

Tʜɪs story seems to show a patient, loving mother and her good relationship with her child. Why do we include it here? Let's take a good look at the *movements* of mother and child. What is Joyce doing? She is sweetly and charmingly *demanding constant attention*. Her behavior is saying, "Unless you pay attention to me, I am nothing. I have a place only when you are busy with me."

Children want desperately to belong. If all goes well and the child maintains his courage, he presents few problems. He does what the situation requires and gets a sense of belonging through his usefulness and participation. But if he has become discouraged, his sense of belonging is restricted. His interest turns from participation in the group to a desperate attempt at self-realization through others. All his attention is turned toward this end, be it through pleasant or disturbing behavior, for, one way or another, he *has* to find a place. There are four recognized "mistaken goals" that such a child can pursue. It is essential to understand these mistaken goals if we hope to redirect the child into a constructive approach to social integration.

The desire for *undue attention* is the first mistaken goal used by discouraged children as a means for feeling that they belong. Influenced by his mistaken assumption that he has significance only when he is the center of attention, the child develops great skill at attention-getting mechanisms. He finds all manner of ways to keep others busy with him. He may be charming and witty, delightful and coy. But as pleasant as he may be, his goal is to win attention rather than to participate.

In our example, it seems that Joyce wants to participate. She wants Mother to play with her. How do we determine that Joyce is misbehaving? Very simply. *Participation im-*

plies co-operation with the needs of the situation. The courageous child with self-assurance senses Mother's need to do something besides play with her. Joyce has a different idea. She feels that if Mother is busy with something else, she has forgotten about her. Joyce believes she can only have status if she gets attention.

If charming means of getting attention fail, a child will switch to disturbing methods. He may whine, tease, dawdle, mark the walls with crayons, spill his milk, or try any of a thousand attention-getting devices. At least when his parents jump on him he is sure that they know he is there! Such a child has a mistaken self-concept. Whenever we yield to his undue demands foi attention, we *reinforce* his erroneous self-concept and *increase* his conviction that this mistaken method will serve to gain the sense of belonging which he desires.

Naturally, children need our attention. They need our help and training and sympathy and love. But if, by watching ourselves, we discover that we are merely prompted by the child's efforts to gain constant and undue attention, then we can be pretty sure that this is what the child wants us to do and that this is his mistaken way of finding his place.

It may seem difficult at first glance to know how to distinguish between due and undue attention. The secret lies in the ability to recognize the demands of the situation as a whole. Participation and co-operation require that each individual within the family be situation-centered rather than self-centered. The parent can mentally step back and observe what the child does. If the action and response seem out of keeping with the demands of the situation—as is illustrated in the story of Joyce—the child is most likely demanding undue attention. Frequently we can determine what the child's unconscious intentions are by observing our own response. Since the interaction between two people takes place on the unconscious level, we just "naturally" respond to the child's design. When we become aware of the interaction and when we develop the skill to interpret it, we bring it to the conscious level and thereby have the means to promote redirection or to offer guidance to the child.

Five-year-old Peggy was watching television. She had been reminded three times that it was past her bedtime. Each time that Mother spoke to her, Peggy whined and pleaded to stay up longer and finish "this one program." Mother gave in because it *was* a good program. At the end of this one, however, when Mother told Peggy again to go to bed, Peggy ignored Mother, changed channels, and settled down for further watching. Mother entered the room. "Peggy, it is way past your bedtime. Come on, now, be a good girl and go to bed." "No!" answered Peggy. Mother bent over her and said crossly, "I said for you to go to bed. Now get going!" "But, Mother, I want to watch—" "Do you want me to spank you?" Mother interrupted. She turned off the television set. Peggy immediately started screaming, "You mean old thing!" She dashed to the set and tried to turn it on again. Mother grabbed Peggy's hands, slapped her, and forcibly drove her from the room. "I've had enough out of you, young lady. Now you get ready for bed. Go on, get those clothes off." Screaming defiance, Peggy threw herself face down on the bed. Mother left the room somewhat shaken. Twenty minutes later Mother came back to see how things were going and found Peggy still dressed and looking at a book. Completely exasperated, Mother spanked Peggy, undressed her, and put her to bed.

To begin with, Peggy knew it was time for her to go to bed. But by dawdling and asking to stay up longer, she could challenge Mother's authority. Therefore, when Mother conceded and let Peggy stay up, she played right into her daughter's hands. Peggy's behavior seemed to say, "My importance lies in making you do what I want." She got what she wanted when she wheedled mother into letting her stay up longer. She successfully showed her ability to win out over Mother.

The *struggle for power*, then, is the second mistaken goal and usually occurs after the parent has tried for some time forcibly to stop the child's demands for attention. The child then becomes determined to use power to defeat the parent. He gains an immense sense of satisfaction from refusing to do what the parent wants him to. Such a child feels that if he were to comply with requests he would submit to a stronger power and would thereby lose his sense of personal value. This fear of being overwhelmed by greater power is a devastating reality to some children and leads to terrifying efforts to demonstrate their own power.

When Peggy's mother insisted that Peggy go to bed after the program was over, Mother and Peggy became involved in a power contest. The rest of the story illustrates how each one tried to show the other who was boss. Every time Mother became upset, every time she slapped or spanked Peggy, she conceded victory to her. The insult and pain of the punishment was a price well worth paying for the victory: for keeping Mother frustrated, causing Mother to declare bankruptcy—which is what we parents do when we feel utterly defeated and lose our temper. Our behavior is saying, "I have nothing left but my superior size and strength." Children sense this and utilize it. Can't you remember the times when you had an inside smile (in spite of outward tears and screams) when you got your folks to the point of complete exasperation and frustration?

It is a grave mistake to try to overpower a power-drunk child. It is also futile. In the ensuing battle, which becomes chronic, the child merely develops greater skill in using his power and finds greater reason to feel worthless unless he can demonstrate it. This growing process may lead the child to the point where he finds his only satisfaction in being a bully, a tyrant.

The problem of the power contest is becoming prevalent in today's society because of the changes occurring in our concept of equality. We will discuss this problem further in Chapter Sixteen. For the moment it is sufficient to be able to recognize that a struggle for power exists when parent and child each attempt to show the other who is boss.

One of the important distinctions between a demand for attention and a demonstration of power is the child's behavior upon correction. If he merely wants to get attention, he will stop his disturbing behavior, at least for the moment, when reprimanded. But if his intention is to demonstrate power, attempts to make him stop only intensify his disturbing behavior. The examples of Joyce and then of Peggy clearly show this distinction.

Mother was in the kitchen, Daddy in the basement. Roy, five, and Allen, three, were playing in the living room. Suddenly Allen screamed out in pain. Mother and Daddy rushed to the scene to discover Allen cowering in the corner, screaming, while Roy continued holding a flaming cigarette lighter under his brother's arm. The damage was done by the time the parents arrived. Roy had succeeded in giving Allen a nasty burn.

The third mistaken goal arises from the intensification of the power contest. When parent and child become increasingly involved in a power struggle and each tries to subdue the other, a transaction of intense retaliation may develop. The child, in his discouragement, may proceed to seek revenge as his only means of feeling significant and important. By now he is convinced that he can't be liked and doesn't have any power; that he counts only if he can hurt others as he feels hurt by them. And so his mistaken goal becomes one of *retaliation and revenge*. Roy, deeply discouraged in his efforts to gain a place, sees himself as a bad and unlikable boy. And because his behavior is so disagreeable he is quite successful in convincing others, too. Such children, who need encouragement the most, get it the least. It takes genuine understanding and acceptance of the child *as he is* to help him rediscover his worth. If Mother or Daddy punish Roy, they will only give him further proof that he is bad. It will also provide him with further incentive to provoke, which will lead to further retaliation, to further mutual infliction of hurts.

The fourth goal is used by the completely discouraged child. He tries to demonstrate his *complete inadequacy*.

Eight-year-old Jay was having difficulty at school. In a conference, the teacher told Mother that he was an extremely poor reader, was behind in all subjects, and didn't seem to get anywhere, no matter how much he tried nor how much extra help she gave him. "What does Jay do to help at home?" Teacher asked. "I quit asking him to do things at home," Mother replied. "He doesn't want to do anything, and if he does, he is so clumsy and does it so badly that I just don't ask him any more."

A completely discouraged child gives up entirely: he feels that he has no chance to succeed in any way, be it by useful or useless means. He becomes helpless and uses his helplessness, exaggerating any real or imagined weakness or deficiency, to avoid any task where his expected failure may be even more embarrassing. The seemingly stupid child is frequently a discouraged child who uses stupidity as a means of avoiding any effort whatsoever. It's as if these children were saying, "If I do anything at all you will discover how worthless I am. So leave me alone." These children no longer put others into their service; they merely give up. Whenever Mother finds herself saying, "I give up! There is no point in asking him to do anything," she can be pretty sure that this is exactly what the child wanted her to feel. It is as if the child said, "Give up, Mother. It is no use. I'm worthless and hopeless. Just let me alone." The child's view of himself is, of course, a mistaken concept brought about through a series of experiences that he has seen as presenting impossible obstacles and so he has become discouraged. No child is ever worthless!

When we are aware of the four possible mistaken goals behind children's misbehavior, we have a basis for action. *Under no circumstances is there anything to be gained by telling the child what we suspect may be his mistaken goal. This could be most damaging.* Psychological knowledge is something to be used as a basis for *our action,* not as a flow of words that become weapons against the child. He is utterly unaware of his purpose. One can make a child aware of his hidden purpose; but such an act of disclosure should be left to professionally trained persons. However, once *we* are aware of the mistaken goal of the child, we are in a position to realize the purpose of his behavior. What seemed senseless now begins to make sense. We are now in a position to act. If we remove the results that the child desired, his particular behavior becomes useless. If the child fails to gain his goal, he may reconsider his direction and choose another course of action.

When we realize that a child is demanding undue attention, we can avoid yielding to his demands. What is the point of demanding attention of a mother who disappears? When we find ourselves involved in a power contest, we can withdraw from the field of battle and not allow ourselves to become engaged in the contest. There is no point in being the victor of an empty field. When a child seeks to hurt us we can be aware of his deep discouragement, avoid feeling hurt, and avoid retaliation through punishment. And we can stop being discouraged by the "helpless" child and arrange experiences where he may discover his abilities. What good does it do to give up if Mother just won't believe one is helpless?

Subsequent chapters will illustrate these four goals in action and describe possible methods of rendering them futile. It is important to recognize, however, that these four mistaken approaches are obvious only in the young child. In his early years, the child's attention is focused upon developing relationships with his parents and other adults. He sees himself as a child in an adult world. During this time the four mistaken goals are rather obvious to the knowing observer. However, by the time he is eleven or so, his relationship to his peers becomes more important and he pursues a wider variety of behavior patterns in order to find his place in the peer group. For this reason, disturbing behavior (which always represents a mistaken effort to find one's place) can no longer be entirely explained by one of the four goals. Provocative actions in teen-agers and adults as well can sometimes be explained in terms of the four mistaken goals, but other forms of mistaken approaches are evident— such as thrill-seeking, excessive attention to masculine attributes, material successes, and so on—which do not necessarily fall within the scope of these goals.

Another important consideration that must always be borne in mind is that we, as parents, can only try to stimulate our child toward a change in behavior. We cannot always succeed, even though we may do the right thing. (And to expect to succeed all the time is an impossible demand upon oneself, anyhow!) Each child makes up his own mind about what he will do. Influences outside of the home, especially those of his peers, impress him very much. Should our efforts to guide him into another direction seem futile, we must remember that he is an individual and makes his own choices and decisions. We cannot take responsibility for this; it belongs to the child. This, also, is part of the meaning of equality.

Life consists only of the present moment, and if we do the right thing at this moment, we move toward improvement. On the other hand, if we do not fulfill the requirements of a given situation or do not know how to deal with it, then the chances for improvement are slim indeed.

Naturally, the solution of our problems cannot always be found immediately. This moment is only one of many in a series of events that either bring solutions, defer them, or prohibit them. With our children, every moment contributes either to his training, to improvement of relationships, or to the opposite—the development of detrimental attitudes and poor social integration.

Many of the problems our children have can be resolved through a step-by-step procedure. In this book, we attempt to indicate which procedure in a given conflict situation may be helpful and which damaging. For most parents and for most situations, it seems sufficient to know what to do and what not to do in a given instance. In past times such knowledge, common to all mothers, constituted what we can call a tradition of raising children that was handed down from generation to generation. Our job now is to clarify the approaches which are effective in a democratic setting, thereby leading to a new tradition of child-raising.

In many cases the child's erroneous ideas and mistaken goals underlying his misbehavior are so well entrenched that it may take more than a correct response to the various acts of provocation. One may have to work toward a deep reconstruction of a child's basic assumptions, of his personality pattern. More comprehensive insight into the dynamics of his behavior may be needed. If such is necessary, parents may find it profitable to attend Parent Study Groups or Counseling Centers or to receive individual counseling. It may also be necessary to study more theoretical books on child psychology.* What we try to offer is some clarification on the day-to-day procedure—some help for the harassed mother who first must discover her tremendous potential for influencing her child if she knows what to do with him. The more parents learn to really understand their children, the more they can help them in reorientating themselves, in developing a more accurate picture of life, and in accepting social values that are necessary for harmonious co-operation—as well as for a satisfactory fulfillment of their lives.

* To counteract the present tendency of mothers to read a variety of books and so become more confused in their efforts to understand and cope with their children, we suggest books that follow the same orientation, such as:

Adler, Alfred. *The Problem Child.* New York: Capricorn Books, 1963.

Adler, Alfred. *Understanding Human Nature.* New York: Premier Books, 1957.

Beecher, Marguerite and Willard. *Parents on the Run.* New York: Julian Press, 1955.

Dinkmeyer, Don, and Dreikurs, Rudolf. *Encouraging Children to Learn: the Encouragement Process.* Englewood Cliffs, N.J.: Prentice-Hall, 1963.

Dreikurs, Rudolf. *The Challenge of Marriage.* New York: Duell, Sloan and Pearce, 1946.

Dreikurs, Rudolf. *The Challenge of Parenthood.* New York: Duell, Sloan and Pearce, 1948, revised edition, 1958.

Dreikurs, Corsini, Lowe, and Sonstegard. *Adlerian Family Counseling: A Manual for Counseling Centers.* Eugene: University of Oregon Press, 1959.

Rasey, Marie. *Toward Maturity: The Psychology of Child Development.* New York: Hinds, Hayden & Eldrige, 1947.

Rasey, Marie, and Menge, J. W. *What We Learn from Children.* New York: Harper & Brothers, 1956.

Wexberg, Erwin. *Our Children in a Changing World.* New York: Macmillan Company, 1938.

CHAPTER 5

THE FALLACY OF PUNISHMENT AND REWARD

Mother wondered why everything was so quiet and decided to investigate. She found Alex, two and a half, busily stuffing toilet tissue into the toilet again. Alex had been spanked several times for stopping up the toilet in this fashion. Furious, Mother yelled, "How many times am I going to have to spank you for this?" She grabbed Alex, took down his pants, and whipped him. Later that evening, Father found the toilet stuffed up *again*.

AFTER so many spankings for the same act, why in the world does Alex continue? Is he too small to understand? Far from it. Alex knows exactly what he is doing. He deliberately repeats this misbehavior. Of course, he doesn't know why! But his behavior tells us why. His parents say, "No—you can't." His actions say, "I'll show you I can—no matter what!"

If punishment were going to make Alex stop stuffing the toilet, one spanking would have accomplished results. Repeated spankings have not made much impression. What is wrong?

In Chapter 1 we discussed the change in our social climate, which has brought a greater realization of democracy as a way of life. Since democracy implies equality, parents can no longer assume the role of the "authority." Authority implies dominance: one individual having power over another. There can be no such dominance among equals. Dominance —force, power—must be replaced with egalitarian techniques of influence.

Punishment and reward belong properly in the autocratic social system. Here, the authority, enjoying a dominant position, had the privilege of meting out rewards or punishment according to merits. It was his privilege to decide who was deserving of rewards and who of punishment. And because the autocratic social system was based on the firm establishment of dominant powers, such judgments were accepted as part of the code of living. Children observed and waited and hoped for the time when they could be the privileged adults. Today, our whole social structure is changed. Children have gained an equal social status with adults * and we no longer enjoy a superior position to them. Our power over them is gone: and *they* know it, whether *we* do or not. They no longer recognize us as a superior power.

We must realize the futility of trying to impose our will upon our children. No amount of punishment will bring about lasting submission. Today's children are willing to take any amount of punishment in order to assert their "rights." Confused and bewildered parents mistakenly hope that punishment will *eventually* bring results, without realizing that they are actually getting nowhere with their methods. At best, they gain only temporary results from punishment. When the same punishment has to be repeated again and again, it should be obvious that it does not work.

The use of punishment only helps the child to develop

* This concept of equality is difficult to comprehend. Despite the fact of accomplished equality, we have no traditional perception of what it implies. We look for single qualities that make one individual inferior or superior to another, although all such evaluations have become obsolete.

greater power of resistance and defiance. Little Alex, at his young age, has already started down a terrifying path of defiance and resistance.

Six-year-old Rita had been cantankerous all morning. She had refused breakfast. Mother had scolded. Rita fought with her four-year-old sister. Mother sent her to her room for a half hour. Rita pulled up flowers by their roots. Mother had scolded and threatened a spanking. Rita had tied the neighbor's cat to the clothesline, nearly strangling it. Mother made Rita sit on a chair in the kitchen. Finally, Rita threw her lunchtime milk on the floor. At this, Mother hauled Rita to her room, spanked her soundly, and told her to stay in her room the rest of the afternoon. An hour later, everything being quiet, Mother thought Rita might be asleep and peeked into the room. To her utter dismay she saw the bedroom curtains cut to ribbons as far as Rita could reach. Aghast, Mother cried, "Oh, Rita! What am I going to do with you?"

Rita hides her discouragement behind a front of "guts." Her behavior says, "At least you know I'm around when I'm bad." Then, when Mother was driven from one punishment to another, Rita finally told her mother with her behavior, "If you have the right to hurt me, I have the same right to hurt you!" A horrible progression of retaliation and revenge ensued. The more Mother punishes, the more Rita retaliates. Such is the result of punishment. Unfortunately, children are far more resilient and tenacious than adults. They can outplot, outfigure, and outlast their parents. The result is that parents come to the end of their endurance, shake their heads, and cry out in misery, "I don't know what to do!"

Punishment, or the authoritative idea—"obey me, or else," needs to be replaced by a sense of mutual respect and co-operation. Even though children are no longer in an inferior position, they are untrained and inexperienced. They need our leadership. A good leader inspires and stimulates his followers into action that suits the situation. So it must be with parents. Our children need our guidance. They will accept it if they know we respect them as equal human beings with equal rights to decide what they will do. The insult to a child's dignity is enormous when he is whacked, and not much of Mother's dignity is left when she is through with the procedure, particularly if she feels guilty afterwards.

We parents can learn to use more effective methods to stimulate a child so that he has a desire to conform to the demands of order. We can create an atmosphere of mutual self-respect and consideration and provide an opportunity for the child to learn how to live comfortably and happily with others. We need to arrange learning situations without showing a lack of respect for the child or for ourselves. And we can do all this without a show of power, for power incites rebellion and defeats the purpose of child-raising.

Should it happen, however, that in the course of retraining ourselves in new methods of child guidance, we find ourselves provoked into punishing or spanking a child, we should be honest and admit that we have relieved our own feelings of frustration and not try to kid ourselves that we have punished the child "for his own good." At the same time, we can acknowledge that the child has really asked for the whipping. His provocative behavior is part of his goal, which is to prove that he is "bad" or to engage us in a power contest or to retaliate for previous "injustices." When we punish him, we fall into line with his intentions— fall into his trap, as it were. The problem lies in the fact that, as humans, we are imperfect. Every once in a while we act like humans instead of educators. The best thing to do is to smile at our own frailty and to keep going, keep aiming at more constructive efforts on our own part. And we must have the courage to be imperfect. When the child constantly defeats us, we are perhaps entitled to the short moment of victory when we beat him down, and we don't need to feel guilty about it afterward. Guilt feelings are a luxury we can ill afford. At such times our feelings are saying for us—"Yes, I hit him. I think it was wrong. But as long as I feel guilty I am not really a bad parent." Oddly enough, a frank admission—"Sure, I hit him. He asked for it. I know it is useless as a training method, but it made *me* feel better. Now I can pick up the pieces and go on again"—adds immensely to our own courage and our own feeling that we *can* cope with the child.

Mother gave Bill, eight, a dollar and asked him to go into the bakery while she went into the supermarket. When they met outside again, Mother asked for the change. "How come ya want the change?" Bill snarled. "Why, Bill! I need it." Angrily, the boy poured the change into Mother's hand. "I don't get it," he snapped. "Did ya a favor, didn't I?" Puzzled, Mother looked at him. "Yes, you did, son. A favor." As they headed for the car, Bill showed his resentment in every line of his body.

The system of rewarding children for good behavior is as detrimental to their outlook as the system of punishment. The same lack of respect is shown. We "reward" our inferiors for favors or for good deeds. In a system of mutual respect among equals, a job is done because it needs doing, and the satisfaction comes from the harmony of two people doing a job together as Bill and his mother were doing. But Bill has no concept of how he has done his bit towards contributing to the family welfare. His attention is centered on himself. He showed resentment when his idea of "what's in it for me" came up against "nothing." What a jolt! And how restricted Bill's outlook is. His inborn social interest has been smothered by his mistaken idea that he only has a place if he "gets." He sees himself as belonging only when he gets something in return for his actions.

Two high-school juniors were talking during the intermission of a concert. "Hey, Mavis is pretty good at Debussy," one remarked. "Aw, she doesn't have much 'go' about her," replied the other. "You know what?" he continued. "Her mother pays her a dollar an hour for practicing." "You're kidding!" "No, I'm not. Mavis said she practiced eight hours a day all summer just so she could get all that money." "That's a heck of a reason to practice! No wonder she doesn't have any 'go.' She doesn't play for the fun of it. Heck. When I practice, I get so lost in it my folks holler for me to stop so they can rest." "Yeah! I know what you mean. I fool around a lot, too."

This is an example of the perspicacity of our youth!

A heavy snow had fallen and Daddy asked Mike, ten, and Stan, eight, to shovel the walks. "What'll you pay us?" demanded Mike. "Well," hesitated Daddy, "what do you think it's worth?" "Aw, about a buck and a quarter apiece," bargained Mike. "Does that price include the driveway?" Daddy asked dubiously. Not wanting to stretch things too far, Mike answered guardedly, "Yeah, I guess so." "O.K., then," Daddy agreed. "Whooppee!" the boys yelled as they dashed off.

Why should children be paid to do chores? They live in the house, eat the food, are provided with clean clothes, and share in the benefits. If they are the equals they claim to be, they are obliged to share in the toil.

Through the system of rewards, Mike and Stan have assumed that they needn't do anything unless there is something in it for them. They can't possibly develop a sense of responsibility under these circumstances. The emphasis has been placed on "what's in it for me?" to the point that we have run out of satisfying rewards. The pathetic part is that there is no reward that totally satisfies.

Children should share in the whole aspect of family life. They also have a share in the spending money, usually in the form of an allowance. This is their share of money and they should be allowed to do with it as they like. There should be no connection at all between chores and allowances. Children do chores because they contribute to the family welfare. They get allowances because they share the benefits.

Mother left her two small girls in the car in the parking lot so that she could grocery shop unhindered. As soon as she got out of the car they started to cry. "Be good, now, and I'll bring you a toy." "What kind?" the three-year-old asked. "Oh, I don't know—something," Mother answered hastily as she walked away.

Mother is trying to win co-operation by offering material gains. Children don't need *bribes* to be good. They actually want to be good. Good behavior on the part of the child springs from his desire to belong, to contribute usefully, and to co-operate. When we bribe a child for good behavior, we are in effect showing him that we do not trust him, which is a form of discouragement.

A reward does not give a child a sense of belonging. It may be a sign of parental approval of the moment, but what about the next moment? Do Mother and Daddy still approve? Or is another reward needed? Considering the number of moments, one soon runs out of rewards! If we withhold a special reward it is interpreted by the child as a waste of his efforts. Parents face a serious problem if the child refuses to co-operate without an answer to the question, "What's in it for me?" Unless he considers the reward sufficient, what is the sense of co-operation? Why should he bother to do as he should if he does not gain anything special in return? And so the attitude of materialism grows monstrous; there is no chance to satisfy the appetite of acquisition. A completely false value has been established, since the child assumes that the world owes him everything. If nothing is automatically forthcoming, he will "show them." Such is the feeling of the sixteen-year-old for whom the simple sense of following highway rules to preserve his life has no place in his set of values. He prefers to aim his car in reckless defiance. Why should he bother to obey highway rules? Where is the reward? He has his car. It is much more fun to see how much thrill he can experience and to show what a clever guy he is in doing as he pleases and still not getting caught. Besides, what's a little punishment if he does get caught? The thrill of defiance is worth it. And Dad will fix it up, anyway.

Here is the end result of reward and punishment. "They haven't rewarded me; I shall punish them. If they punish me, I'll punish back. I'll show them!"

Satisfaction comes from a sense of contribution and participation—a sense actually denied to our children in our present system of rewarding them with material things. In our mistaken efforts to win co-operation through rewards, we are actually denying our children the basic satisfactions of living.

CHAPTER 6

THE USE OF NATURAL AND LOGICAL CONSEQUENCES

Since punishment and reward are ineffective, what can we do when children misbehave? Well, what happens if Mother forgets about the cake in the oven? It follows by logic that the cake is burned. This is the natural consequence of her forgetfulness. If we allow a child to experience the consequences of his acts, we provide an honest and real learning situation.

Ten-year-old Alfred frequently forgot to take his lunch to school. As soon as Mother discovered the lunch, she would take it to school and make sure that it got to him. Every time this happened she bawled him out for his forgetfulness and reminded him how much it put her out to take his lunch to him. Alfred responded to these lectures with bad temper—and kept on forgetting his lunch.

What would be the natural consequence of forgetting one's lunch? One would go hungry. Mother can tell Alfred that she no longer feels responsible for his lunch. Then when he forgets it, she simply ignores his complaints. After all, it is not *her* problem. Alfred will be angry, to be sure, because he thinks it is Mother's duty to see to it that he has his lunch.

But Mother can answer quietly, "I'm sorry that you forgot it, Alfred." (It may be necessary to enlist the co-operation of the school in this matter so that someone else doesn't supply lunch money.) If, however, Mother were to add, "Maybe this will be a lesson to you," she would immediately turn the "consequence" into punishment. It is most important that we use words which convey to the child that he has it in his power to take care of his problem, and not that he must do what we decide.

The idea of letting a child go hungry is horrifying to many parents. Actually, it *is* unpleasant to be hungry. But one missed lunch now and then is not going to cause bodily harm, and the discomfort may be effective in stimulating Alfred to remember to take his lunch with him. It will help to eliminate the friction and lack of harmony between Alfred and his mother, which is more damaging than hunger. We do not have the right to assume the responsibilities of our children, nor do we have the right to take the consequences of their acts. These belong to them.

Alice, four, is underweight and catches cold easily. Both Mother and Daddy are convinced that her health will improve with proper nourishment.

Alice sits in front of her plate eating the first few bites with relish. She drinks a little milk; and as the conversation between Mother and Daddy starts, she gradually loses interest in her food. She leans her elbow on the table and supports her head on her hand. Listlessly, she pushes the food around on her plate. "Come on, darling," prompts Daddy. "Eat your good dinner." He speaks gently and lovingly. Alice smiles winsomely, puts a bite into her mouth, and holds it there. Daddy is again talking to Mother. Alice's jaws move once or twice. "Come on, sweetheart. Chew it up." Mother interrupts her conversation with Daddy. "You want to be a big, healthy girl, don't you?" Alice chews vigorously. "That's my girl," Daddy encourages. But as soon as Mother and

Daddy talk again, Alice stops eating. The whole meal is one of continually coaxing Alice to eat.

The purpose of Alice's poor appetite is to keep her parents busy with her. This is easy to discover when we look at what the parents are doing

Eating sustains life. It is a normal function. There is always a misbehaving parent when a child becomes a feeding problem. It is the *child's* business to eat. The parents should mind their own business and not the child's.

The simplest way to teach Alice to eat properly is to "let" her eat. If she refuses, the parents should maintain a friendly attitude, abstain from verbal reminders altogether, remove the unfinished food from the table when everyone is finished, and allow Alice to find out what happens. If we don't eat, we get hungry. At the next meal, *and not before,* food is again offered. If Alice still dawdles, nothing is said; friendliness prevails at the table. The implication is, "If you wish to eat, here is food. If you don't wish to eat, then I must assume that you are not hungry." The food is casually removed if the child plays with it. There is no threat of punishment and no bribe of reward (dessert.) Alice may complain of hunger an hour later and beg for milk and cookies. Mother replies, "I am sorry you are hungry. Dinner will be ready at six; it is too bad that you will have to wait so long." Regardless of how piteable Alice's hunger may appear, Mother must allow Alice to be hungry because this is the natural consequence of not eating. The suffering inflicted by a spanking is punishment because it is inflicted by the parent. The discomfort of going hungry is not imposed by an adult but is the result of not having eaten at mealtime.

Why is it that parents feel no compunction about inflicting pain with a spanking and yet are horrified at the idea of hunger pain that the child inflicts upon himself? It seems that the parent feels deeply responsible for providing food and feels accused of being a bad parent if she sees her child hungry and does nothing about it. However, our overconcern with eating, the deeply felt anxiety over thinness and health, are often a mask. Parents may fully believe in their sense of responsibility when in truth they camouflage their real intention to dominate: "I intend to have my child eat the way I want her to." It is a desire to control which prompts many parents. It is this very authoritative control that Alice is fighting. When the "authority" is removed and Alice no longer has anything to fight against, there are no benefits in not eating, and she will probably eat. It may take a little time. It certainly takes patience.

If logical consequences are used as a threat or "imposed" in anger, they cease being consequences and become punishment. Children are quick to discern the difference. They respond to logical consequences; they fight back when punished.

Alice's parents have decided to use logical consequences. She dawdles. Mother is annoyed but says nothing. Daddy and Mother converse, but without animation. Their problem sits there right under their noses, dawdling, pushing food around. Mother and Daddy have almost finished their lunch. Daddy turns to Alice with loving patience. "Alice, come on, eat your lunch. If you don't, you know you will be hungry before dinner and you can't have anything between meals. You don't want to go hungry, do you?" "I don't want any more lunch," Alice replies. "All right you'll be hungry. And remember, nothing till dinner."

This is not logical consequence: it is still punishment. Alice is "threatened" with hunger. Mother and Daddy are still concerned with her eating and have subtly shown it. They still want to "make" Alice eat. Clever Alice. She senses how bad they will feel if she is hungry. So she denies herself her lunch and will "suffer" hunger to punish her parents.

The only way out of the dilemma is for Alice's parents to be actually and genuinely unconcerned with her eating. It is her problem. She has to solve it. She may eat or not; she may feel hunger or not—it is her choice. Let her take the consequences for herself.

When we use the term "logical consequences," parents so frequently misinterpret it as a new way to impose their demands upon children. The children see this for what it is —disguised punishment. The secret lies in the manner of application. It comprises a judicial withdrawal on the part of the parent that allows room for the logical sequence of events to take place. It works both ways. The natural consequence of not eating is the discomfort of hunger. The natural consequence of eating is the comfort of satisfaction.

Lunchtime was a daily hassle for Mother, who was having trouble getting Carol, six, off on time for afternoon kindergarten. Then she heard about the system of applying logical consequences. Mother admitted that it was a matter of pride to her that Carol should be on time. It was hard for her to allow Carol to disgrace her by being late. However, one day she showed her daughter where the hands of the clock would be when it was time for her to leave for school and then sat down to lunch with her. Carol dawdled. So, when Mother was finished, she left the table and sat in another room with a book. (No matter that the words went in one eye and out the other; she *appeared* to be absorbed in her own affairs!) Carol finally left for school a half hour late. When she returned, Mother casually discovered that nothing had happened as a result of the tardiness. However, Mother continued with the same procedure the next day. On the third day she wrote a note to the teacher asking for her co-operation. Carol was forty-five minutes late that day. When she came home she was crying because she had been late. "I'm sorry you were late, dear. Perhaps you can manage better tomorrow." From that day on, Carol watched the clock like a hawk, and

Mother ceased being concerned with getting her off to school on time.

This same technique can be applied to children getting up and off to school in the morning. They can be given their own alarm clock. Mother explains that she no longer will be responsible for getting them up and to school on time. (Mother is not going to school!) She ceases to be after them and lets the children dawdle and forget books and homework. If a school bus is involved, the children will have to walk to school—even if it is a very long way. They have the energy.

Many times a logical consequence to fit the act will occur to us after a little thought. We merely need to ask ourselves, "What would happen if I didn't interfere?" Homework not done brings the teacher's wrath. Toys destroyed are gone— not replaced. Clothes not put into the hamper don't get washed. And so on. At other times it may be necessary to subtly arrange the consequence.

Three-year-old Kathy refused to stay out of the street when she played in the yard. Mother had to watch her constantly and bring her back into the yard. Scoldings and even spankings did no good.

What would the logical consequences be in this case? Naturally, we wouldn't give the child free rein until she got hit by a car—the natural result of playing in the street. So we have to arrange a consequence that will fit the disrupted order. The first time Kathy goes into the street, Mother asks her if she feels she can stay in the yard. If she wanders away, Mother picks her up quietly and firmly carries her into the house. "Since you do not feel like playing in the yard, you may not be out. When you are ready, you may try again." It is best if Kathy has a definite play area in the house. In removing Kathy from her outdoor play there must be no evidence of rancor. When Mother says, "Since you do not feel like staying in the yard . . ." she indicates Kathy's right to her own feelings. Mother cannot *make* Kathy feel like staying in the yard. But she can establish limitations and consequences. As soon as Kathy expresses willingness to try again, she may go out. If she runs into the street, she is brought back into the house for the rest of the day. To prevent this from becoming a power contest, after the third successive time, Mother may keep Kathy in for a few days. It is most important to constantly give children a chance to try again. It allows them to feel that they still have a chance, and indicates Mother's faith in the child and his ability to learn. Kathy may protest being brought in and express her rebellion at not getting her own way. At this point, Mother remains calm. She does nothing at all about the rebellion, since we can deal with only one problem at a time.

Betty, three, neglected to brush her teeth. In order to get the job done, Mother had to go with her and force her each time. This quarrel upset both Mother and Betty. Then Mother thought of a consequence. She told Betty that she need not brush her teeth if she didn't want to. But since candy and sweets destroy unbrushed teeth, Betty could have no sweets. Thereafter, Mother avoided any mention of tooth brushing. For a week Betty neither brushed her teeth nor had any sweets. The other children had candy and ice cream. One afternoon Betty announced that she wanted to brush her teeth and have some candy. "Not now, Betty. Morning is the proper time to brush teeth." The girl accepted this without complaint. The next morning she brushed her teeth of her own accord.

Many of the things children do which annoy us are done for that very purpose, and to keep us busy with them. Logical consequences work very nicely here.

Guy, four, consistently put his shoes on the wrong feet. This annoyed Mother considerably. "For heaven's sake, Guy. When will you learn to put your shoes on right! Come here." Then Mother sat him down and changed his shoes.

Guy knows that his shoes are on wrong. Mother can be pretty sure of the purpose of her son's action when she considers her response to it. He is showing Mother that he will use his shoes to put her into his service. When Mother says, "When will you learn..." she implies that Guy is dumb. This is far from the truth; if anyone is dumb, it is not the child. Mother can get herself and Guy out of this conflict situation by ceasing to care how Guy wears his shoes. They are his feet, not hers. If she does not interfere, Guy will experience the discomfort which inevitably follows shoes worn on the wrong feet. The first time that Mother notices that the shoes are on properly, she can quietly express her pleasure that he now knows what to do. This is quite enough to say. It gives Guy recognition for his accomplishment and encouragement to continue his efforts.

Ten-year-old Allen left his catcher's mitt at the playground, and when he went back for it, it was gone. He cried brokenheartedly. Daddy scolded, "This is the third mitt you've lost this summer. Do you think money grows on trees?" After a long sermon on the need to take care of belongings, he extracted a promise from Allen to take care of the next mitt. "All right, I'll get you another one tomorrow. But remember, this is the last one this summer!" (Daddy had said all this after the loss of the second mitt, including the last remark. But he just couldn't stand to see Allen so heartbroken!)

There are many times when a parent has a golden opportunity to allow the consequence of misbehavior to take effect; but due to their pity or their desire to "protect" the child, they deprive him of the consequence and punish him in their own way with a scolding or a sermon.

Daddy can say, "I'm awfully sorry you lost your mitt,

Allen." "But I've *got* to have a mitt," Allen explodes. "Do you have the money for a new one?" "No—but you could give it to me." "You will get your regular allowance at the regular time." "But that's not enough!" "Sorry, but there is nothing I can do." Daddy must remain firm, although friendly.

The use of logical consequences means a reorientation of our thinking. We must realize that we no longer live in an autocratic society that can "control" children but in a democratic society that needs to "guide" them. We can no longer impose our will on our children. We must now "stimulate" proper behavior, which we can no longer enforce. Until we have lived with these new techniques long enough for them to become second nature, we will find the process of reorientation rather difficult. It will require an extraordinary amount of thinking and regular exercise of our imagination. At times it is possible to let the natural flow of events occur without any interference from adults. This is known as "natural consequences." For instance, if the child oversleeps, he will just naturally be late to school and have to face the ire of the teacher. At other times we may need to structure events which logically follow the misdeed. (These are "logical consequences.") Natural consequences represent the pressure of reality without any specific action by parents and are always effective. In contrast, logical consequences cannot be applied in a power struggle except with extreme caution because they usually deteriorate into punitive acts of retaliation. For this reason, natural consequences are always beneficial but logical consequences may backfire.

There is no logical connection if Mother denies Bobbie a favorite television program because he failed to take out the garbage. No matter how Mother says it, Bobbie will hear, "You did not remove the garbage, therefore I will punish you by not letting you see your program." The logic of this situation could be that Mother is unwilling to cook in a kitchen that is offensive with garbage. On the other hand, if Bobbie fails to complete his Saturday chores by the time the ball team gathers, it is quite logical that he cannot join the play until he finishes his job.

Accurate and consistant application of logical consequences is often remarkably effective and may result in amazing reduction of friction and an increase in family harmony Children are very quick to see the justice of logical consequences, and they usually accept them readily without resentment. The less the parent talks about "consequences," the less it will appear as punishment. At times, of course, there is no possible consequence and we must wait for another occasion. Sometimes the problem can even be solved by discussing it with the children and seeing what they have to offer.

If, however, the parent is engaged in a power struggle with the child, he is inclined to use logical consequences as punishment and thereby forfeit the effectiveness of this method. It is most important that we be constantly on guard not to fall into this trap. We must repeatedly remind ourselves, "I have no right to punish a person with status equal to mine, but I do have the obligation to guide and direct my child. I do not have the right to impose my will—but I do have the obligation not to give in to his undue demands."

CHAPTER 7

BE FIRM WITHOUT DOMINATING

IT IS difficult at times to understand the difference between firmness and domination. Children need firmness. It provides limits without which they feel uncomfortable. If there are no limits, the child keeps reaching to see just how far he can go. The usual result is that his behavior gets to the point of outrage and then the axe falls. An unhappy scene follows and the harmony is disrupted.

As Mother drove, Judy and Jerry, five-year-old twins, merrily romped in the back of the station wagon. They became more and more noisy. The distracted mother asked them several times to quiet down. They would stop for a minute and then return to their roughhouse play, which became wilder and wilder. Suddenly Jerry pushed Judy in such a fashion that she was thrown against Mother's head and shoulders. "This is the utter end," she screamed as she stopped the car at the curb. Both children looked panic-stricken and frightened. Mother gave each a sound spanking. The twins were completely astounded, since Mother rarely used violence.

Mother is very lenient with the lively spirits of the twins, who in turn feel that "anything goes." If we permit violation of order at one time and blow up at another, we teach our children to mind us only if we get violent.

A car is not the place for wild play at any time. Mother can establish order in the car without any force; she can be firm without dominating. How can this be done? The secret lies in knowing *how* to be firm. Domination means that we try to impose our will upon the child. We tell him what he should do. If Mother attempts to impose her will upon the twins, she will succeed only in evoking their rebellion. Firmness, on the other hand, expresses *our own action*. Mother can always decide what *she* will do and carry it out. She simply will not drive while the children are unruly. Every time that they cut up, she stops the car. She may say, "I will not drive as long as you misbehave." Then she sits quietly until they are orderly. No other explanation is necessary. Mother has taken her stand and is firm in her decision.*

Firmness without domination requires practice in mutual respect. We must respect the child's right to decide what he intends to do. Respect for ourselves is gained by our refusal to be placed at the mercy of the unruly child.

Seven-year-old Eric, a middle child, was a very finicky eater. As Daddy served generous portions of beef stew—a family favorite—Eric slumped down in his chair and petulantly announced, "I don't like any of that stuff." "Eric, please try it," Mother pleaded. "You know I don't like things all mixed up together," Eric whined. "I simply won't eat it." "Well, all right, I'll fix you a hamburger." While Mother prepared the food, Eric dawdled with his knife. Father and the other children finished their meal and left the table. As Mother and Eric ate, they talked of his day at school.

---

* One mother who had used this technique was able to make a two-thousand-mile trip in the car with her two children, ten and seven, in complete ease and enjoyment. At no time during the trip was there any friction or disorder in the car.

Eric manipulated the whole situation so that Mother not only gave him special food but also her undivided attention. He had Mother fully in his service.

Eric has the right to refuse to eat the stew and Mother must respect this right. But in her desire to be a "good" mother, she has assumed the role of a slave. Mother and Daddy can be firm about what *they* will do, and let Eric take care of himself. Let us see what happens if the parents are firm.

Eric announced that he didn't want the stew. "All right, son. You don't have to eat it," Daddy replied. He continued to serve, but omitted Eric. "Well, aren't you going to get *me* something?" the boy asked. "We are having stew tonight," Mother answered. "If you aren't, you may leave." "But I don't like stew," Eric shouted. "There is nothing I can do about *that*," was Mother's only reply. At this point, both Mother and Daddy firmly avoided a verbal battle. They ignored any further comments from Eric about food, hunger, and so on and ate their dinner. Eric left the table in a temper. Later, Eric came to the kitchen for milk and crackers. "I'm sorry, Eric. I do not have a restaurant; I serve only at mealtimes." Eric was not given any food until the next meal, despite all his remonstrations, which got no further reply from Mother. Both parents remained firm in their stand on several successive occasions. Eric soon joined the family in eating what was served.

Respect for a child's needs and wishes is essential. We need to develop sensitivity to recognize the difference between his needs and his whims. The needs of the total situation can be our guide.

Kathy, three and a half, had been ill for several days and had required care during the night. After she was well, she continued to demand nocturnal service. Several nights later, Mother decided to call a halt. She and Daddy agreed on a course of action. Mother kissed Kathy good night and said, "Daddy and I are going to sleep tonight and will not respond if you call us." When Kathy awoke and called, neither parent answered. After this one experience, Kathy slept through the night.

Mother stated what *she* would do and let Kathy make her own decision. When Kathy tested her, Mother remained firm.

Mother and Sharon were on their way home from the playground when Sharon decided she wanted to stop at Auntie's house. Mother said no, they were going home now. Sharon whimpered and begged. Mother continued to walk. The child threw herself onto the sidewalk, screaming. Mother calmly and quietly walked on without looking back. Suddenly, Sharon jumped up and ran to her mother, smiling and jumping. They walked happily the rest of the way home.

Mother indicated by her action that she had decided she would go home. She did not press Sharon with arguments or explanations, nor did she give in to her demands. When the child saw that Mother really meant to go home, she respected her mother's decision and joined her.

Firmness is our refusal to give in to the undue demands of the child or to indulge him in his every whim. Once we have made a decision in line with order, we must maintain it. The child soon catches on.

The maintenance of order may require a certain amount of firmness and even quiet pressure, particularly with younger children. When Mother says "No," she has to see to it that the restriction is carried out. Scolding, threatening, or spanking will not succeed because any one of these hostile moves, while they may temporarily stop the undesirable act, usually shifts the conflict into another area causing added misbehavior. Children can learn limitations only through firm insistence. If the child is not willing to dress properly for school, Mother can prevent his going. If he is too noisy and does not want to stop, he can be asked to leave the room. However, such acts of pressure must always be accompanied by giving the child a choice. "You can stay if you are quiet." If he is not quiet, Mother can give him the choice to go by himself or to be taken out. To ask him to leave may appear dictatorial. However, the child does not see it so if he is given a choice and if the request is justified. If the relationship between parents and child is at all friendly, the child is likely to respond, provided the parents do not make a big issue of the matter, with long explanations and apologies or preaching. Quiet insistence is particularly effective and necessary with younger children. Sometimes a steady glance is all that is required. Children sense when parents *mean* it. As one mother in a discussion group put it: "Whenever I am not sure I mean it, Barbara gets by with what she wants. But when *I* know I mean it, she doesn't even bother to tease. She simply drops it."

CHAPTER 8

SHOW RESPECT FOR THE CHILD

Democratic living is based on mutual respect. If only one person in a relationship is granted respect, there is no equality. We must be very sure that we show our respect for the child and his rights. This requires sensitivity in reaching a balance between expecting too little and expecting too much.

Mother and Daddy are extremely proud of two-month-old Gregory, their first child. Whenever the occasion arises, they awaken Gregory and display him to admiring friends.

Gregory has a right to sleep. Mother and Daddy show a lack of respect for him when they ignore his rights.

Gregory cries often and sleeps poorly. He is fed whenever he cries, even if he was fed only an hour before.

Gregory's bodily health and growth depend upon regular rest and food. Under regular routine, the stomach adjusts to a pattern of the work of digestion and then of rest. This promotes the full utilization of food, and establishes a basic order which lasts a lifetime. At first a baby seems to be all stomach. His first contact with a system of order comes through his feeding routine. Baby and stomach have a right to regularity and orderliness. Baby can even participate in the regulation of feeding times.

Pediatricians vary in their advice about feeding schedules. The mother who is following a "demand feeding" program will find that her baby will develop a regular time interval between feedings if she is relaxed and confident in what she is doing. However, if she is filled with anxiety and indulges the baby whenever he stirs, she fails to assist him in developing a schedule and stimulates him to make undue demands. Irregular feeding schedules show a lack of respect for baby and for order.

Peter, nine, is an only child and deeply desires to please his parents. They have extremely high standards for behavior and scholarship. A broad program of activities was arranged for him, and excellent performance in all fields was expected from him. Any grade less than "A" was a calamity. He must be a leader in Scout activities, shine in athletic programs at the "Y," master his piano lessons to perfection, know the proper name for each rock in his collection, make his model planes perfectly, and memorize his Bible passages without error. He must at all times show impeccable manners and tidy grooming. Peter is considered a brilliant and extraordinary child by all who know him. But he has one fault which his parents have been unable to correct: he bites his fingernails to the quick. He also has nightmares and a nervous habit of shaking his shoulders.

Mother and Daddy are unknowingly brutal in their "great expectations." Since Peter is driven by the desire to please, he is easily led into any endeavor. Since he is above average in intelligence and tries very hard, he manages to meet these expectations. But he shows signs of inner rebellion and apprehension. He feels that he only has significance as long as he pleases his parents and is on top. He doesn't dare to lose his position by rebelling openly against their demands.

He can only protest in his sleep. Peter is headed for disaster. Mother and Daddy display a deep disrespect for Peter as a person; they use him merely as a means of enhancing their own prestige. Peter cannot respect himself when his whole life is directed into serving his parents' desire for his greatness.

Only when we have confidence in a child and his ability can we show respect for him. But this does not mean that we may make demands that serve our ambition.

Eighteen-month-old Pam tried to climb up into a chair in the living room. She slipped, bumped her chin, and bit her lip. Mother remained calm when she saw the blood start trickling. She said cheerfully, "Try again, Pam. You can do it." Pam licked her bleeding lip and returned to the business of learning.

Cruel? Not at all. If Mother had made an issue of the injury, Pam would have lost courage. Since Mother was unimpressed by blood, Pam could afford to take it in her stride —an extremely valuable lesson!

Jeff, nine, traded a valuable geode in his rock collection for a much less valuable, but to him much more interesting, fossil. When Daddy discovered the trade he was furious—first, because the other boy was fourteen and knew more of the relative values of the rocks, and second, because Jeff had not consulted him. Daddy "straightened out" the affair, causing a rift in the friendship between the boys and making Jeff feel belittled and inferior.

The trade decision was Jeff's; this decision should have been respected. The situation can be handled so as to show respect for Jeff and allow him to keep his self-respect. When Jeff showed Daddy the fossil, Daddy could have shown the same interest as usual and dropped the matter for the time being. On another day Daddy could help Jeff to discover the relative value of his items with no mention of the trade. Jeff will see for himself that he has been "taken" without being subjected to humiliation. When Daddy "straightened out" the affair, he implied that Jeff should have known better and that he was deeply at fault. Yet, never having had an experience of this nature, how could Jeff know? Daddy expected too much of Jeff. The boy must also be shown that having made a decision, he is honor bound to abide by it. In this manner, a conflict situation is turned into a teaching situation, and friendliness is maintained.

On a family outing at the amusement park, Robert, eleven, pestered Mother for another ride on the bumper cars. Ruth, nine, and Betty, seven and a half, wanted to go to the Penny Arcade. The group started walking toward the Arcade while Robert continued to beg. Mother crossly refused. Whenever Robert got excited or tense, he developed a speech defect and sounded like a babbling baby. The more he begged, the more obvious his speech defect became. Finally, Mother turned on him, imitated his speech, and made fun of him. Ruth and Betty burst into laughter Robert pressed his lips together, fighting back tears, and lagged behind the group.

Humiliating a child for any reason whatsoever shows intense lack of respect and is certainly not a training device. The fact that Robert has developed a speech defect when under stress shows that he is already in trouble. Mockery reinforces his faulty self-concept that he is helpless in the face of adversity and that there is no hope for him. Respect for Robert can be shown if Mother refuses to accept his mistaken evaluation of himself. A quiet, "We are going to the Arcade now, son," will solve the problem of the begging.

Family dissension at amusement parks is a frequent sight. It can be solved so easily. Before the family leaves home, a definite decision is reached as to how much money each may spend. Each must understand that he has this much money and no more. Restrictions, for reasons of safety, about what may be ridden are also understood before leaving home. If

parents have established respect for their firmness, the outing can now be fun. The children are then allowed freedom
to decide what to ride and how fast to go from one ride to
another; in this way, they quickly learn how to budget their
money and their time so as to make the fun last longer.
Constant parental reminders and admonitions, on the other
hand, will turn the situation into one of conflict, bickering,
and disappointment for all.

Respect for the child means that we regard him as a
human with the same rights to make decisions as we have.
But similar "rights" does not mean that the child may *do*
what the adults do. Everyone in the family has a different
role to play—and each has the right to be respected in that
role.

CHAPTER 9

INDUCE RESPECT FOR ORDER

ONCE we have established respect for parental firmness and shown our own respect for the child, it is much easier to guide the child further into learning respect for order.

A child has no respect for order if he is shielded from the results of disorder. He develops respect for a sharp knife if he cuts himself, for fire that can burn if mishandled, for a bicycle that tips if he doesn't keep it balanced, for a moving baseball if he doesn't duck. All these represent an irrefutable order that he can't escape. He demonstrates compliance with the order of gravity when he throws his foot out as his bike tips. He shows deference to the force of a flying baseball when, up at bat, he ducks a badly thrown ball. He learns to live within the limitations of his physical world and to put the physical laws to his use. No amount of talk can teach a child how to balance a bicycle. He learns through experience. We aid him by putting training wheels on his bike, but he learns the art of balancing it by himself. So, in every field where respect for order is needed, the child must learn through experience—through action, not through words. We are obligated to add the training wheels and to remove them gradually as his skill develops. We must take advantage of situations that provide training experience.

Grace, nine, sat at the desk in the living room, writing. Wilma, seven, was on the floor cutting out paper dolls. Scraps of paper lay all around. "Clean up when you're finished, girls," Mother commented as she passed through the living room. "We will," Wilma answered with heavy disgust. Her face had an expression that signified "Here we go again!" The next time that Mother went through the living room both girls were watching TV. The desk was a mess of papers, and the scraps and paper dolls lay ignored on the floor. "Be sure to clean up, girls," Mother admonished again. "Yes, Mother," came the chorus, automatically, and still with a drop in voice to indicate disgust. A little later Mother noticed that the girls had had a snack and had left their glasses on top of the TV set. Cookie crumbs were on the floor. "For heaven's sake, will you pick up after yourselves? Look at the mess you've made!" "All *right*, Mother," said Grace in an exasperated tone. "We will."

Not long after this, Mother found Grace lying on her bed reading and Wilma outside playing. The living room was a shambles. She called Wilma in and burst forth angrily, "Get busy and clean up. We have company coming for dinner. You know I want this room to look decent. You yourselves helped me to clean it up this morning. Why can't you pick up when you're through? Before you go on to something else, you should put away what you've been doing. You know that." On and on Mother went with her angry preaching. Grace and Wilma sullenly gathered things up and put them away while Mother hovered wrathfully over them.

Of course Grace and Wilma know that they should pick up. But they have no respect for Mother's words, nor for the needs of the situation. The fact that Mother is still reminding the girls to pick up after themselves at their age indicates that many years of talking and preaching have done no good. At seven and nine, the girls still disregard order. And the minute Mother speaks, they placate her with promises which they don't intend to keep, visibly resenting the reminder.

Lack of respect for order is one of the most common

complaints of parents today. It seems that children in general take this form of rebellion against adults. Putting things away is a demand made by all parents and resented by most children. The more Mother shows her concern for tidiness, the more vulnerable she becomes to the effective resistance of her children.

Children need to experience order as a part of freedom. Where there is disorder, there is loss of freedom for all.

This consitutes a problem in mutual respect. Respect for the girls denies Mother the right to "force" her concept of order upon them. Her respect for herself denies her the right to pick up after them, to run after them, and to allow them to put her into their service, doing their jobs for them. Instead, she can induce in the girls a respect for order. How can this be done? She can determine what *she* will do.

If she finds things belonging to the girls out of place, she may pick them up and put them away—not for the girls, but for herself, because they are in her way. However, she alone knows where they are, since she picked them up. Since the girls didn't put their belongings away, how can they know where they are? Mother remains firm about this, although friendly. This is not punishment. The logical result of not putting something away is that one doesn't know where it is. The paper dolls disappear. The pen and paper likewise. Since snack dishes and glasses aren't put away, there can be no snacks in the living room. All of these actions are done with cheerfulness and without rancor, and without the usual stream of words. In no way must these actions appear as punishment or retaliation. The girls may be as disorderly as they like—in their own room. Mother need not concern herself about the disorder they create in their own room, but she may allow them to experience the consequences. Instead of feeling defeated because she can't "make" the girls be tidy, she can refuse her co-operation in changing bed linens or cleaning up as long as the room is a shambles. The girls may soon be fed up, especially when socks get lost or blouses can't be found. In order to avoid overwhelming discouragement over the disorder, Mother may offer to help clean the room once a week if the girls *want* her help. When she cleans *with* the girls, she must refrain from any remark concerning disorder—any comment of "See how awful this is—how can you stand it," etc. All conversation should be pleasant and concerned with anything except the disorder. Gradually, as the girls discover that their disorder does not upset Mother and that she refuses to make an interesting game of "who wins?" they may decide that order is more comfortable. If their disorder in the rest of the house results in the disappearance of items belonging to them, they may be more careful to put them away.

Jean, three, left her tricycle in the driveway. Mother called to her to bring it to the back yard. Jean ignored her and continued to play in the sandbox. Mother angrily yanked the girl up, spanked her, and followed her to the tricycle. "I've told you to put that tricycle away when you are through riding it. And I mean for you to do it." Then Mother pulled the tricycle with one hand and her crying daughter with the other.

Mother's use of force fails to teach Jean the need for order: it merely creates a feeling of hostility and rebellion. Quiet insistence will prove more effective. Mother may bring the tricycle in and put it where it will be difficult for a three-year-old to get it out without help. When the child wants it again, Mother may say, "I'm sorry, Jean. Since you did not feel like putting your tricycle away the last time you rode it, you may not have it out this time. You may try again this afternoon." This last remark gives Jean encouragement so that she may want to put the tricycle away herself the next time she has it. Or Mother can quietly take her child by the hand and both of them can put the tricycle away.

Eleven-year-old Clay is frequently late for dinner. He gets so involved in his healthy boy activities that Mother pardons him every time. When he does get in, she heats up his dinner for him and waits to clean up the kitchen until he is finished.

Clay has it made! Mother is his devoted servant who cheerfully puts herself out to serve his interests. He feels that this extra service is his due. But he has no respect for order since none is demanded of him. He has learned that good play relations with the guys and healthy activities that develop strong bodies are values which Mother holds very high. Why should he respect the dinner hour? It gets moved around to suit his desires.

Clay's healthy body and his relationships with his friends *are* important. But these won't suffer any loss if he also learns to respect order. Mother can tell Clay that dinner will be served at six o'clock hereafter and then refuse to serve him later. He has the choice as to whether or not he wants to be home on time for meals—and this may become important to him if Mother is unconcerned about his food intake.

Mother was having a very difficult time getting Doris, four, to see that she must put her things away. The family, which also included fourteen-month-old Kevin, was crowded into a tiny apartment. One day Mother attended a Child Guidance Center. That evening she discussed with Daddy an idea she had received. He agreed to follow through. The next morning Doris left her pajamas on the floor and strewed her toys about as usual. Near noon Mother asked, "Do you want to put your things away?" "No." "Well, how would you like to have a day when you didn't have to put anything away?" "That would be swell!" Doris exclaimed. "All right. But may I have the same kind of day and not put anything away?" "Sure," answered Doris with a shrug. For the rest of the day Mother left everything she touched out of place. Otherwise she talked and played with her daughter as usual. She proposed to Doris that they look through all of her clothes to see what needed mending. Doris joined her and they worked together. However, Mother left all the clothes on the child's bed. Kevin's clothes, toys, and bottles were likewise left out of place. When Daddy came home the apartment was a complete mess. He draped his coat over the doll carriage, hung his tie on the lamp, kicked his shoes off and left them in the middle of the floor, and he settled down to play with the children as usual. He acted as if nothing unusual were going on. While dinner was cooking, Mother fed Kevin. The table was littered with Doris' papers, crayons, and paints, so there was no place to set dinner. Mother went into the living room and started reading a magazine. "What about dinner, Mother?" Daddy asked after a bit. "It's ready," Mother replied. "Well, how about it? Shall we eat?" "Can't," said Mother from behind the magazine. "Why not?" "No place to put the dishes." Daddy settled down with the paper. "I'm hungry, Mother," Doris said. "I am, too," answered Mother. Doris studied the situation silently, walked into the kitchen, looked at the table, and came back into the living room. She pushed her blocks around with her foot for a minute and then returned to the kitchen. Mother and Daddy continued to read, knowing full well that Doris was clearing the table. Pretty soon she came back and said quietly, "Mother, we have a place to eat now." Mother immediately set dinner out, and they all enjoyed a gay conversation.

When Doris got ready to go to bed she couldn't find her pajamas. "I'm sorry that you can't find them, honey." "And how am I supposed to get into bed with all that stuff on it?" the child demanded. "That will be awkward, won't it?" "Mother, I don't like this!" Doris burst into tears. "What should we do about it?" asked Mother. "I guess we better put everything away," her daughter replied.

Three things made this experience a success. First, Mother remained friendly and kept the atmosphere pleasant. Second, she refrained from any preaching. She rarely spoke about the matter at hand—almost to the point of verbal shorthand. But she talked about everything else. Third—and most important—Mother *felt* the spirit of the teaching experience. She had no hidden intention of *making* Doris put things away nor any sense of getting even.

A maneuvered situation such as this must be used very rarely. Its value lies in the dramatic impact of an experience with disorder shared by the whole family. This impact would be lost if the teaching experience were repeated too soon.

Another method for dealing with children's belongings left out of place is to have a large cardboard box into which everything goes. Mother picks up what is in her way—not what the children leave out of place in their own rooms. Everything from rubbers to toys goes into the box. Fishing things out of this box can become quite exasperating.

If the children's rooms become too bad, Mother can simply avoid going into them. When the clean clothes are ready to be put away, she leaves them somewhere else because she doesn't like to go into so much disorder. Besides, how can she tell where to put the clean clothes?

Imagination will aid us to find friendly ways to avoid forcing children to obey order and yet to provide experience with disorder, which may induce them to comply with the needs of the situation.

In most cases of a gross disrespect of order there is a profound disturbance in the relationship between parents and children. This cannot be corrected by any one means such as the use of logical consequences. The parents need to develop a plan to rectify their faulty relationship.

CHAPTER 10

INDUCE RESPECT FOR THE RIGHTS OF OTHERS

Six-year-old Cary seemed to have a keen sense for music and enjoyed playing his records on his own player. One day Mother was quite dismayed when she discovered her son playing her records on the hi-fi in the living room. He had scratched several good records by mishandling the needle. Mother explained to him the value of the records, how they should be taken care of, and how much they meant to her. The boy wiggled restlessly. She finally extracted a promise from him never to touch her records again, but to wait for her, and they would listen to them together. However, the next day Cary broke his promise and again played records on the hi-fi.

Cary has no right to play Mother's records. Mother must be firm about this. All the explaining is not only futile—as is the obtaining of a promise—but it also misses the point. All Mother should say is, "Cary, these are my records. I am the only one who plays them." Every time that Cary attempts to use the hi-fi, Mother may ask him if he wishes to leave the room himself or be taken out. This approach displays respect for the child's right to make a decision. Mother is firm in her decision that Cary must leave the room, but leaves the manner of his going up to him.

This illustrates the subtle line between being a dictator and demanding one's own rights. The difference lies in the intent. Mother does not demand that Cary play his own records. She shows him her intention to demand respect for her own rights.

Every time Ellen, four, was displeased by what her mother did, she would slap or kick or even bite her mother. Mother did not believe in striking children and was dismayed by her daughter's behavior. She tried to make Ellen feel sorry enough to stop it by showing how deeply hurt she was. The child was unimpressed.

Poor Mother! She believes that the children have all the rights! In a situation between equals, each one has the same rights. If Ellen has the right to slap or kick or bite, Mother has the same right. Mother is obligated to demonstrate this to Ellen. The secret lies in the manner in which it is done. When Ellen slaps, Mother can say cheerfully, "I see you want to play a slapping game." Then Mother slaps Ellen—and doesn't pull her punch. She really slaps. The child may become hotly incensed and slap again. Still in the attitude of a game, Mother slaps again—hard. Mother continues this game until Ellen quits. It has been our experience that few children wish to play this game a second time! They may forget and slap impulsively again, but when presented the second time with the statement about a slapping game, they beat a hasty retreat.

Occasionally a parent may assume what a child believes to be his own special right. This works delightfully in many situations. Without saying a word at all, when Mother sees her six-year-old sucking his thumb, she starts sucking hers! He resents this! He feels that he has a right to do this, but Mother doesn't. We have seen these children give up thumb-sucking when Mother took up the habit. (But one cannot rely on this alone!)

Penny, seven, and Pat, five, became obnoxious whenever Daddy and Mother had friends in for bridge. They ran about the house in their night clothes, "showed off" in every conceivable manner, and refused to go to bed. Mother and Daddy would put up with it for a while, but eventually Daddy spanked both of them and angrily plopped them into their beds.

Mother and Daddy have a right to an evening with their friends without interference from the children. Before the guests arrive, the children can be told, "We want to see our friends without trouble from you. You may be polite and tell them 'hello,' but then you must stay out of the living room. Now, do we take you over to Auntie's tonight,* or will you manage so that you can remain with us in the house?" The decision of the children must be respected. If they decide to remain at home and fail to behave, they should be removed upon the next occasion without being consulted first. The next time after this, they are again given a choice.

On pages 88–89 we showed how Kathy was taught respect for her parents' right to sleep.

* If no aunt is available, one can employ a baby sitter to stay with the children in their room.

CHAPTER 11

ELIMINATE CRITICISM AND MINIMIZE MISTAKES

Eight-year-old Charles had just finished his thank-you letter to Grandmother. Mother asked to see it. Reluctantly, the boy pushed it toward her. "Oh, Charles, look at your awful penmanship. And why can't you make your lines straight? You have three words spelled wrong. Here! Copy it over. You can't send a mess like that to Grandmother." Mother printed the correct spelling over the words and Charles started over again. He kept making more mistakes, discarding one page after another until finally he burst into angry tears and flung the pen down. "I can't get it right at all," he yelled. "That will be enough of that," Mother commanded. "You may do something else for a half hour and then come back to this."

OUR EMPHASIS ON MISTAKES is disastrous. Charles enjoyed writing his letter, and Grandmother would have been delighted with it, mistakes and all. As it is now, he hates the letter and the anguish it causes him. When Mother centered her attention on the mistakes, she directed her son's attention from the positive to the negative. He became afraid of making mistakes. This fear squeezed him so badly that he only made more mistakes. Now he is really discouraged. And here is the disaster. When we pay constant attention to mistakes, we discourage our children. *We cannot build on weakness—only on strength.*

How much Charles would gain if Mother would commend his thoughtfulness in writing to Grandmother! This would put the emphasis on the positive and give him a surge of pleasure. He would be inclined to want to do more thoughtful things. Furthermore, Mother can find some well-formed letters and acknowledge them. "I see you have made a very nice letter C here. That is good. You are learning." Charles would then feel stimulated to make better letters because his confidence in his ability to do so has had a boost. Mother could let the misspelled words go. His desire to communicate is the important thing for now. Mother expects too much of Charles.

We spend a great deal of our time with our children, watching to see what they do wrong and immediately hopping on them for it. Our prevailing system of training our children seems to be based on the idea that they must be "trained" out of faults and into virtues. However, anyone who stops to think will realize that we really do follow our noses. If our nose points at mistakes, we arrive just there. If we center our children's attention upon what they do well, express our confidence in their ability, and give them encouragement, the mistakes and faults may die from a lack of feeding.

As it is, however, we live in a sort of fear that our children will grow up badly, learn bad habits, develop wrong attitudes, do things the wrong way. We watch over them constantly and try to prevent some mistake. We are constantly correcting, constantly admonishing. Such an approach shows lack of faith in our children; it is humiliating and discouraging. With all this emphasis on the negative, where can we expect the child to find the energy to proceed toward achievement?

When constantly corrected, the child not only gets the feeling that he is always wrong but may become fearful of making a mistake. Such fear may lead to his reluctance to do anything, since he might do it wrong. Fear may press upon him so much that he loses his ability to function. He gets the impression that unless he is perfect, he has no value. However, perfection is an impossible goal, and striving for it seldom leads to improvement, but more often to giving up in despair.

We all make mistakes. Very few are disastrous. Many times we won't even know that a given action is a mistake until after it is done and we see the results! Sometimes we even *have* to make the mistake in order to find out that it *is* a mistake. *We must have the courage to be imperfect*—and to allow our children also to be imperfect. Only in this way can we function, progress, and grow. Our children will maintain their courage and learn more readily if we minimize the mistakes and direct their attention toward the positive. "What is to be done now that the mistake is made" leads to progress forward and stimulates courage. Making a mistake is not nearly as important as what we do about it afterward.

Margaret, ten, burst into tears as she took the burnt cookies out of the oven. She had had no trouble following the instructions on the mix box, but now her cookies were ruined. Mother, smelling the burnt odor, came to the kitchen. "What happened, darling?" "I burned the cookies," Margaret sobbed. "Yes, I can see that. Let's find out why. I know you didn't do it intentionally. It isn't going to help to cry, honey. Of course you feel bad, but let's see why it happened." Faced with a direction in which to go from here, the child stopped sobbing and examined the situation. She and Mother checked back over the instructions and what had been done until they discovered that Margaret had miscalculated the time on the automatic timer. "Oh, I see what I did wrong." "Good," said Mother. "Let's clean up this mess and then you can try again."

Mother turned disaster and the evidence of failure into a teaching situation. She offered no reprimand over the lost food and no criticism for error. She matter-of-factly demonstrated to Margaret that a mistake isn't the end of everything —that the thing to do is to find out where there was a misjudgment. She acknowledged her daughter's dismay without being overly concerned and led her out of it by joining with her to search for the reason for the mistake. Then she immediately encouraged Margaret to try again. Discouragement was dissipated by Mother's support and sympathy.

Many times when a child makes a mistake it is the result of inexperience or faulty judgment. He may already be distressed over the results. To scold him or condemn him further adds insult to injury.

Daddy went to his workbench to get a screwdriver. His anger rose at what he saw. A model plane lay on his bench, with screwdriver, pliers, hammer, and wrenches scattered about. The model plane, together with the whole surface of the bench and all the tools, was covered with a coat of aluminum paint. The can of spray aluminum paint lay on its side on the floor. Furious, Daddy called his ten-year-old son. "Just look at the mess you've made," he exclaimed when Stan arrived. "Why can't you learn to be tidy? What right have you got messing up my bench like this? All my tools covered with paint! What did you do it for? Answer me," he yelled as Stan stood tongue-tied and frightened.

Stan fought back tears. "Daddy, I just wanted to paint my model. I didn't know it would spray so far. Then I didn't know what to do about it." "Why didn't you tell me about it at the time, instead of waiting till I found out?" "I was scared you'd get mad," Stan muttered. "Well, I certainly am mad! You knew you did wrong. That's why you sneaked away. I'm going to thrash you for this, young man."

Daddy's anger is understandable. However, the coat of aluminum paint over the tools didn't affect their function. In his anger, Daddy didn't hear the distress in Stan's voice, nor did he recognize the dilemma the boy was in. When Daddy reacted as he did, he reaffirmed Stan's fear of his father's anger and moved him even further away from coming to him for help. The thrashing didn't restore the bench to order nor teach Stan how to use a can of spray paint.

What approach would be helpful?

First, Daddy's immediate impulse of anger should give way to the realization that Stan didn't intend to paint the whole bench. One look could have shown what happened. Daddy then can use the situation as a teaching opportunity. The fact that the boy went ahead on his own shows that he has courage.

Suppose it had gone this way:

Daddy called Stan to the workroom. "I can see that you got into difficulty here, son. Can you tell me what happened?" Stan, embarrassed, answered, "Well, I was trying to paint my model. I didn't know the paint would spread so far." "So you learned that spray paint is different from brush paint, didn't you?" "Yeah, I sure did," Stan answered, feeling relieved by Daddy's friendliness. "Have you any ideas about how to manage spray paint the next time?" "Well," the boy considered. "I guess I could spread papers around." "How would it be if you took the side out of a carton, put your plane inside and sprayed from the open side?" Daddy suggested. "Hey, that would work keen!" "Now how about the tools on the bench?" "Well, gee, I don't know. They aren't hurt any, I guess." "What would have happened if they had been hanging on the board where they belong?" "They couldn't have got all painted," Stan acknowledged with a small grin at this subtle reminder to put things away. "Have you any ideas about what should be done with the tools, now?" "I guess I'll have to use some turp to clean them up." "Turp won't affect dry paint, Stan." "Well, what else?" "The handles will have to stay aluminum-colored, I guess. But I think a good polishing with steel wool will clean up the metal." "Okay, I'll try it."

Stan willingly went to work to repair the damage. His father and he are friends; harmony is maintained, and he has learned from his mistake.

Mother was putting spaghetti sauce into the serving dish. "Can I help?" asked June. "Oh, June, I don't know. You are so clumsy! Well. All right. Here. See if you can get this onto the table without spilling it. Be very careful now." Mother handed June the dish full of sauce. June walked very slowly, her eyes focused on the contents of the dish, watching it carefully so that it wouldn't tip. Her foot caught against the leg of the chair; the bowl tipped; the contents splashed over onto the table, down the front of her dress, and onto the carpet. "June! You clumsy thing! What *is* the matter with you? Didn't I just get through telling you to be careful? Why can't you do anything without being so clumsy?"

June was trying so hard not to be "clumsy" and spill the sauce that she walked right into the chair and succeeded in doing the very thing she was afraid she would do. If Mother had shown real confidence in June's ability to carry the dish full of sauce, June would have been able to steer her course more accurately. Now her opinion of herself as being clumsy has again been reinforced, and she has another failure to her credit.

Naturally, children make many mistakes and do many things wrong. If we have a general critical attitude, we may unknowingly promote an incidental deviation from desirable behavior into a starting point for a serious and often permanent deficiency or fault. For instance, many young children stutter occasionally, but the defect disappears if no issue is made of it. However, since we feel so dreadfully responsible for preventing or correcting any undesirable act—since we feel *something has to be done*—we are prone to hop on the child at the first sign of any "wrong" behavior. Far from correcting it, we actually increase the difficulty because the child finds it to his benefit to continue, either because he gains extra attention or because he can be victorious in defeating our pressure. Criticism, therefore, does not "teach" children; it only stimulates them to maintain their objectionable actions or deficiencies.

In order to guide our children effectively we need to be alert to what is going on. Is this a mistake? Is discouragement or poor judgment or lack of knowledge at the bottom of the wrongdoing? Or is there a hidden purpose behind the act? The stories of Margaret (pages 108–109) and of Stan (page 109) illustrate a lack of experience and of poor judgment. Charles (page 106) and June were discouraged. The first two children need instruction without criticism; the second two need encouragement to discover their abilities.

However, as we have shown, an act of wrongdoing could be the result of a mistaken goal—it could have a purpose. If this is true, it is no longer a *mistake*, but a *fault*.

Mother met a friend in the park where she and five-year-old Sharon where having a picnic lunch. The child clung to Mother with her finger in her mouth as she was introduced. "Come on, now, Sharon, don't be shy," Mother begged. Then, turning to her friend, "I don't know why she is so shy. No one else in the family is." The girl withdrew further. The friend stooped down and tried to get her to respond. Sharon continued unsmilingly to look at Mother's friend from under lowered eyebrows. When the friend finally gave up and started talking to Mother, Sharon stood silent for a while and then tugged at Mother, climbed onto her lap, and put her face up for a kiss.

Since Sharon has a purpose in her shyness, it is futile to tell her to stop. Paying attention to her fault (or mistaken approach) merely reinforces it. Sharon identifies herself as "the shy one" of the family. This gives her a certain distinction. When we examine what the result of her shyness is, we discover that Sharon becomes the center of considerable concern. People try hard to get her to respond, and she becomes the center of their attention. (Sometimes one gets the impression with shy children that they are secretly laughing at the antics of the adults!) Shyness pays off. Why *should* Sharon stop it?

If Sharon failed to get all of these interesting reactions there would be no point in continuing to be shy. Mother can introduce her with pride but in a casual manner and, when she fails to respond, continue the conversation with her friend. Sharon's shyness would be minimized and ignored. If the friend upsets things by saying, "My, she's shy, isn't she" (as friends are apt to do), Mother can respond, "No, she isn't shy. She just doesn't feel like talking right now. She will later."

If we want a child to overcome a fault, we must discover the purpose behind the behavior, then, *without talking about it* at all, act in such a way that the purpose is no longer fulfilled. Most of the time this action on our part consists of *not acting*, of failing to respond, of avoiding our first impulse.

Isobel, six and a half, had an eight-year-old brother, Fred, who was a charming, happy-go-lucky roughneck. Isobel was in tears most of the time. Mother, Daddy, and Fred called her "crybaby." They scolded her outright for crying, and Fred teased her, made her cry, and then showed his contempt. One day the family went to the swimming pool. Both children jumped from the car and raced ahead. Isobel fell down and skinned her knee slightly. She burst into sobs and was inconsolable. "Aw, she's always crying!" Fred exclaimed in contempt as he walked off. "That's not a bad hurt, Isobel," Daddy said sternly. "Now stop your crying and come on in the pool." "It hurts! Put something on!" the girl sobbed as she hugged her leg. "Stop your crying, now," Daddy admonished. "It isn't bad enough to put anything on. Once you get in the pool you'll forget all about it." "Stop being a crybaby, Isobel," Mother added in disgust. "Come on, let's swim." Isobel continued to cry and refused to move. A favorite aunt came running up and was enthusiastically greeted. Isobel's sobs increased. Aunt Edith noticed her, bent over her, asked what was the trouble, and offered her comfort. But the child's sobs continued. Daddy finally spoke up. "Edith, you can sit there and give her sympathy for three hours and she'll keep right on crying. That's what she wants. She's just a crybaby. Let's go swimming and just let her sit there and cry." The family all jumped into the pool and left Isobel to her own devices. A little later she joined the group, reluctantly at first, but soon enjoying the water.

A crying child usually gets our sympathy. Our hearts are deeply touched by the suffering of a child. Isobel discovered this advantage very early. The trouble is that she overworked it, and her family became disgusted. However, crying still had its advantage. They all *notice* the crying, comment about it, scold, and generally fuss over her. As the poor abused baby, she continues to maintain her place. Her view of herself is reinforced every time someone calls her a "crybaby." The family finally caught on, left her to cry and went swimming without her—but not before they had satisfied the purpose of the crying. Isobel squeezed all she could out of the situation.

If Mother and Daddy want to help Isobel to grow up and stop being a "crybaby," they must first recognize that the purpose of her crying is to gain undue attention. Then they must stop talking about the crying, stop identifying Isobel with her crying, and finally ignore it. In this particular instance, *one* parent (whoever happened to arrive first) can casually examine the injury, evaluate the seriousness of it, and, finding it minor, say, "I'm sorry you hurt yourself. It will feel better in a minute. Come on in the pool when you are ready," and they all go in. As soon as Isobel sees that crying isn't going to produce results, she may decide to change her behavior. The same procedure should be followed every time she cries—casual acceptance of her right to cry together with a statement that she may join the rest of the family when she is ready. This technique of minimizing the fault and removing the results must be accompanied by paying attention to her when she is happy and co-operative.

We must make a particular effort to separate the deed from the doer. This is especially important today because we have developed such a complex of name-calling—"cry-baby," "tattletale," "scatterbrain," "liar," etc. Children need to be recognized as good children who misbehave because they are unhappy or have found that it pays off. When we label a child, we see him as we have labeled him. So does he. He identifies himself with his label. This reinforces his faulty self-concept and prevents his moving in a constructive direction. When we realize that it is not the *child* that is bad, but only what he does, the child senses it and responds to this distinction. He becomes aware of our faith in *him*, which gives him added encouragement toward overcoming his difficulties, which seem less to him now that we minimize them.

CHAPTER 12

MAINTAIN ROUTINE

"Where's Penny?" Daddy asked as he sat down to breakfast. "I thought she ought to sleep late this morning, dear." "How come?" "Well, she was up so late last night. She wanted to see you before she went to bed." "But I told you I would be very late." "I know, but she doesn't understand that. So I let her stay up until she fell asleep." "What about school today?" "Oh, it won't matter. It's only kindergarten. I'll write a note that she wasn't well this morning." "I don't know, Meg. It seems to me that Penny ought to follow some sort of rules." "Oh, there's plenty of time for her to learn about rules. She's so little!"

D<small>ADDY</small> is right. Penny does need a routine to follow. Routine is to a child what walls are to a house; it gives boundaries and dimensions to his life. No child feels comfortable in a situation in which he doesn't know exactly what to expect. Routine gives a feeling of security. An established routine also provides a sense of order from which freedom grows. Allowing Penny the "freedom" to stay up late at night denied her her right to proper rest, cluttered the next day and threw it off balance, and denied her the right to her school experience. This is not freedom, but license. Penny is in no position to develop wisdom about her decisions if Mother deprives her of the consequences by giving a false excuse to the school. Penny, like many children, searches for the comfort of limitations and boundaries. She seeks to find how far she can go. And when the sky is the limit, she becomes bewildered, demands the right to do as she pleases to see if she can find a limitation; and then, suddenly, one day she behaves in such an outrageous manner that someone in her environment drops the axe and she is left stunned, wondering what happened.

It is the obligation of the parents to set up a routine within which the family can function comfortably; to establish and maintain a daily order and then let the children fall into line. No child is ever too young to experience order. Once this has been established, children sense it and will know what to do as a matter of course.

If you wanted to travel from Chicago to Los Angeles, you wouldn't get into your car and start driving freely down any road that happened to appeal to you. You would follow a definite pattern of highways. So it is with our children's education in living. Los Angeles is the goal we set for our car journey; social integration and self-sufficiency are the goals of parental guidance. We can only arrive there by following definite patterns of highways. We have a choice as to what routine we wish to establish for the family, just as we have a choice of several highways by which to reach Los Angeles. But a routine is needed. It should not be so rigid that there is no room for flexibility. There are always occasions when a routine has to be broken to fit an unexpected need. However, such breaks should be the exception, rather than the rule; and they should not be made for the convenience of the parents nor for the satisfaction of a child's whims.

During the summer months, Ginny and Lynne did just about as they pleased. They stayed up late at night, ate breakfast whenever they got up, had snacks and soft drinks whenever they desired, dodged household tasks by having urgent play plans with their friends, and kept Mother hopping with their demands to be taken here and there in the car. By mid-July Mother frequently sighed, "I'll be so glad when school starts again and things settle down around here."

It seems to be a widespread practice to allow children freedom from the pressures of time schedules during summer vacation. Naturally, the schedule and routine will change; but it does not have to lead to anarchy. A laissez-faire approach to summer vacation gives the child the impression that school—or work—is obnoxious and that to be "free" from such demands is desirable. This is a false concept. Going to school is the child's function in life, just as going to work is Daddy's and homemaking is Mother's function. All of these functions need routine or they become disturbed. Vacations are necessary. A vacation is a time of change in routine, a means of refreshing ourselves; a change in pace, in activity. But it cannot mean an abandonment of routine altogether. Summer routine may vary from the school-year routine; bedtime hours may be arranged so that the family has more time for fun together, rising hours adjusted to the sleep needs, mealtimes shifted to adapt to new summer activities— all make the change from school routine to summer vacation obvious. And yet we have to maintain a system of order; otherwise co-operation and social harmony are impossible.

Let us return to the story of Joyce on page 57. Joyce demands constant attention from Mother. If Mother had an established routine for playtime, it would give her an "out" when she wishes to resist her child's undue demands. When she is sure of a given playtime with Mother, Joyce will be more ready to accept the demand for order implied in Mother's refusal to give in to her constant requests.

Children do need our attention. What better method of establishing harmonious, happy relationships than a definite and unchangeable playtime? This time belongs to the child. He knows he can count on it. If both Mother and child are aware of this period in the day as a time for having fun together, both will be inclined to drop whatever conflict situation may have developed in order to make the most of the fun-time. What a delightful relationship ensues! (Sadly enough, some children are so deeply entrenched in their non-co-operative attitudes that they do not even wish to play with their parents. They don't consider them as their friends.)

Or let us consider the situation of Peggy on page 60. Mother and Peggy got into a power contest that could have been avoided if a "routine" had been strongly felt and Peggy had known that Mother would be firm about it. Bedtime is bedtime. Period. If children experience the firmness of a routine, they seldom feel inspired to transgress in an attempt to find the boundaries. Naturally, if a power contest has developed, the child will use each routine as a point of his attack. Only when routine is experienced casually, as a matter of course, with quiet insistence and without verbal battles, can the parents win compliance to a system of order within the family. Naturally, where common activities are involved, it will be easy to have one routine for the children and adults. An example of this is mealtime. However, the different function of each member of the family may well require different routines; but these differences must be clearly within the range of the different functions and must not occur in areas where all members function in the same way. The one-year-old has a much earlier bedtime than the nine-year-old, and his is earlier than that of his parents.

Again, in the situation with Clay on page 100, Mother could resolve the difficulty if there were an established routine about dinner time and all members of the family ate at that time. It is only reasonable to assume that one would not arbitrarily set the established dinner hour at a time inconvenient to the members of the family. Each family must work out the pattern that will serve the interests of the family as a whole. There can be no stereotyped routine which fits all families. But it is usually up to Mother to establish the routine and to set the boundaries within which her family will grow and develop. Whenever a child transgresses the order, Mother is obligated to insist quietly that it be maintained. Serious disruption of family routine results only when parents permit constant transgressions.

Also, it is usually up to Mother to establish the standards by which the family lives. Such practices as beds made before going about daily tasks, living room tidy before Daddy comes home, appearances at the table, Sunday dinner in the dining room, the manner of celebrating holidays—these are all part of the cultural values that we hand down to our children. They become part of the routine under which we live.

Once, in a Parent Discussion Group, it was discovered that there was a common problem of deplorable table manners. It came out in the discussion that the habit of casual dining in the kitchen might be a factor. Each of the eighteen mothers present decided to try serving dinner more formally in the dining room and to report the results at the next meeting. Those who lacked dining rooms were going to be more formal in the dining area of the kitchen. The following week each mother was astonished to find that the others reported similar improvements in table manners. Each felt that the added work involved was more than compensated for by the improvement in the family atmosphere. (Could this have anything to do with the present demand of homemakers for a dining room in new home construction?)

These patterns for living that we establish make up part of the family routine. Daily small bits add up to an enriched and more pleasant life.

CHAPTER 13

TAKE TIME FOR TRAINING

CHILDREN need definite training for the many functions of living. Naturally, the child will pick up much knowledge through observation. But we can't depend upon his learning everything this way. He needs training in how to dress, how to tie his shoes, how to eat, how to wash and bathe, how to cross the street; and, gradually, as he grows older, how to perform the tasks around the home. These can't be learned by incidental remarks nor through scolding or threat of punishment at the time when these tasks must be done. Time for training should be a part of the daily routine.

Every morning Wendy, four, sat helplessly until Mother dressed her. Buttons dismayed her, front and back confused her, and shoelaces were impossible. Every morning Mother scolded and eventually dressed her and then sent her out to play.

Wendy has discovered the usefulness of being helpless. Mother waits on her. Mother needs to take time to train her child to dress herself.

If we fail to take time for training we will spend a great deal more time correcting the untrained child. Constant corrections fail to "teach" because they are criticism and as such discourage and provoke the child. As a consequence of the conflict, the child becomes determined not to learn. Besides, the so-called "corrections" often misfire because children regard them as a means of getting special attention, and they love to provoke repetitions.

The undiscouraged child displays interest in doing things. Alert parents recognize such attempts and encourage them. However, definite periods should be set aside for such experiences. The morning rush hour is scarcely the time to teach a child how to tie his shoes. The pressure of the moment only produces impatience in the mother and rebellion in the child. Afternoon playtime is usually an ideal time for training in a new skill, which can be part of a game. Countless training aids can be found on the toy market. Or Mother can devise her own—a row of large buttons and buttonholes from a worn-out dress can be tacked to a board as an aid for Wendy. Large holes punched in a cardboard upon which a shoe has been drawn can serve to teach lacing and tying. If the children participate in the creation of such items, they are doubly interested. It is always fun to watch Mother make something to play with—and more fun to help. Mother can also appeal to the child's ingenuity and thereby foster his creativity.

Table manners can be taught with doll tea parties. At the same time, introductions and the manner of greeting guests can become part of the party. Behavior on train, bus, or streetcar can be taught with pretended rides. Acting and role-playing are excellent training aids, since children are born actors.

Training in any skill should be taken up in a repeated routine until the particular skill is mastered. Each skill should be learned separately. Patience, confidence in the child's ability to learn, encouraging phrases such as "Try again—you'll get it," a pleasant, happy atmosphere, and acknowledgement of an accomplishment make the learning process a joy to both child and parent.

It is also wise to provide children with training in and understanding about unpleasant contingencies.

Gwen and Bobby were scheduled to have their tonsils removed. Mother felt that some knowledge of what to expect would be helpful. Several days before the scheduled event she devised a game. "Let's pretend the dolls are going to the hospital to have their tonsils out," she suggested. "Now, what do we need first?" "Suitcase," Bobby answered and brought a toy one. "What goes into it?" The children selected items and placed them in the suitcase. The dolls were dressed. Bobby, in the role of Daddy, drove the car. The reception by the nursing staff and the procedure of getting to bed in a hospital were acted out with appropriate conversation. Then Mother took the role of the doctor, speaking to the dolls. Using the wagon, she explained that it was a stretcher. Then, using a tea-strainer covered with an old white sock, she pretended to give an anaesthesia, explaining to the doll as she went along. "Now this will smell funny, Betsy [the doll's name], but you just take some nice long breaths and count for me. Very shortly you will be sound asleep." At this point in the game Mother adroitly avoided the actual surgical procedure since the children would be unaware of what went on later. "Now Betsy is sound asleep. I'll take her tonsils out and put her back on the stretcher." While saying this, Mother removed the "mask" from the doll's face, wrapped her again in her blanket, and placed her back in the wagon. "Here she goes back to her room. When she wakes up she can have some ice cream." "Does it hurt her to have her tonsils out?" Gwen asked. "She can't feel anything at all, Mrs. Grogan," Mother answered, continuing her role as the doctor. "You see, she's sound asleep." "Will it hurt after she wakes up?" "Her throat will be a little sore, Mrs. Grogan, but I know she can handle that. It won't last very long." Then Mother asked who wanted to play doctor for the next doll. Bobby took over and repeated the story.

The next day the children played "tonsils out" using each other as patients. Mother provided a larger strainer.

When Gwen and Bobby went to the hospital they displayed confidence and were very co-operative. When Mother had suggested that the doll could deal with the sore throat, she honestly admitted that there would be pain, but she showed her confidence in the ability of the children to cope with it. She also casually pointed out something very important about pain—it won't last forever (even though it seems as if it will to one in pain!)

Training in self-sufficiency is explained on page 40. Barbara needs to learn to be self-reliant and to play by herself. Here is a teaching situation in reverse. In this case, Mother must teach by getting out of the situation. Countless times it is necessary for parent to step back and let the children practice by themselves—work out a tough spot alone.

Jane, two and a half, screamed in angry frustration because the wheel of her wagon was caught against the leg of a chair. "What is it, Jane?" Mother came to investigate. Jane stamped her foot and kept on screaming. Mother sat down and waited. The girl yanked. The wagon stayed stuck. "What else could you do besides yank?" Jane pulled another way. Still stuck. "What would happen if you pulled the back of the wagon?" Jane tried. The wagon was free! Off she ran, pulling the wagon after her. "You got it loose by yourself, didn't you?"

Mother took time for her training program, which will continue for many years—showing her daughter that there are many ways to cope with a problem. Mother refrained from pulling the wagon free, utilizing this situation to teach Jane that she can be self-sufficient.

Mother put ten-month-old Bruce into the sand pile and sat down nearby to watch over him. Bruce dug his hands into the sand, fingered it, looked at Mother, grinned, and stuffed a handful into his mouth. "Bruce. No, no." Mother jumped up and ran to her son, who was scampering away on hands and knees, grinning delightedly. She caught him, dug the sand out of his mouth, and replaced him in the sandpile. This performance was repeated many times in the course of an hour.

Bruce has discovered a delightful game of keeping Mother busy with him. Mother doesn't dare to read while Bruce plays outside. She must watch him constantly.

Mother needs to take time to train Bruce not to put everything in his mouth. Most babies do this: it is part of their method of exploring the world around them. How does it feel? How does it taste? Simply because this is natural behavior is no reason not to train them in self-restraint. Mother can take Bruce out of the sand and put him in his carriage or his stroller every time he puts sand into his mouth. Since Bruce doesn't feel like playing properly in the sand, he must be removed. Bruce may howl and scream his protest. Mother reads and lets him howl. She respects his right to display his chagrin. When Bruce is quiet—and not before—Mother may let him try again. As soon as sand goes into his mouth, she quietly lifts him and and puts him in his stroller again. He will soon catch on. Sand in mouth—sit in stroller. No words are necessary. Bruce wouldn't understand them. But he does understand the action.

As the family grows, the training needs of the younger children may easily be neglected. The older children may do for the younger ones what they should be doing for themselves. This needs to be watched, since the older child may use this opportunity to establish his own superiority over the baby. Each child deserves his training period, which leads to a sense of personal accomplishment and skill.

Training should not be attempted when guests are present

or the family is out in public. In such circumstances the child acts as he is accustomed to act. If a parent wishes a child to behave in public, he will have to train him at home. If his behavior is out of keeping with the situation, the only practical solution is to remove him quietly.

CHAPTER 14

WIN CO-OPERATION

During diaper changes, eight-month-old Lisa kicked, rolled, and twisted so much that the procedure was nearly impossible. Mother frequently became exasperated to the point of administering a light slap. Lisa would burst into the pitiful sobs of deeply hurt feelings.

Astonishing as it may seem, this eight-month-old baby, operating on unverbalized perception alone, has discovered a means of frustrating Mother. We never seem to be quite willing to give credit to infants for their cleverness. We are inclined to take very bright children, treat them like little idiots, and raise them to be stupid adults! But any mother who learns to see will have to admit that babies are darned clever! * Right now, Mother has to train Lisa to do

---

* Nine-month-old Norman was a normal child of deaf-mute parents. He was crawling on the floor one day and bumped his head against the table. He sat up, turned toward his mother, and started to cry. His face puckered up, his mouth opened wide, tears poured from his eyes—but the astonished observer heard no sound! She stood watching for a moment. Mother rushed over to Norman, picked him up, and comforted him. Infants size up situations. Norman didn't bother with the sound effects because he sensed that his parents were deaf. Older children of deaf-mute parents display a loss of temper by stamping their feet rather than by futile screaming. The parents feel and react to the vibrations.

her share in the business of getting her diaper changed. Mother can win Lisa's co-operation, first, by recognizing Lisa's purpose; then she will know what to do and be free from exasperation. Second, she can rearrange her schedule so that she has added time at the routine bath time, which she will utilize for a training period. Then, every time that Lisa moves in a manner that obstructs the dressing process, Mother quietly, and with a warm smile, can hold her still with her hands, at the same time talking to her. "My precious will learn to hold still. Such a big girl. How lovely and quiet she can be ... " etc. It doesn't matter that Lisa doesn't understand the words. She gets the meaning! It is very easy to put admiration into a smile. Lisa will sense this admiration and will respond. It is also very easy to put aggravation into a frown. The baby will sense this, too, and will respond— with further demonstration of her power to aggravate. If Mother *feels* no rancor, but only loving firmness, her daughter will understand. Mother can let go of Lisa as soon as she stops resisting. As soon as she wiggles again, Mother can hold her again. Thus, Lisa will be trained in co-operation.

In our increasingly democratic social atmosphere we frequently find it necessary to re-evaluate what we mean by some of the words we use. "Co-operation" is certainly one of these words. In former times, when authority was invested in those who were in control, co-operation meant doing as one was told. The inferior was required to "co-operate" with his superior. Democracy brings a new meaning to this word: *we* must work together to meet the demands of the situation. While we have greater equality and greater freedom in a democratic social atmosphere, we also have greater responsibilities. Having lost the power of superior status, we need techniques to stimulate co-operation. We no longer can demand from children, "Co-operate with me," nor say, "Do as

I want you to." We must recognize the need for winning their co-operation.

In addition to having them make their beds every morning, Mother assigned daily tasks to each of her four children. Stewart had to clean up the bathroom, Genevieve had to wipe the dishes, Roberta had to dust the living room, and Ronnie, take out the garbage and papers. Daily, Mother first reminded, then scolded, finally shouted, and frequently punished in order to get the work done. Her favorite comment directed to all four children was, "We'd better have some co-operation around here, or there will be four kids in serious trouble."

It is pretty obvious that Mother means, "Do the jobs I have told you to do—or else!" She has authoritatively decided what each child should do and is trying to "make" them do it. All four children are stimulated into rebellion against this oppressive approach and at the same time are permitted to succeed in their rebellious defiance. Mother's attitude when assigning the tasks shows her determination to be the boss. The children respond with an attitude of "try and make me!" This is a power contest—not co-operation. Mother is trying to impose her will upon the children instead of winning their co-operation in the business of living together. How can Mother stimulate the children into real co-operation? She can take time for a discussion with all members of the family. They can list the jobs which are to be done: Mother states which she is willing to do and then asks what is to be done about the rest of the jobs. Daddy and the children may then select those jobs they are willing to undertake. In this way Mother shows her respect for the children. She allows a choice—and a decision. If one or another neglects his chosen chore, nothing is said—nor is the chore done. After a week of neglect, Mother has another conference. "Stewart chose to keep the family room tidy this week. He hasn't done it. What are we to do about it?" The "we" puts the responsibility onto the group, where it belongs, takes Mother out of the authoritative role, and puts her into the role of leadership. All suggestions are carefully considered and a group solution is reached. Group pressure is effective, while adult pressure only stimulates rebellion. This method of dealing with a problem usually takes the form of a Family Council, which will be discussed later. The point we wish to make here is that today's family functions as a group; the group as such stimulates each individual to co-operate with the others for the benefit of all. The attention of each member in the group becomes focused on the needs of the family as a whole. Co-operation means that each and every member moves along together to accomplish that which is best for all.

Co-operation in a family of four can be compared to a four-wheeled self-propelled wagon. Each member is a wheel, while family-living-together is the wagon. All four wheels must roll together to get the wagon going smoothly. If one wheel is stuck, the wagon jerks or even turns from the desired direction. If one wheel falls off, the wagon cannot even go on without readjustment. Each wheel is as important as the other, and yet none is all-important. The direction that the wagon takes is determined by the four wheels working together. If each wheel is determined to take off by itself, the wagon would be split and useless. The size of the family makes no difference. The family body of the wagon can be supported by any number of wheels.

When we speak of training children to co-operate, we presuppose our own co-operation. We don't mean that one person should "give in" to another, but there should be a sense of all moving together in harmony toward a desired goal. When the harmony of family living is disturbed we can be sure that there is a disruption in co-operation—one or the other of the wheels is stuck. It might even be us!

Every one in the family can learn to think in terms of what will be best for the group. "What does the *situation* demand?" We can no longer think in terms of what *I* want someone else to do. This is imposing our will upon another and violates respect for him. Neither may we give in to undue demands of the others just to have peace. This violates self-respect. In helping our children to learn to co-operate, we must always be aware of the real meaning of co-operation, which implies the acceptance of common ground rules.

One of the detrimental stunts we parents pull is deciding at what age we want our children to help around the house. When the toddler wants to help set the table, we say, "No, you are too little," and then when she is six, we *demand* that she set the table. By this time she figures that we have gotten along without her this far, so why should she help now? We waste untold opportunities to allow our children to contribute. However, if a child is *allowed*—not requested! —to contribute from the very beginning, he enjoys it and has a sense of pride in his accomplishment.

Ward, seven, had been ill with the flu for a week. Donna, five and a half, and Lorraine, four, had had the playroom to themselves. Saturday morning was house-cleaning time, and everyone helped until the job was done. Today was Ward's first day up again. When the time came to clean the playroom, Ward said, "I don't see why I have to help. I haven't been down here all week. I didn't mess it up." "No, I guess you didn't, Ward," said Mother. "But I'll bet Donna and Lorraine would let you help if you asked them." Ward considered this for a moment and then helped the girls to put toys away and to dust while Mother used the vacuum cleaner. Ward noticed that the top toy-shelf seemed untidy. "Let's fix that up so it looks nicer," he suggested. The three children worked happily along with Mother. When they were finished, Donna exclaimed, "Gee, it looks nice in here!" "Sure does," Ward agreed. "And we helped do it!" he added proudly.

Ward had a point, and his resistance was understandable. However, this family already has a good relationship. Mother's brainstorm helped to win Ward's co-operation, since she acknowledged his point but deftly turned his attention to the needs of the situation and the help he could give his younger sisters. She also implied that it would be an honor to help, which appealed to Ward, since he is the oldest. Ward discovered for himself that he could take the role of leader in suggesting that the play-shelf be straightened. All had a good time together, getting something essential done.

Sometimes, in order to win co-operation, it may be necessary to help a child regain his place in the family. Let us return to the problem of Beth on page 15. Beth is unaware of her new place in the family. She needs help. Mother sought professional advice. It was explained to her that Beth assumed that only a tiny, helpless baby had value. Mother also was helped to see her own mistake in refusing Beth's proffered help. A program was devised for Beth to regain her sense of value.

Mother's first step toward correcting the situation was to enlist Beth's help in the nursery. She asked Beth to bring the bottle to her from the warmer in the kitchen. Beth angrily stormed out of the house. Later, Beth came back with wet pants. Realizing how serious the problem was for Beth, Mother didn't scold or fuss. She held Beth in her arms and asked her if she wanted to be her baby girl again. Beth burst into sobs and cuddled closer. Deeply sympathetic, Mother comforted her. Then she suggested that Beth return to her crib from which she had graduated. Mother was willing to change her diapers and to feed her a bottle and to do everything for her just as she did for baby brother. Beth was delighted when Mother came the next morning to change her before taking care of the baby. She enjoyed her six o'clock bottle. She was given only the same food that the baby received. As the day wore on and Beth asked for toys to play with in her bed, Mother gave her infant toys. When she asked for her crayons, Mother replied, "A tiny baby can't color. You are my tiny baby." Every time that Beth expressed a wish for something beyond the infant stage, she got the same kind of an answer expressed in a tone of voice that showed warmth and sympathy. At noon on the second day Beth vehemently declared that she was a big girl and didn't want to be a baby. "Fine. Do you feel big enough to help with baby brother who can't do anything for himself?"

Beth responded immediately. Her mother continued to encourage her toward being big, and the infant behavior disappeared. In this situation Mother demonstrated to Beth through action much more than she could ever tell her in words. She allowed Beth to discover for herself that being a baby wasn't all it looked to be. Beth found out for herself that the advantages of being big and capable were more satisfactory than the advantages of being an infant. Through her action, Mother redirected Beth's motivation and helped her to re-establish her place as a big girl who could help.

Mother and Eddie, five, got into the car to pick Daddy up at the train station. It was a bitter cold day, but Eddie rolled the window down. Mother said, "We will go when you roll the window up." Eddie waited. Mother sat impassive. Eddie said, "I'll roll the window up when you start the car." Mother said nothing but continued to wait. Eddie said, "All right, I'll roll the window up when you put the key in." Mother still continued to wait without a word. She showed an attitude of interior withdrawal. Eddie finally rolled the window up. Mother started the car, smiled at Eddie, and asked, "Isn't the sun lovely on the snow? Look how it sparkles like thousands of diamonds."

Mother avoided making a demand, "Roll up the window," and thus stayed out of a power struggle. She expressed immediately what she would do in the situation and held firm without rancor. When Eddie still tried to tease her into giving him his own way, at least in part, she merely waited. When Eddie complied with the demands of *the situation*, Mother acknowledged it with her smile and directed his attention elsewhere in friendly fashion. Eddie's rather quick co-operation shows that he already has respect for Mother's firmness.

Pat, nine, and her friend were making macaroni necklaces. Mother entered the room carrying ten-month-old Randy. "Pat, take care of the baby for me," she demanded. "I have to go pick up Daddy." "Aw, Mother, he'll mess everything up! Why do *I* always have to look after him?" "That's enough of that. Do as I ask you to." As Mother left, Pat glared at Randy, who was already crawling toward the interesting objects. She yanked him back and handed him a teddy bear. Randy tossed it aside and crawled rapidly toward the dishes of macaroni. When Mother returned, Randy was screaming and Pat was yelling. Mother joined the commotion. "Can't you even look after him for fifteen minutes without a fight?"

Mother's tone of voice and hurried demand instantly provoked Pat to reluctance and resentment. If she stopped to think a moment, Mother would realize that her back would be up instantly were a friend to hurl a demand at her.

Our tone of voice and manner of approach are important factors in winning co-operation. So many times we are aware that the child may resist our request, either because it is badly timed, as it was with Pat, or because the nature of what must be done is distasteful to the child. On such occasions, we are inclined to raise our voices and be emphatic, hoping thereby to overcome resistance. Actually, we increase it.

Politeness alone can go a long way toward winning co-operation from children, and we can phrase our request to indicate that we understand the child's point of view. "I'm sorry to interrupt you," or "I realize you may not want to, but it would help me out so much if . . ." or "I'd appreciate it very much if you feel you could . . ." tend to support harmony, reduce reluctance, and win co-operation.

Ardith, ten, lived in a suburb where there was no public transportation. Her very best friend, Pat, with whom she felt quite close, lived beyond walking distance, and biking was inadvisable in winter weather. The two girls wanted to be together every spare moment. It soon developed that one or the other mother was almost daily driving her daughter back and forth. Conflicts of engagements frequently resulted in disappointed girls, and the situation began to get tense.

This called for co-operation. One night while Ardith and her mother were doing the dishes and the atmosphere was friendly, Mother discussed the problem with her daughter. She explained her position; she understood Ardith's right to see her friend, but at the same time felt that she was too involved in running back and forth. "Can you think of what we could do about it?" "Well, I suppose we could cut down some." "How many times a week do you feel it is fair for me to take you over to Pat's?" The girl thought for a moment. "Well, I guess two times a week. Then if Pat comes here twice a week, it would even up." "All right," Mother replied, "I'll be very happy to take you over two times a week." "Which days, Mother?" Mother thought for a moment. "Well, Tuesday evening and Saturday afternoon I'm usually free. How would that be?" "I think I'd like it that way, 'cause then I know for sure when I can go."

The situation is now resolved in a co-operative manner; neither Mother nor Ardith feels imposed upon and each recognizes the other's rights. Of course, it is understood that Mother is now obligated and must forego making other arrangements for these times without advance consultation with Ardith.

Fred, eleven, had recently lost his father. He and Mother lived in a suburb and went to the city on Saturday for a music lesson. Fred wanted to change his lesson to Wednesday afternoon—his only free time—so that he could join a ball team on Saturday. However, Mother met with her circle of friends on Wednesday and resented Fred's request. A bitter deadlock resulted, and each felt abused by the other. Mother sought our advice.

Fred presented his point of view, which we understood but did not agree with. However, there was no point in fighting or pressing him into submission: this would have increased his sense of injury and further damaged his relationship with Mother. We suggested to him that since Mother had sought our advice, we would recommend that he have his lesson on Wednesday. Fred was not quite sure. He felt that Mother would not give in—she was too stubborn for that. (It is amazing how many children think that parents are stubborn while parents are convinced that only the children are.) We assured him that Mother would accept our advice. Fred suddenly expressed reluctance. He was not sure Mother should be asked to give in. "Why not? Your benefits from the ball team on Saturday are greater than Mother's on Wednesday." "No," the boy pondered, "that's not true. Since Dad died, these friends are very important to Mother. It would not be good for her to miss their get-together." "Well, what is to be done, then?" "I guess we better leave things as they are."

Why did Fred suddenly capitulate? As soon as it was obvious to him that his reasons and rights were understood and appreciated, he lost the feeling that he was being imposed upon and was free to examine the needs of the total situation.

Anyone becomes unreasonable when he feels imposed

upon. We cannot win co-operation by trying to impose our will upon someone else.

Actually, there *is* co-operation at all times in any interpersonal relationship, but we seldom see it for what it is. Sometimes parents need to rearrange the co-operation. David and George on pages 27–28 actually co-operate with each other to maintain the status quo. When "good" David provokes George into being "bad," the latter co-operates by responding! "Good" David would be considerably upset were his "bad" brother to behave as a "good" boy. David would feel his position to be threatened. Both boys co-operate to keep Mother busy in praising David and scolding George. A shift anywhere in this established interaction or mutual co-operation will change the total picture. To tell George that he, too, can be good would be futile. He must be silently stimulated to change his form of co-operation. George will never believe that he can be "good." Also, if George should be "good," his brother will redouble his efforts to make him "bad." However, Mother, through her understanding, can alter the interaction by changing her response to what the boys do. First, knowing that George sees himself as "the bad one," Mother can refuse to accept his evaluation. She can stop *all* comments about "good" and "bad." Every time that David demonstrates how good he is, Mother can accept it quietly and say, "Fine. I'm glad you enjoy doing it." Every time George misbehaves, Mother can hug him and say, "I understand." But this is hard to do, you say. Sure it is. Who said being a parent is *easy?*

CHAPTER 15

AVOID GIVING UNDUE ATTENTION

The family was staying at a summer cottage. Daddy was out fishing and Mother was working in the kitchen. Two-year-old Hilda stood at the front door. "Mommie?" "Yes?" "Mommie?" "Yes, dear?" "Mommie—" "Yes, dear. What is it?" "Mommie!" Mother went to her child. "What?" "Walk?" "In a little while." Mother returned to the kitchen. Hilda remained at the door with her nose pressed to the screen. "Mommie?" "Yes?" The same routine was repeated three times. When the child started the fourth time, Mother went to her again. "Oh, all right, Hilda. We will go for a short walk. But I do have to get dinner ready." Mother took her hand, helped her down the steps, and they went for a walk.

Hilda doesn't go to Mother. She makes Mother come to her. Mother responds. She yields to Hilda's undue demands.

The child who seeks constant attention is, of necessity, an unhappy child. He feels that unless he gets attention he is worthless, has no place. He seeks constant reassurance that he is important. Since he doubts this, no amount of reassurance will ever impress him. Mother notices him. A few minutes later, he questions, "Is Mother still aware of me? Do I still count?" This is a never ending circle of doubt. What a miserable situation! How can Mother help?

When Hilda succeeds in getting Mother to respond to her every whim, the response becomes a confining wall. There is no room to seek another set of values. What Hilda does, works. Suppose Mother drew back and refused to respond to undue demands. Then, not finding the satisfaction to which she is accustomed, Hilda would—after an initial rebellion—explore different ways to acquire her sense of belonging. She may need help to find constructive means, otherwise her search may lead her into more destructive behavior. Mother can be aware of and acknowledge proper behavior. As things are now, Mother shows a lack of self-respect when she allows her daughter to enslave her. She also shows a lack of respect for Hilda by demonstrating, through her response, that she doubts her child's ability to get along without her service.

Mother can stop going to Hilda whenever she calls. She can answer the first call pleasantly, without going out of her way, and say that she is busy right now. Then when Hilda calls again, she can simply not answer. Two can play this game! The child may scream, but Mother can assume that since she is busy with what she must do, Hilda will have to come to her. Mother has the right to go on with her work and the obligation to train her child to respect the needs of the situation. Hilda does not have the right to go for a walk whenever she likes. In justice to Hilda, Mother does not have the right to give in to her whims. Hilda must discover the benefits of accepting order and the needs of the situation. A certain time is set for a walk, and that is when they go. Should Hilda come to Mother and ask to take a walk, Mother may say, "It is not time to go out now, Hilda." Period. No matter what else Hilda does, Mother remains firm and goes on with her work.

Mother's friend stopped for coffee in the afternoon. As they visited, Mary, the youngest of three, came running in with a tale of injustice from her playmate. Mother commented, "Well, I suppose she doesn't feel well this afternoon." "Why, Mommie?" Mother attempted to answer the "why." Every time Mother finished, the child asked another "why." Finally Mother asked Mary to return to her play so that she could visit. Mary went out but was soon back with more "whys." Much of the visit time was thus occupied. At last Mother admitted to her friend, "That's just her way of getting attention when we have company."

Mother knows exactly what Mary is up to! Mary is the baby and feels that she needs all attention centered upon her. It is much more important to her to keep Mother busy and to prevent Mother from becoming absorbed in a friend than to develop her own friendships with her peers. And yet Mother doesn't seem to realize that her daughter is misbehaving. She excuses her. Mother sees what she is doing but is unaware of the meaning of Mary's behavior. As soon as Mother realizes that the child keeps her busy only because she feels lost unless she is the center of attention, she can help her by refusing undue attention, so that Mary can grow up and become self-sufficient.

It is difficult to train a child when guests are present. However, at the first interruption Mother can say, "We are visiting now. Do you feel you can play with *your* friends and leave us alone, or would you like to go to your room?" This gives Mary a choice and may elicit greater willingness to co-operate.

We can always be suspicious of the child with a constant flow of "whys." How many times is the child really seeking information? We underestimate our children. Countless times a child asks "Why?" although he knows the answer. In order to keep the parents' attention he is getting he may be busy figuring out the next "why." What does his face show? Interest? Did the question reveal reasoning? Take a good look. Chances are that most of the time a constant "why" is idle. The child uses "why" to keep the parent busy. He senses the parent's desire to "teach" and uses it to get attention, not to learn! We can easily tell the difference if we stop and look. If we find pat phrases, illogical sequence of questions, and repetition of the form and content, and if a new question is asked before the previous one is answered, then we can be sure that we have fallen into the trap. We can smile a knowing smile and say, "I enjoy playing a 'why' game with you. But now I must go on with something else." Or a mere knowing smile and a buttoned lip may be sufficient. Children don't like to be caught in the act. Don't be surprised if the child shows marked innocence, resentment, or even redoubled efforts to regain attention. About this time, departure from the area is smart.

John, five, next to the youngest of four, is the "good" child in the family. However, he does one thing which drives Mother to distraction. Every time she is on the phone, he finds ways to interrupt her. He has to show her something, asks to go outside, asks to have a friend in, wants something to eat, wants an object out of reach, or wants to know where certain toys are. Sometimes Mother stops her conversation to answer John. Other times she scolds, "Let me alone till I'm through!" At this point John usually starts to tease his little sister and make her cry!

John is in the position of a middle child. He feels more or less left out. But he has found a wonderful way to prove his importance. He may find it hopeless to get Mother's attention when she is busy with the baby. But when she is on the phone, he can get her away from another adult!

John is overambitious. He wants to be noticed all the time.

He is "good" only for the purpose of winning Mother's approval, not for the benefit of usefulness. Mother needs to lead him away from seeking undue attention. First, she has to recognize that the "good boy" is actually unsure of his place. She must show her interest in him, but not at the time he makes undue demands. At the phone, Mother continues to talk as if the child simply weren't there, even if she can't hear a word said at the other end of the line. Her friend, having been clued in, will understand what might otherwise sound insane! At no point during the conversation should Mother give in. This takes a lot of fortitude and a lot of determination, especially when John starts teasing his sister. Don't worry. Sister can handle it! Training John to become self-sufficient and not to depend on attention and approval is well worth the effort.

Whenever we stop responding to a child's undue demands for attention, we must be sure to notice him when he is co-operative; this will help the child to re-evaluate his methods. When Hilda plays happily alone, Mother can comment, "How nice that you know how to take care of yourself." When Mary gets along well with her playmates, Mother can say, "I'm so glad that you had a good time playing." When John is nice without any special aim for his action, Mother can be pleased. "I'm so glad you enjoy being with us."

Children need our attention. But we must become aware of the difference between due and undue attention. If we find ourselves overly busy with the child at a time when the situation fails to justify it, when we feel annoyed or distressed, we can be assured that we are confronted with undue demands. Study the situation. What does it require? Could the child handle it if we didn't interfere? How does our response affect the child's self-concept? Does it prove to him that he can do it without us, or does it induce him to remain the helpless, feeble, or needful person he sees himself to be? In order to help our children to learn that they gain satisfaction in life from contributing according to the needs of the situation, we need to stop making it possible for them to reap results from short-sighted "getting."

CHAPTER 16

SIDESTEP THE STRUGGLE FOR POWER

"Empty the dog dish," Mother sternly demanded of Suelynne. "Aw, heck. Why should *I* do it?" "I said to empty the dog dish, young lady. Now do it." "I don't see why I have to." "Because I told you to." The girl shrugged her shoulders and subtly avoided doing what Mother had asked. A few hours later Mother found the dog dish still dirty, with ants crawling all over it. She called Suelynne. "I thought I told you to empty this dish several hours ago. What is the reason for your not doing it? Now look at it! All covered with ants. Now take care of it. Right away!" "Okay, okay." Suelynne, having placated Mother, who had turned away, still disregarded the dish. A while later Mother found it still dirty. This time she slapped Suelynne, who took it stony-faced. She refused to cry. "If you don't take care of this right now, you will go to bed early, and there won't be any television for you tonight. Besides that, you'll get your little tail whipped, but good. Now get at it." "All right, I will." Suelynne bent over the dish as Mother turned away, but she didn't clean it. Late that evening Mother found the dish still dirty and unemptied.

Suelynne and Mother are engaged in a power struggle. Mother attempts to force Suelynne to mind. Suelynne will show who is boss!

145

Evidence of such struggle for power is increasing at an alarming rate. Power-mad children are brought to guidance centers and counselors' offices by despairing parents in greater and greater numbers. Why? What is the matter? Children dare to do today what we would never have thought to do to our parents. How can this be?

The problem is stimulated by the general cultural change which is now taking place. Children sense the democratic atmosphere of our times and resent our attempts at authority over them. They show their resentment through retaliation. They resist our attempts to overpower them and show us their power instead. A vicious round develops in which parents attempt to assert themselves and the children declare war. They absolutely will not be dominated or coerced. All attempts to subdue them are futile. Children are by far more clever in a power contest. They aren't inhibited by social consequences of "appearances" or dangerous consequences of their actions. The home becomes a battlefield. There is no co-operation and no harmony. Instead, there is anger and fury.

Mother had succeeded in making Patty, twelve, agree that she would clean up her lunch box and rinse out the Thermos as soon as she got home from school. Things went nicely for a few days. Then one day Patty neglected to take care of her lunch box. Mother was angry when she found it on the counter with scraps of food in the box and souring milk in the Thermos. She scolded and preached. Patty promised to remember. A few days later she again failed to assume her responsibility. This time, Mother remembered that she had considered the use of logical consequences. So, she ignored the situation, but was angry inside. She thought to herself, "I'll show her!" The next morning she packed a lunch in a paper bag and laid milk money on the table. Patty knew what was up. Mother left the lunch box on the back of the counter. "I absolutely will not clean it up," she thought rebelliously. The moulding food scraps and souring milk stayed right on the back of the counter. Patty continued to carry her lunch in a paper bag. Mother became more and more furious as the days went on. Finally she landed on her daughter in terrible wrath. Patty glowered with lowered eyes and still made no move to clean the box. Finally, in desperation, Mother shoved her into the kitchen, stood over her, struck her repeatedly until she finished cleaning up the box. "Do you intend to remember from now on?" Mother shrieked. "Yes, Mother," Patty promised. However, the next day she again left the box dirty. In complete despair, Mother decided to abondon the whole project. "You can just carry your lunch in a sack." "That's okay by me. Hardly any of the kids bring their lunch in a box, anyway."

The day that Patty neglected her lunch box and Mother became angry was the height of the power struggle. Mother, in spite of herself, was still trying to "make" Patty clean up her lunch box. She actually used logical consequences as punishment—"I'll show her" is retaliation, which is the same as punishment. Patty sensed Mother's anger, although Mother tried to hide it. Mother didn't really consider the nature of a logical consequence. When she put the lunch in a paper bag and provided milk money, she avoided the real consequence: she continued to serve, despite the girl's unwillingness to co-operate. Had she followed logically, she would have prepared the lunch as usual but, not having a clean container in which to place it, would have left it on the counter. The sequel would have been up to Patty.

Patty intended to show Mother that she could not be made to clean her lunch box. She would take anything rather than submit to this demand. How could Mother handle the situation without a show of power?

Mother has to be *really* unconcerned about the lunch box. It belongs to Patty. If she doesn't want to clean it up, then she will have to do without it. Mother can only decide what *she* will do. First, moulding food and souring milk certainly have no place in the kitchen. To leave it there is rebellious retaliation on Mother's part. To stand over Patty and "make her clean it up," is using force and continues the power struggle, as was evidenced when, the next day, in spite of her promise, the girl again failed to clean her box. Mother got angry because Patty had defied her. She felt her position of authority threatened and wanted to show Patty that she was not going to let her get by with defying her. How much better it would have been if Mother had tried to find out what made Patty adamant and had changed her tactics so that there was no need for defiance! In this case, the child resented carrying the lunch box, since very few children in junior high carry lunches in a box. Why didn't she say so in the first place? Because she used this situation to engage Mother in a power struggle. And she won. Mother gave up. A friendly talk with Patty could have shown Mother how her daughter felt about the lunch box; then she could have avoided this long and agonizing struggle. "I see that you have neglected to take care of your lunch box today, Patty. I must assume that you don't want to take your lunch in the box. Would you prefer that I put it in a sack and give you milk money?" This would have ended the power struggle right there.

Any time we "order" a child to do something, or try to "make" him do it, we invite a power struggle. This does not mean that we cannot guide or influence our children into proper behavior. It only means that we must find a different and effective approach. We must abandon the obsolete, futile attitudes and methods and assume those which will be effective.

Five-year-old Jimmy was driving Mother crazy. She said so to him and to others in front of him. Mother fought with him about one thing or another all the time. Jimmy simply would not mind, no matter what. And when Mother resorted to spanking, it only helped for a short moment, if at all. Today, for instance. Jimmy is not regular with his bowel movements, and Mother had been trying to train him for years. This morning she sent him to the bathroom after breakfast, but he came back and said that he couldn't go now. She let him go out to play and went on with her work. About noon, while putting some clothes away in the closet, she noticed a fecal odor. She investigated and found that Jimmy had had his stool in his Daddy's hat! She raced out, found him, brought him in, confronted him with the hat, and whipped him hard. He wet his pants immediately, but she figured that was because of the whipping. However, Jimmy wet his pants the rest of the day, and wet his bed that night.

Mother has been concerned about Jimmy's bowel movements from the time he was an infant. She indicates, "You will move your bowels when I say so." Jimmy's action says, "I will have my own movement where and when I please." Very early the boy used this as one method to defeat an overpowering mother. The daily lives of Jimmy and his mother were a constant power struggle. It will not be easy for Mother to change the interrelationship unless she knows what the trouble is and what she can do about it.

So many parents create similar difficulties for themselves when they exhibit overconcern about toilet training. The difference between normal concern and overconcern lies in our attitude. If we "insist" that the child learn proper toilet habits, we invite resistance. If we anticipate and encourage proper toilet training, we invite co-operation. If, after reasonable time taken in training, the child seems to use these functions to gain undue attention, or to resist the pressure of the parent, it is time to withdraw and to show no concern; to let nature take its course. In all such cases we find a general struggle for power. We can resolve it first in other areas, where the situation is more favorable for the maintenance of order without fighting. As far as urination and defecation are concerned, Mother can allow the child to lie in a wet bed or to change his own linens if he is uncomfortable. If he is way past what she considers the diaper age, she can place him in training pants and let him remain wet. Of course, he cannot be allowed to wet the living-room carpet or furniture. So, until he is ready to stay dry, he will have to remain where a puddle doesn't hurt things. All of this can be done in a casual manner, with the attitude of "This is your problem. You will solve it when you are ready. Meanwhile there are limitations." If the satisfactions of extra attention or winning a contest are lacking, the child may possibly choose to abandon the discomfort.

At this point many readers may feel puzzled. There *are* times, such as an imminent life danger, when we must use force. We also use a kind of pressure when we are firm, or when we are in a position where physical force is needed to maintain order.

Peter, five and a half, had been kept home from kindergarten because of a severe cold. One afternoon the weather turned pleasant, the snow started to melt, and Peter wanted to go out. "No, son. You are still coughing too much." The boy pouted sullenly. A short while later Mother heard the door slam. Peter, dressed in snow suit and boots, had gone out to play. Mother went out after him, took him by the hand, and told him he had to come in again. He resisted. Mother picked him up and carried him in. "I'm sorry, Peter. You cannot play outside today." The boy stormed and cried. Mother took off his snow suit forcibly; she knew that being overheated would be inadvisable. Peter, in a temper, dashed to the door. Mother stood quietly and firmly held the door. She said nothing further, nor did she attempt to restrain Peter in his display of anger. He started coughing violently as a result of the screaming and exertion. Mother said nothing, merely continuing to block his way out. Finally Peter burst out, "I hate you, I hate you, I hate you!" He dashed to his room and flung himself onto his bed. Mother went on about her work, leaving Peter to finish his temper tantrum.

To the untrained observer, this looks like a power struggle. Peter wanted out and Mother used force to prevent him. However, Mother was *not* engaged in a struggle for power. She meant to maintain the order demanded by the situation. How do we tell the difference? It lies in Mother's *attitude*. Mother was obligated to be firm and to maintain order. She did both—without any feeling of anger, frustration, or authority. In this case, order meant obeying the rules of health. The struggle between Peter and his mother was not one of power because *Mother had no stake in it*. This is an important clue. Whenever we wonder if a situation is or is not a power struggle, we can ask, "What is my personal stake in the affair?"

Many parents delude themselves into feeling that they do things for the sake of the child. Come, now. Are we sure? Is our prestige involved? Do *we* gain anything? Will there be a personal satisfaction if the child complies? Do we want the world to see an obedient child? Do we want to be known as "good" parents? Successful parents? Do we seek the "upper hand"?

Another way to discover whether or not we are involved in a power struggle is to look at the results. Does the child continue to do the same thing in spite of our "training"? Does he show defiance? Are *we* angry? Resentful?

A third test is our tone of voice. This is a dead giveaway. Do we sound imperious? Angry? Insistent? Demanding? Firmness is usually expressed quietly, while power contests are generally accentuated by verbal battles and angry words.

Peter had a temper tantrum because he couldn't have his

own way. Mother ignored his "I hate you"; she knew it was only momentarily true and was part of his reaction. Having maintained order, she was no longer concerned. Peter worked out the rest of the problem for himself. Had Mother been engaged in a struggle for power, she would have been deeply involved in the subsequent reactions.

Mother parked the car outside the doctor's office. Gene, two, refused to get out. Mother begged. Gene refused. "Gene, it's time for my appointment. Come on now, be a good boy." Gene slumped further and refused to get out. Mother turned to her friend. "What can I do?"

Mother can take him out! Firmly, quietly, as a matter of fact, to maintain order and comply with the needs of the situation. Mother does not need to be angry. No power contest is involved if Mother remains cool and calm.

In order to understand the power struggle fully and to develop techniques for dealing with it, we must re-evaluate our position as parents. We must become very much aware of our new role as leaders and give up completely our ideas of authority. We simply do not have authority over our children. They know it, even if we don't. We can no longer demand or impose. We must learn how to lead and how to stimulate. The following chart will indicate the new attitudes which are needed to promote harmony and co-operation in the family. On the left we have listed the autocratic attitudes and on the right those attitudes which must now replace them.

Once the attitudes listed in the right-hand column become more or less our second nature, we will be less vulnerable to getting involved in a power struggle. If our attention is centered upon the needs of the situation rather than upon "making him mind me," we may discover ways to stimulate the child to respond. Whenever we approach a child with determination to "make" him do something, he senses it and immediately stiffens into rebellion. This may take the rather passive tack which Suelynne took when she avoided emptying and cleaning the dog dish, or it may take the active form of revenge which Jimmy took when he used his father's hat for his stool.

Autocratic Society	*Democratic Society*
Authority figure	Knowledgeable leader
Power	Influence
Pressure	Stimulation
Demanding	Winning co-operation
Punishment	Logical consequences
Reward	Encouragement
Imposition	Permit self-determination
Domination	Guidance
Children are to be seen and not heard.	Listen! Respect the child.
You do it because *I* said to.	*We* do it because it is necessary.
Prestige-centered	Situation-centered
Personal involvement	Objective detachment

Our prestige takes the greatest beating when our children defy us. Here we can make the greatest change. We have a chance if we concern ourselves with what the situation needs and forget about the assault upon our own dignity.

Many of the rules already discussed apply to the power struggle. Most important is to be firm—about what *I* shall do, not about what I'm going to make the child do. Then, the parent, as a leader, decides what the demands of the situation are and works toward fulfilling those demands, not his own preference. Understanding, encouragement, logical consequences, mutual respect, respect for order, routine, and winning co-operation, all come into play as a means of resolving a power struggle. Of course, when a power struggle has already evolved, the use of logical consequences is usually impossible. The best structured consequence then degenerates into punishment—because the parent is using it as a weapon on his side of the contest.

Above all, the most important step for any parent to take is to recognize his own part in the power struggle. This is not easy to accomplish. It requires a constant alertness; otherwise we get involved without realizing it. It requires constant self-reminders. "I really can't *make* my children do anything. I cannot force them to do anything nor stop them. I may try all the tricks in the book, but I cannot force my child into co-operative action. It cannot be forced; it must be won. Proper behavior must be stimulated, not demanded. However, I can utilize my ingenuity, tact, and my sense of humor to promote willingness." This actually gives parents much more to work with than the mere use of force. The development of these skills brings into play the creative force inherent in all of us. Once we know the rules, all sorts of variations occur to us. The important thing is that we become aware of the fact that we *can* do something besides the futile attempts at force.

CHAPTER 17

WITHDRAW FROM THE CONFLICT

THERE are always two sides to any unpleasant situation between parents and children. The disturbance is the result of a conflict between two people. If one person withdraws the other cannot continue. If the parent removes himself from the battlefield he leaves the child in a vacuum. He no longer has an audience or an opponent—nothing and no one to defeat; no one to lord it over. "The sail has been taken out of his wind." *

Every evening at seven thirty the battle of bedtime started. Four-year-old Harry was a master in prolonging the battle. "Come, Harry, it's time for bed," Mother said quietly. "Not yet, Mother, I'm not sleepy." "But it's your bedtime," Mother persuaded. "After a while, when I've finished coloring this picture," the boy argued. "You come right now," Mother said harshly. "You can finish your coloring tomorrow." As Mother tried to put things away, Harry screamed and gathered the crayons within the curve of his arm in an effort to prevent them from being picked up. Mother, hesitating to fight bodily, yielded. "All right, then, finish the picture." Harry again concentrated on the book,

---

* This phrase is more accurate than the customary one; one cannot stop the child from blowing—therefore his "wind" is uncontrollable. But one can remove one's self from his wind, which thus becomes futile and ridiculous!

a tiny smile at the corner of his mouth. Mother sat down on the bed to wait. The child's crayon moved more and more slowly. Mother became impatient. "You're just fooling around. Come on, finish it." "I want it to be real pretty. I have to be careful," was the boy's smug reply. Mother waited impatiently a while longer, then said that she would put away the crayons that were no longer needed. Harry protested. Mother insisted. Harry reluctantly let Mother put some of the crayons away, teasing her all the while by holding back or pretending to lose some. Once things were put away, Harry found many more ways to delay bedtime. He dawdled in his bath, romped on the bed, wanted a drink of water. Finally Mother got him tucked in and returned to the living room. A few minutes later her son was up again to go to the bathroom, then wanted another good-night kiss. At nine o'clock he was still active. Mother lost her temper and whacked him. Harry burst into screams. Daddy came to the door and scolded Mother. "I don't see why you have to have all this ruckus every night. Harry! Shut up. Get in that bed and stay there." Finally there was peace.

Harry's immediate goal is power. He displays his ability to do as he chooses and to engage Mother in a battle. He is fortified in his belief in his own power by Mother, who tries to impress him with her demands and then gives in. Harry should go to bed. However, Mother does not know how to induce him to go.

There are several ways to solve this problem. One is to withdraw from the conflict situation. Perhaps Mother and Daddy can reach an agreement as to what to do. Let us see how that could work.

During the afternoon play-hour Mother says to Harry, "Eight o'clock is your bedtime. I will tell you when it is time for your bath. Daddy and I will tell you good night at eight o'clock. After that we will no longer be concerned with what you do." At seven thirty Mother starts Harry's bath water and calls him. "I want to play some more," the boy answers defiantly. "Your bath water is ready, dear," Mother answers and returns to the living room. At eight o'clock Mother and Daddy go to Harry's room. Harry is still playing. "Good night, my big boy." Daddy picks his son up and gives him a hug. "I'll see you in the morning." "Good night, darling. Have pleasant dreams." Mother kisses him. The parents return to the living room and turn on the television. "But I haven't had my bath," Harry yells, running into the living room. Mother and Daddy act as if Harry were already asleep. Harry climbs into Mother's lap. "I want a bath, Mother," Harry whimpers as he puts his face in front of Mother's. "George, let's make some popcorn." (This ruse gets rid of the lap to sit on.) Mother gets up, allowing Harry to slide off her lap. Harry does everything he can think of to get attention. He screams, stomps, stands on his head, drags on his parents' legs; but nothing avails. Finally, he goes to his room and undresses. Next he comes out asking to have his sleepers fastened. Mother and Daddy are absorbed in television and act as if he were already in bed and sound asleep. About nine thirty Harry climbs into bed unassisted, with his sleepers unfastened, and cries himself to sleep.

Mother and Daddy have been firm. They have said good night and then been responsible only for what *they* would do. They have withdrawn and left Harry the field. He desperately redoubles his efforts to engage them in fighting to get him to bed. He even plays on their pity by crying. Still their firmness holds. A new way of training has begun that fundamentally alters the boy's relationship to his parents and to order. The following night Harry could be ready for his bath and Mother and Harry would enjoy the half hour together. At eight o'clock Mother and Daddy would tuck Harry in, say good night, and leave him. If, a few minutes later the boy were to get up to go to the bathroom, demand a drink and another kiss, Mother and Daddy would again act as if he were asleep. He might then go back to bed. Chances are that within a week Harry would readily accept eight o'clock as the end of his day.

Another way to avoid a power struggle while putting a four-year-old to bed would be to firmly but quietly—without words!—take him by the hand at the proper hour, undress and bathe him, and then remain totally aloof when he disturbs—even to the point of retreating to one's own bedroom and locking the door.

Sarah, three and a half, ran into the kitchen where Mother was cooking dinner. "I want a drink, Mommie," she whined. "Stop that whining, Sarah. You won't get anything until you ask for it right." "But I want a drink," the child whined harder. "I can't stand that whining! Stop it." Sarah whimpered, holding onto Mother's legs and burying her face. "Are you going to ask nicely?" "Please can I have a drink?" Sarah whined. "Oh, for heaven's sake. Here!" Mother got the water.

We are told that all children go through a whining phase. We are advised to be patient and told that they will outgrow it. However, it isn't really necessary to "endure" whining. Sarah showed her power to do what she wanted in spite of what Mother required. Mother demanded, "stop it." Sarah continued, and Mother gave in.

There *is* something we can do. We can refuse to meet a whining demand. But we have to withdraw—and without talking! We are sure to yield if we stand there as a ready target. Mother must take time out for training. She can turn off the gas and go to the bathroom!

We call this the "bathroom technique." This is the one place in the house that, by custom, symbolizes privacy. It is an absolutely ideal retreat. We should have a magazine rack stocked with literature for such times and a radio to shut out the noise. Every time that Sarah whines, Mother disappears into the bathroom. She says nothing—it isn't necessary. Sarah may soon change her tone of voice.

Mother heard noises in the kitchen and investigated. She found Larry, four, on the counter, reaching for the candy supply on the top shelf. "You can't have any candy now, Larry. It's almost lunchtime." Mother took her son down. "I want candy now," he screamed. "No, Larry. I'll make lunch now." "Candy!" the boy screamed. "Larry, please behave yourself." The child threw himself on the floor and screamed and kicked. "You want me to spank you?" Mother stormed. "Stop that racket!" "I hate you, I hate you." "Larry! What a thing to say!" The boy's tantrum increased. "Larry, stop it. Here. I'll let you have *one* piece. Now stop screaming." Larry gradually subsided and finally took the candy that Mother held out to him.

Mother refused at first, but Larry forced her to give in. Larry won the contest and strengthened his trust in his own power. Mother can make temper tantrums futile by retreating from the scene. Take the candy away and go to the bathroom at the first scream. Let Larry have his tantrum in a vacuum. No tantrum is meaningful without an audience.

Mother and Allan, five, had visited a friend that afternoon. He had been fascinated seeing Chuckie, the friend's son, get his own way by throwing a temper tantrum. During dinner, Allan left the table to go to the bathroom. It was a well-established custom of the house that if anyone left the table during the meal, they could not return. While he was away, Mother hastily told Daddy about the visit. He understood. Mother removed Allan's plate. Allan returned. When he saw that his plate was gone, he threw himself on the floor in a vivid imitation of Chuckie. Mother and Daddy continued their meal as if Allan were not there. Presently they heard him mutter, "Oh, what's the use? They aren't paying any attention!" Mother had trouble stifling a giggle.

Allison, ten months, had been crawling on the floor while Mother ironed. The ironing finished, Mother put the baby into her playpen. She objected and cried. Mother attempted to distract her attention, but Allison threw herself backward, arched her back, and screamed lustily. Mother went to the bathroom. Ten minutes later she returned to find Allison contendedly playing with her ball.

Even a ten-month-old baby will try to get her own way. Mother is training Allison to accept order. She respects Allison's decision to try a temper tantrum and yields the *field* to her, but does not give the desired attention or service.

Withdrawal from the conflict situation is a most impressive step. It by no means implies withdrawal from the *child*. Love, affection, and friendliness continue. Withdrawal *at the time of conflict* actually helps to maintain friendship. When a child is particularly provoking, we usually feel far from friendly—we feel much more inclined to bop him one. The hostility on both sides does a great deal of harm to the relationship. When we become skilled in immediate withdrawal, we find that our children respond to an amazing degree. Since they have a deep desire to belong, they find an empty battlefield most disconcerting. It doesn't take them long to modify their behavior to avoid the useless exhibition of ill temper. Once this practice is established in the home, children very quickly sense their limits. If they go beyond the limits and the parent withdraws from the situation, the children very quickly abandon the conflict and indicate their desire to co-operate again. Since training our children in co-operation is our goal, we have here an excellent procedure by which to win co-operation.

It may be difficult to see how this procedure can be right. On first examination it looks as if we are letting a child "get by" with something. However, if we look closer at the motive of the child, we discover that in most conflict situations he wants our attention or wishes to engage us in a power contest. If we permit ourselves to become involved, we succumb to the child's scheme and strengthen his mistaken goal.

Therefore, our training must be aimed at the base of the problem rather than at the surface. It is futile to "correct" a child's bad behavior verbally. If we wish to train a child toward better behavior, we must act so as to induce a change in his attitudes. If he finds that his attempts to have his own way yield him only an empty field, he soon will move into a new direction, eventually discovering how much more he can gain through co-operation. If he can't have his own way, he learns to take the requirements of the situation in his stride. Thus he develops respect, both for reality and for his parents, who represent the existing social order.

Once training through withdrawal has been established in the home, it is easier to deal with conflicts in public. We can develop a mental withdrawal-to-the-bathroom which is also effective. Children are extremely sensitive. They feel the withdrawal, the noninvolvement of the parent. We saw the effect of just such an attitude in the story of Sharon on page 89. When Mother quietly walked ahead as Sharon displayed her temper, she withdrew from the conflict. Sharon recognized this, gave up, and rejoined her mother, who immediately accepted her without reproach, and the rest of the walk was pleasant. We meet a severe test when our children misbehave in public. We feel a sense of shame and humiliation because they put us in a position of seemingly inadequate parents. Children behave in public as they are trained to do at home. If they are "out of hand" at home, they will misbehave in public, and we get what we deserve. The trouble is, children do more misbehaving in public because they sense our vulnerability. However, we can use our mental withdrawal-to-the-bathroom to include all the bystanders also. Again, once our attention is focused upon the demands of the situation and not upon our own personal prestige, we have the key to the solution of the problem.

CHAPTER 18

ACTION! NOT WORDS

"How many times do I have to tell you to wash your hands before you come to the table? Now beat it, all three of you. And don't come back to this table until you're clean!" Three chairs scraped back; three children left the table as Mother continued to feed the one-year-old.

How many times do I have to tell you . . . ?" Said thousands of times by thousands of parents, in a tone of complete exasperation. The phrase serves just that purpose: an expression of exasperation. It is useless as a training device. The fact that we even ask, "How many times?" indicates that "telling" has not served the purpose of instruction. Children learn very quickly. One "telling" usually will indicate to the child that a given action has met disapproval. From this time forward he knows his continued behavior in this direction is out of line.

So why do the three children continue to come to the table with dirty hands? What is their hidden purpose? Well, what happens as a result? What does Mother do? She makes a fuss about it. There is the baby getting Mother's attention. Suddenly she is aware of the dirty hands. Now the other three have her attention. They have defied a rule and gained a response. Mother plays right into their hands and serves their purpose. It would be silly to wash their hands as they have been told! Then they couldn't keep Mother busy with them.

If Mother really wants to change the behavior of her children, she will have to *act*. Words are futile. Out of respect for the children she cannot decide what they will do. But she can decide what *she* will do. "I will not sit at the table with you when you have dirty hands." Mother removes the plates and serves no food to people with dirty hands. The second time that Mother finds dirty hands at the table she doesn't even have to say why she does not serve. Now the situation is changed. The children no longer have Mother busy with them. What purpose can dirty hands serve now?

Mother glanced out of the kitchen window to see Bryan, eight, the oldest of four, taking aim at the neighbor's window with his BB gun. "Bryan, come here, honey. I want to talk to you." The boy lowered the gun and strolled slowly toward Mother, who held the screen door open for him. She led him to the den, sat him on the footstool and herself on the chair. "Now, you know, dear, that when we gave you the BB gun we taught you about the dangers of it. We built a special shooting lane in the 'rec' room where the BB's wouldn't hurt anyone or break anything. Isn't that right?" Bryan looked at Mother with wide-eyed innocence and gave the impression of keen interest in this little conference but failed to answer. "Do you know that the BB could break Mrs. Ward's window?" The boy's eyebrows went up. "You see, dear, there *is* quite a bit of force behind those pellets. Just the right angle, and the window would be broken. You wouldn't want to do that, would you?" Bryan lowered his eyes. "After all, honey, you know, if you did break the window, we would have to pay for it. You wouldn't want that to happen, would you?" Bryan again glanced up at Mother with earnestness but still said nothing. "Don't you want to take your gun downstairs now and shoot in the lane we fixed for you? I think that would be very nice." The boy tipped his head, wagged his foot, and said, "I think I'll play outside." "All right, son. But leave the gun inside. Okay?" "Okay," with a shrug.

A few days later Mother found her son shooting at bottles and cans at close range. She again called him in for a conference. Mother repeated the cautions which should be observed with the gun. She reminded him again of the dangers of ricochet. Bryan again gave the appearance of earnest attention. Again after the "talking to" he left the gun in the den and returned to other play outside.

Mother, guided by the concept of "reasoning with the child," did not believe she should punish or "repress" Bryan. So she had nothing left but words. Many parents pile up words in an unending array. The child, who has a purpose behind his behavior and therefore has no intention of changing it, finds all this talk a mere bore and quickly develops immunity to it. He becomes "mother deaf." This deafness eventually includes anyone who offers words as a means of guidance. Parents and teachers all know a great number of children who "don't hear a word I say." And yet they continue this futile approach, redoubling their vain efforts!

Words are supposed to be a means of communication. In a conflict situation, however, the child is unwilling to listen, and words become weapons. Nothing can be conveyed to a child by means of words at a time of conflict. At this point his deafness is total. Whatever is said to him will be ammunition for his own verbal retorts. A verbal war is on. Even if the child says nothing in retort, he is rebellious nonetheless and carries out his rebellion in action. Deliberate defiance or merry mischieviousness are the child's most common forms of action.

Bryan gave the appearance of listening because it served his purpose to do so. He really didn't hear a word that was said. He had no intention of carrying out the instructions he was receiving. To appear to listen was a small price to pay to get his own way. And had Mother really observed and interpreted the facial expressions, she would have seen that Bryan was mocking her.

If reasoning does no good, and Mother doesn't believe in punishment—what can be done? Mother can act: she can take the BB gun away from Bryan. "I am sorry you do not feel like following the rules. You may have the gun when you are ready." This should be done once or twice; after that the gun should be removed. Absolutely nothing more needs to be said.

There is a tragic sequel to the story of Bryan. He continued to use his gun as he pleased. One day he aimed at a bottle at close range. A pellet ricocheted and entered his eye, destroying it.

"Janet, pull up your pajamas. You will fall, walking on the legs like that. And go on upstairs to bed." Mother turned back to her guests and explained, "I got those pajamas on sale yesterday. They are too big for her, but you know how children love anything new. She just had to wear them now. I meant them for next year." By now everyone was looking at the girl who still stood on the stairs and smiled happily at everyone. She glanced down at her feet, which were hidden in the too-long legs of the pajamas, and gave each foot a tenative wave. The extra length flopped enticingly. She looked up again with a happy mischievous smile and surveyed the group. Mother again commanded, "Janet, please pull up the legs before you fall on them. Go on upstairs, now." The child slowly turned and flipped the pajama leg up one step, brought the other up to meet it, turned and again stood looking at the group. Mother's back was turned toward her and she stood for a few moments listening to the adult conversation. Then she sat down, extended both legs, and waved them. Mother, observing the smiling glances of her guests, turned again. "Janet! Do you want to fall? Pull them up, now, and go on upstairs. Carl, come get Janet." Janet turned and rapidly climbed the stairs unmindful of the flapping legs, arriving at the top just as Daddy appeared.

How many times we see potential danger surrounding our children and caution them against it! If they listened to us in earnest, they would be quite fearful of moving in any direction! Mother talks too much. She uses words as threats, fear as a threat.

Janet knew exactly how to control the legs of her pajamas. Her movements were much too studied to show unawareness of the danger involved. She had the pajamas, and her mother, under her control. She found it agreeable to have Mother express so much concern for her. She knew that she belonged in bed, but she took advantage of this opportunity to get Mother's attention away from her friends and onto herself. For Janet, this is a proof of her skill in keeping Mother concerned with her. The more challenging the situation, the greater her victory. And Mother has responded as Janet sensed that she would.

Many times the parent's action should be nothing more than keeping the jaws together. Parents who try this for the first time may find the effort very great indeed. They feel so terribly pressured to *do something* about the situation. It doesn't take long to discover that their very silence reduces the tension of the situation and often restores family harmony. However, some mothers can shout with their mouths closed!

Mother should have said nothing at all to Janet about the pajamas. She should have acted, giving the child a choice of going to bed by herself or being carried up.

One Sunday, Terry, five, stood in the corner of the Sunday-school classroom, crying. Mother coaxed and begged him to stop. "If you don't stop crying, I'm going to go off and leave you." The boy cried louder. "Now I'm *really* going to go." Terry screamed and edged toward the door after Mother. She slipped out of the door and right back in again when Terry let out a piercing wail. "Now, Terry, you must stay right here and stop crying immediately." The teacher stepped in. "Mrs. X., why don't you just go on. Terry will be all right." "I'm afraid he'll leave the church. We had trouble before we left home." "I'm sure Terry will join us when he is ready. We'll be glad to have you work with us, Terry. Remember, we are friends." Mother left, and Terry stopped crying but remained in the corner for a while. The teacher returned to the class. Before long, the boy joined the group.

Faced with a screaming, rebellious child, Mother felt helpless and tried to pressure her son into submission with words, more words, and finally threats, which she didn't intend to carry out anyway. She wanted to "make" him stop his crying instead of extricating herself from his pressure. Crying is often mere "water power."

George, five, climbed over the shopping carts in the supermarket, then scooted onto the rails and sat on the turnstile. "George, get down. You're going to get hurt." The boy ignored Mother and hung by his knees from the rail. "Come on, George, get down before you get hurt." Mother pulled a cart from the line. Her son pulled himself up and impishly sat on the turnstile to prevent another woman from coming through. Mother called, "George, get down so the lady can get through." George climbed down, then scrambled up onto the carts. "George, come on!" Mother proceeded down the aisles without him. George played on the rails and the turnstiles until his mother had finished shopping and went after him to say she was ready to leave.

So many times a parent feels that the words themselves will have a punitive effect. When the child still fails to respond, the parent usually manages a strategic retreat, leaving the child the unrestrained, uninhibited, and uneducated victor. Nothing has been accomplished toward training the child in co-operation. The parent is vaguely aware of this and at the next occasion redoubles his efforts to "teach" the child by "reasoning with him," with the same results.

In order to pull ourselves out of this dilemma, we must learn to substitute action for words. We must adopt the motto, "At the time of conflict, keep your mouth shut and act."

George is mother-deaf. Mother should keep her mouth shut and act. Instead, she hopes to win co-operation with the threat of danger. George knows better. He is completely aware of what his body can do and how little danger is involved. Very few children get hurt climbing over the rails and turnstiles in the markets.

When Mother found that her words made no impression, she retreated, leaving George the unrestrained victor. But in the end she went to tell him that she was ready to leave so that he would not be left stranded. George apparently has Mother better trained to take care of what he wants than she has him trained in proper behavior.

The misbehavior of children in the supermarkets has become so common that it is accepted as normal. Actually, a grocery store is not a playground. Children can be trained to understand this difference and to behave accordingly.

Before they enter the store, Mother can say, "George, the store is not a playground. You may walk down the aisle with me and help get the groceries." When George jumps up onto the carts, Mother may immediately lead him by the hand out of the store and to the car. "I'm sorry you don't feel like behaving in the store. You may wait for me in the car."

With such firm behavior, Mother can show George that she means business. She follows through by not taking him on the next shopping trip but, on the subsequent one, allows him a choice of coming with her if he thinks he can behave himself. She must resist the temptation to use words as threats—"If you don't behave, you'll have to stay in the car.

You don't want that to happen, do you? So you'll be good, won't you?" He won't.

The only two forms of action that do not express—and therefore do not increase—hostility are the use of natural consequences or, if this is not possible, removal from the situation.

Four-year-old Johnny was running over the rows in the garden that Mother had just planted. "Johnny, get out of my garden!" The child continued to run back and forth over the newly seeded beds as if he hadn't heard his mother. "Johnny! Get out of my garden. You're ruining it!" He continued, unheeding, to run back and forth. Four times more Mother yelled at him. He continued to run until he was tired, then, with a laugh, he ran to the bushes and sat down in the shade. Mother glanced at him and went on with her work.

A few days later Johnny ran over a newly seeded bed in a neighbor's yard. With deliberate intent he took short stomping steps over the fine earth in the rows. The neighbor firmly took his hand and led him to the gate of her fence-enclosed yard. "See here, young man. You are not welcome in this yard. Stay out." Looking up, she saw Johnny's mother coming for him and realized that she had been overheard. "Did he hurt something?" Mother asked. "Of course he did," replied the angry neighbor. "He's too little to have enough sense to stay off the flower beds, and I don't want him in this yard, now or in the future." "Well, I'm sorry," huffily replied the mother. The neighbor continued, "He doesn't mind me any better than he minds you. He'd better not come back in this yard." Johnny burst into sobs. "My poor darling," Mother comforted and picked him up. She walked back to her own yard with the child sobbing against her shoulder as she comforted him against "that mean old woman."

Johnny is a misguided boy who feels that unless he has his own way he has no place. He is a tyrant. He does as he pleases, and no one can stop him—at least not with words! He stopped tromping on Mother's garden when *he was ready*, after he had sufficiently annoyed her. Mother's continued admonitions fell on deaf ears. Since she does nothing but talk, Johnny continues to do as he pleases.

The neighbor, on the other hand, acted. She led him out of her yard. Of course, she displayed her anger at both Johnny and his mother in her comments about Johnny's size and his lack of obedience. In return, Johnny's mother felt that he was under attack and instantly offered her sympathy, which was certainly unwarranted. If her son has acted in such a way as to provoke anger and hostility, he should be allowed to experience rejection of his behavior rather than to be shielded against it with ill-advised sympathy. By feeling sorry for him, Mother encouraged Johnny further in his role as a tyrant. He now knows that not only can he do as he pleases at home, but that Mother will protect him from any unpleasant results of doing as he pleases abroad. But Johnny's tyrannical behavior will not find acceptance anywhere in society. Tyrants have no social function. Actually, Johnny wants to belong. He lives alone in an adult world, and he is so much the beloved child who came later in life that his parents indulge his every whim and make themselves his abject servants. In so doing, they have undermined his natural inclination to belong through usefulness and have encouraged him in his mistaken assumption that he can belong only if he can overpower all the large-looming adults.

In order to help Johnny out of his mistaken approach, his parents must first realize their own mistaken concept of how to express their love. Then they must act, rather than talk.

Johnny would have been much more impressed in the garden scene if Mother had taken his hand and led him into the house. "I'm sorry you don't feel like behaving. You may come out again when you are ready." Mother need not offer any further explanation about his behavior or why it is wrong. He knows very well that he shouldn't run over the newly seeded bed. Inasmuch as Johnny is already a tyrant, this new treatment will meet with hot resistance. When he again starts to tramp over the garden, Mother may again remove him to the house, saying again, "You may come back out when you want to behave." Johnny should always be offered another chance to try again and always be returned to the house when he shows unwillingness to comply. As long as Mother remains cool and quietly establishes her right to maintain order, there is no power contest involved. Her firmness will be understood, and eventually her action will bring respect. Johnny badly needs to learn respect. Action, not words will bring this about.

CHAPTER 19

DON'T SHOO FLIES

As Mother pushed Connie, almost two, in her stroller, the child stuck her foot out and dragged the toe of her shoe along the sidewalk. "No, no, Connie." The girl put her foot back onto the tray but, a few minutes later dragged it again. Each time that this happened, Mother said, "No, no, Connie." Finally, in a temper, Mother reached down and slapped the child's leg. "I said to stop that!" she yelled. Connie kept her foot in place for the rest of the stroll.

"Harry, hurry up. You'll be late." Mother called her seven-year-old and continued to prepare breakfast. "Harry! Come on!" she repeated a few minutes later, and again a few minutes after that. Finally, she went to his door and raised her voice. "Will you get out here this minute!" Harry jumped into action and arrived at the table.

"Stop sniffing, Scott," Daddy addressed his eight-year-old, who suffered from hay fever. The family was watching television, and Scott, absorbed in the story, presently sniffed again. Daddy, annoyed, again asked him to stop. The sniffing continued intermittently until Daddy turned his full attention to Scott and demanded, "*Will* you get a tissue and stop that sniffing?" Scott resentfully did as he was told.

In each of the foregoing examples, the child has provoked his parent into an irritated reaction that can be described as "shooing flies." Exasperated by disturbing behavior, we are inclined to brush it aside with "don't," "stop that," "no, no," "hurry up," "be quiet," and so on, as we would wave aside a bothersome fly. In each of these examples, the parent finally became forceful or violent. While this is a completely "natural" reaction, it is ineffective as a training method—or rather, it trains the child to believe that he does not have to mind us until we become violent! Since this is not what we really want, it behooves us to watch what *we* are doing when we are concerned with his behavior. Our "shoo fly" reaction is our response to the child's demand for attention. Our indiscriminate use of admonitions has little meaning to the child and is of no value to us, since we wish to do more than to provide attention for such transgressions. If we wish to stop a child from doing something or to request that he comply with order, we need to give the matter our full attention from the beginning and then stand by until the requirement has been met.

Sometimes it is a matter of taking time to train a child. Connie's mother can stop pushing the stroller whenever the child drags her foot. No words are necessary. Connie will soon understand and keep her foot in place if she wants to ride. Mother's quiet insistence will be much more effective as a training method than her continued "No, no," and the final slap.

At other times it may be more effective to use logical consequences. Harry's mother could explain to him that she will no longer see to it that he gets to the breakfast table on time and let him take over from there. If words, and finally force, are stopped, Harry may catch on that Mother really means what she said: it is up to him to get to breakfast on time—or go to school without it. She cannot influence Harry to change his behavior by nagging; he merely becomes "mother-deaf."

Scott *does* have a problem with his hay fever. And it keeps his family aware of him and his problem if he sniffs. Besides, who wants to run for a tissue in the middle of an absorbing story? However, Daddy realizes that sniffing can easily become an obnoxious habit, and he doesn't want Scott to develop it. So he shoos the fly. And Scott continues to sniff. Daddy can turn his full attention from the television to his son and get his attention with a quiet "Scott." Then just look at him. Chances are that the boy will go and get a tissue. In this way, Father can establish his influence through quiet insistence. Words are not our only means of communication. Often they are the least effective. If we want to influence a change in our child's behavior, we need to watch our own. Is what we are doing bringing the desired results, or are we merely brushing aside an annoyance?

CHAPTER 20

USE CARE IN PLEASING: HAVE THE COURAGE TO SAY "NO"

"Mother, buy me a new pool," Steve demanded. "What on earth for?" "I don't like this one any more. Take me now to buy a new one." "Steve, I'm too tired. We can get it tomorrow." "Now!" The boy stamped. "Steve, please. We have been out so many times today. First swimming, then to your riding lesson, then swimming again. Can't a new wading pool wait until tomorrow?" "I want to go right now and get a new pool." Mother continued to plead that she was too tired. Her son cried, screamed, cursed, then kicked her. Finally, she gave in, drove to the store, and bought a new and larger wading pool.

MOTHER has a deep feeling that Steve has been cheated because she and Daddy are divorced. To make up for this misfortune, she wants to provide Steve with every possible advantage. Steve senses this attitude and takes advantage of it to get everything he wants. If Mother were to say "no" to Steve's completely unreasonable demands, he would be frustrated. Mother thinks he has enough to bear and should not be "deprived" to boot.

There really is no reason why Mother shouldn't satisfy

Steve's every whim as long as she is sure she will be able to do so until his death. There is no need for Steve to learn how to cope with frustration as long as Mother can guarantee that she will be there to prevent frustration forever. Under these conditions, Mother may continue her role of abject slave, continue to accept abuse and kicks from her tyrant, continue to allow him to disrupt order, to disrespect her, to see himself as a powerful person who demands and receives, and to develop even greater skill in using anger to control.

"Mother, please, can I go to the show tonight with Linda?" Carla asked from the phone. "Her mother will take us." "No, Carla. You know you can't go on a school night." "But, Mother, this is a real special good show and it won't be there Friday." "What's so special about it?" "It's a real good dog story—you know, Mother—from the book. You saw the ads. Please, just this once. I won't be tired tomorrow—I promise." Mother considered. I hate to deny her something that means so much to her. She loves animal stories so! And it *is* a good story. I suppose it won't hurt this once. Besides, if I don't let her go, she will be so ugly all evening that I won't be able to stand it. "All right. But come home immediately after the show is over." Carla returned to the phone. "She says I can go!" she yelped in glee.

Carla has Mother well trained. She is winsome and logical in her request and plays upon Mother's desire to please. But if Mother should actually refuse, Carla would punish her by being unbearably ugly. Carla gets what she wants. Mother allows Carla to disrespect order and break routine. When Mother can't say "no" she shows a lack of respect for herself, for Carla and her health needs, for routine, and for order. If Mother were to keep account, she would be astonished at how many "just this once" requests are filled. Each one by itself may sound perfectly reasonable; but the regularity of such "victories" should cause Mother to reconsider. It is the implied threat in the request that makes it a dictatorial demand.

Feeling obligated to please a child as much as possible is a mistake, because it is a servile attitude that promotes self-centeredness in the child. Carla regards life as a business of getting her own way—or else. Her attention is fixed upon herself and her desires, not upon the needs of the situation. Her ability to develop co-operativeness is undermined. When she can't have her own way she makes everyone miserable. Carla is spoiled. She has no idea how to handle frustration, how to accept "no" graciously and to make the best of it. The sad part of it is that Carla will be horribly handicapped in life when she meets situations where no one is concerned with pleasing her.

Our shortsightedness makes it difficult to see the long-term results of yielding to the child's every whim, since pleasing him usually brings temporary harmony to the home. Therefore it is wise to use care in pleasing. Children need to learn how to manage frustrations. Adult life is full of them. It is sheer nonsense to assume that the child will be able to meet frustrations when he is older. What magic in growing older could provide a skill that should be developed in early life? Balance between pleasing and not pleasing needs careful consideration. If the routine and order of the home require denial, and if Mother has the courage to say "no," Carla can acquire the desperately needed skill to tolerate frustration.

Four-year-old Paul accompanied his mother to the grocery store, carrying a loaded water pistol. Mother turned just in time to see him squirt a woman in the face. "Paul! Shame on you. You know better than that! Put that thing away now." The child lowered the gun as if to put it in the holster, pouted, and gazed at the floor. A few minutes later he saw the same woman and again squirted her in the face. Horrified, Mother grabbed the gun and apologized to the woman. Paul screamed and stomped. People turned to stare. Mother quickly handed the gun back to Paul. "All right. Let's go now."

Mother lacked the courage to say "no." She couldn't stand to have people hear her child scream. Mother has trained Paul to feel justified in his demands and to get his own way no matter how outrageous it is. He in his turn has trained Mother so well that she is ready and willing to submit to his tyranny.

A great many children will violently express their resentment at being denied what they want. Nonetheless, Mother is obligated to maintain order: she cannot let Paul squirt people. Since he is unwilling to restrain himself, Mother cannot let him have the pistol. "When you are ready to keep the pistol in the holster and leave it there until we get home, you may have it again." Mother must respect his right to express his resentment, but also respect her right to say "no" —and mean it! If people stare, that is unpleasant; but the training and development of the child are more important. We must learn to be concerned with the demands of the situation and to be unconcerned with "what people think." Here Mother must make a choice between her vanity, which is hurt, and her obligation as a mother.

Willie, three, stood at the toy counter in the dime store whining. "What is it you want, Willie?" "That." Willie pointed to a toy accordion he had been trying to reach. "No, Willie. It is too noisy. You can't have it. I'll buy you a little car." The child whimpered, "I don't want a car. I want that." Mother ignored him and continued looking at some merchandise on the opposite counter. Willie clung to Mother's leg, crying, "I want it, I want it, I want it." "Oh, for heaven's sake. Here, I'll get it for you." When the clerk handed Mother the package, the boy reached for it. "When we get home. It is too noisy for the store." Willie cried tempestuously, "Now! Now! Now!" "You can carry it, then. But don't take it out of the package." Willie immediately tore the wrapper off the toy. Mother looked on helplessly. He pulled the toy back and forth, producing a hideous noise. "All right, now, Willie. You know how it sounds. Wait till we get home or I'll take it away from you." He pulled and pushed. Mother grabbed the toy. He screamed. Mother gave it back. The child pulled and pushed. Mother became furious. "Will you wait till we get out of the store?" Willie was unimpressed. Finally, Mother pushed her son out of the store. "You make me furious. Why couldn't you at least wait till we were outside?"

Mother lacks the courage to say "no" and face Willie's displeasure. By all means, he must be pleased and kept content. Willie has his mother under his thumb.

There is absolutely no reason why we should buy a child every toy that he sees and thinks he wants. Nor is there any good reason to buy him something every time he goes shopping with us. Such actions pamper a child's whims and make him feel that these purchases are his right. "If Mother won't buy me something, she doesn't love me any more." The child is not nearly as interested in the toy as he is in proving that Mother must constantly give. The toy itself has little value; it may soon be discarded. Making Mother *give* becomes all-important.

Toys should have a useful purpose or meet a given need. They should be given on days when presents are expected— or seasonally, such as jump ropes in the spring, baseball mitts and water toys in the summer, indoor games for winter, etc. Shopping should be purposeful. The child forms ideas about money and about shopping when he goes with us. If there is no limit to what he can demand, he assumes that the supply of money is limitless, and his sense of the value of material things becomes distorted.

Willie's mother would show much greater love for him and greater concern for his welfare if she were more careful in pleasing him and maintained an attitude of "no" to random buying. As it is, she is completely unable to establish order because she lacks courage, is afraid of the child's reprisal, and therefore cannot say "no" and be firm.

"We need cereal today, Laura. Would you like to choose it?" Happily, Laura, six, regarded the array of boxes, chose one, and put it in the shopping cart. Mother accepted the choice, whereupon the girl ran to the candy counter, selected candy, and brought it back to Mother. "No, Laura. Not today. We have enough candy at home." "But I want this kind today." "You may get that kind the next time we shop," Mother said, smiling. "Come help me pick out some oranges." Laura returned the candy and joined Mother at the fruit counter.

Mother shows a reasonable desire to please Laura. She offered her a choice of cereal. The child shares some of the responsibility. However, when Laura made an unreasonable request, Mother said "no" in a friendly manner, and won co-operation by suggesting a future time for the satisfaction of the desire and, even more important, another area in which Laura could help now. Laura is learning how to shop with a purpose.

It is natural that we want to please our children. It gives intense satisfaction to satisfy their desires. However, if we reach the point where we try to please the child at the expense of order or give in to his demands unduly out of fear, then we need to be alert to the dangers in these actions. We need not be arbitrary in refusing to give a child what he wants. But whenever the child's desire or request is contrary to order or to the demands of the situation, then we must have the courage to stick to the "no" that expresses our own best judgment.

CHAPTER 21

AVOID THAT FIRST IMPULSE:
DO THE UNEXPECTED

Every time that three-week-old Donna cried, Mother rushed to see if she was all right. She picked her up, checked her all over, held her, and waited for her to fall asleep again. Then she gently put her back in her crib.

Donna cries—Mother picks her up. This ritual is repeated every time she cries. As a consequence, whenever the baby wants to be picked up she cries. Isn't it a successful technique? Even an infant senses his environment and what he can do with it. Picking Donna up every time she cries encourages her in demanding attention and service as a means of feeling wanted. Tiny babies are wonderfully cuddly and there is such a delightful feeling in holding them that it is very easy to respond to this impulse. However, if we were aware that we were depriving our baby of her right to rest and were giving her a mistaken idea of how to find her place in the world, wouldn't our parental love prompt us to act differently in the interests of the child? A set routine providing time for rest and time for cuddling helps an infant to discover regularity in life and the comfort of an established order. It is therefore essential to avoid that first impulse. Instead, stop and consider—what does the *situation* demand?

Daddy, Bevin, eight, Mary, six, and Sarah, three, were building a snow man. Bevin lost interest and started a game of his own, running and sliding on the packed snow. As Daddy reached out to put the head on the snow man, the boy slid into him, knocking the ball of snow out of his hands. "Gee, Dad, I'm sorry. I didn't mean to!" "Well, watch it," Daddy said crossly. A few minutes later, Bevin slid into Mary and knocked her down. Her foot jammed into the base of the snow man and spoiled it. She burst into tears. "Bevin, go into the house. We'd rather not have you out here."

Daddy, acting on impulse, did exactly what Bevin wanted him to do. Bevin, twice dethroned, and by girls at that, assumes that he has no place in this family. This is the reason for "losing interest" in the common activity. He behaves in such a way that he can prove to himself the veracity of his assumption, although he is not aware of the reason for his behavior. He manages to get himself rejected. Actually, he really isn't very nice. No wonder Daddy and his sisters don't want him around.

Bevin needs someone to understand and help him. If Daddy had understood Bevin's doubt about having a place in life, and knew why he prompted rejection, he could have avoided that first impulse to send Bevin away. He would not as easily have fallen into Bevin's trap. (Of course, it is often most difficult to resist the child's provocation!)

The whole situation would have taken a different turn had Daddy done the unexpected. Since Bevin wants to slide, he could suggest that they stop building the snow man for a while and join Bevin in a sliding game. Daddy could ignore Mary's howls and enthusiastically suggest, "Bevin, you lead us, and we will tramp the snow down in a wide path so that we can all slide." Since Bevin is in high spirits, he probably will co-operate. Such action will forstall the boy's attempt to be rejected, reverse his role into that of leader, and promote family fun. Disturbing behavior can thus be turned into constructive, useful activity.

"How long has your throat been sore, Robert?" the office nurse asked the four-year-old. Mother answered for him. "He complained of it yesterday morning." "He gets sore throats real often," chimed in Becky, eight. The nurse again directed her question to Robert. "Do you feel hot?" Again, Mother replied, "He didn't seem to have any temperature this morning." "Did you eat any breakfast?" "He drank a little milk." "Does Mother always answer for you?" Mother laughed. "Not too much. At least, I try not to. His sister does it all the time, and it drives me crazy."

Robert skillfully gets others to do his talking for him. He is the baby, who has no chance to talk for himself. Discouraged in the beginning, he has discovered that he can sit back, mute, unresponsive—even in facial expression—and let the capable and voluble women take over. He may resent this; but if one watches closely, one can see that, time and again, he lets them serve him. The apparent masters are actually his servants!

If Mother wants Robert to grow up, she will have to shut up. Her first impulse to talk for him gets her—and the boy —into trouble. She must also ignore Becky's answers for Robert. Again, Becky may think that she displays her superiority over the baby; but actually, she has been put into his service.

"Which cereal would you like, Robert?" He could answer, but he waits. Someone will answer for him. Sure enough, Becky pipes up, "He wants corn flakes." "Robert can talk for himself. Why don't we wait until *he* says what he wants?" No cereal is served until the boy states his preference.

Whenever we respond on impulse to what a child does, we can be pretty sure that we are merely doing what he wants us to do, although the child himself may not be aware of this. If he wheedles and whines when we are on the phone, we respond to his desire for our full attention. If we are provoked into scolding him for tracking mud in on the freshly scrubbed floor, he probably has succeeded in involving us in a power contest. If we fasten his coat for him because he is having trouble with it, we reaffirm his self-concept of helplessness and place ourselves into his service, which is the strength of the "weak" child.

Charles, six, had come in from school and found the dinner dessert pudding cooling on the window ledge. He stuck his fingers in the dish and licked them off several times. Mother caught him in the process. "Charles! Now you can't have any pudding for dinner." At the table, Mother served Daddy his pudding first and then served the others but omitted Charles. Daddy asked why. Mother explained the situation while Charles hung his head and sat with a sad expression on his face. Finally Daddy said, "Aren't you going to give him any pudding?" "No. I said he couldn't have any as a punishment." "Don't be so strict; after all, he only tried to taste the pudding." And at Daddy's insistence, Mother weakened and let him have his dessert.

Daddy felt so sorry for Charles, who looked sad and hurt, that he joined him in alliance against mean old Mother, who was unreasonable. Clever Charles! He got Daddy to join him in making Mother feel miserable because she had punished him. What a wonderful retaliation—subtle revenge! Daddy followed his first impulse and reinforced Charles's scheme of revenge, signified by his deeply moving expression of sadness. Daddy should avoid his impulse and, in this case, mind his own business. The conflict is between Mother and Charles. He has no part in it. (See Chapter 26.)

"Milton, come back here and pick up your clothes. How many times do I have to tell you to leave your room neat before you go to school? Put your dirty clothes in the hamper. Get your shoes

into the closet. Put your jacket on a hanger. For heaven's sake!
A nine-year-old boy should know how to keep his room neat. I
can't understand why you have to be so darned messy! What on
earth is all this junk doing on your desk?" Et cetera, et cetera,
et cetera.

Mother's attempt to control through words is utterly futile.
Milton is messy because it defeats Mother, who wants him
to be neat. He has Mother involved in a power contest in
which he wins a thousand victories to her one. She does what
Milton wants—keeps up the conflict so that he can continue
to defeat her. He may eventually pick up now, with a great
display of resentment (which infuriates Mother), and tomorrow, it will be just the same game again.

There are several unexpected things Mother could do. He
certainly would not expect her to withdraw from the contest.
At a friendly moment Mother could say, "Milton, I shall no
longer be concerned about how your room looks. You may
have it just as *you* want it. After all, it *is* your room and
really none of my business." It would be a mistake to say
this just as Milton leaves for school. Then she is angry at the
mess and Milton would see in it a new tactic to force him,
and no good will be accomplished. Mother must actually
feel no concern. It is his problem. Let him solve it. She
washes *only* the clothes in the hamper. Let the logical consequences follow. No need to talk! On house-cleaning day,
she may ask Milton if he would like her to help him clean
his room and then abide by his decision. At no time should
she mention the mess in his room, comment on it, or be
irritated by it. This will not be easy, but it is essential if
Mother wants to extricate herself from the power struggle
and stimulate her son into proper behavior. Should Mother
feel that one way or another she *is* going to *make* Milton
keep his room tidy, she continues the power contest, defeats
herself, and fails to win co-operation.

From early infancy children are engaged in exploring ways and means of finding their place, of being significant, important. As they discover a technique for reaching this goal, they cling to it, regardless of how many times they are scolded or punished. The unpleasantness of parental reaction does not diminish the satisfaction of feeling important. As long as the method they have chosen brings results, they will stick to it and continue their bid for attention or power.

The child is seldom aware of the purpose of his misbehavior and disturbance. Often neither he nor his parents are aware that it is part of his attempt to find a place and to belong to the group. If his behavior violates order and disrupts co-operation, he is using faulty methods to reach his basic goal, and our impulsive response usually reinforces his mistaken assumption. He not only becomes further discouraged but also more convinced that there is no other way for him to behave.

If we look at our response, we can discover what the child gains from it. If we cease to respond as formerly, his efforts may appear to him to be futile, and he may seek a better and more useful method, particularly if we diligently provide attention and a means for gaining status in a more constructive way.

CHAPTER 22

REFRAIN FROM OVERPROTECTION

"Johnny. Johnny!" Mother stood at the front door calling her seven-year-old, who was playing a half block away. Getting no answer, she walked up to where he was. "Johnny, don't you think you should have a sweater on? It is a bit chilly this morning." "No, it isn't Mom. I'm warm enough." "Well, I think you should have it. I'll bring it to you." Mother returned to the house, got the sweater, went back to Johnny, and put it on him.

AN overprotective mother plays the high authority who decides when Johnny is warm and when he is cold. Johnny accepts her decisions because, in doing so, he keeps Mother constantly occupied with him. Mother provides services that are not necessary. Since Mother decided he needed a sweater, he remained where he was; through his passivity, he forced her to walk home and back to him again. Mother, completely unaware of the interaction, thinks that she has the situation well in hand.

"Hey, Mom. Can we go to the store and get some stuff? We want to make a lemonade stand." "No, Jimmy, I can't let you go to the store alone." "Aw, Mom. It's only four blocks. Please," begged Jimmy, seven. "Please, Mom. Please let us. It's a hot day and we could sell a lot," added Marvin, five and a half. "I can't take you now, and you are too little to go by yourselves. Besides, you would have to buy so many things! Paper cups and lemons and all. And where would you make your stand?" "Out front. A lot of people would buy." "No, I don't think so." And Mother talked her boys out of the idea. As they walked out of the house, Jimmy said scoffingly, "Aw! She's just scared!" Marvin nodded.

Mother *is* "scared." She is afraid that something might happen to her boys if she lets them out of her sight. She is trying to protect them from harm, which is a natural and normal desire. But Mother overdoes it. She sees potential danger lurking everywhere. She is overprotective.

We cannot protect our children from life. Nor should we want to. We are obligated to train our children in courage and strength to face life. Mother's desire to protect her boys from possible harm may have a discouraging effect. It may keep them helpless and dependent upon her. And here is one clue to Mother's mistaken attitude.

Under the pretext of concern for their welfare, we keep our children helpless and dependent so that we may appear big and powerful and protective, in the eyes of the child as well as our own. It places us in a superior dominant position and keeps our children submissive. However, today's children will not tolerate such efforts. They rebel.

The second reason behind our overprotective efforts is our own doubt that we have the ability to tackle our problems; therefore, we have much less confidence in the ability of small children to take care of themselves.

For the time being, Jimmy and Marvin have accepted Mother's dictum—but with scorn, not with respect. They frown on her timidity.

The manner in which the child deals with the overprotective parent depends upon the child's goals. The most dangerous response is that of the fourth goal—helplessness. Completely discouraged, the child may give up and expect to be protected forever from all of life's difficulties.

Two months ago it was discovered that Joe, six, has diabetes. He is given a daily dose of oral insulin which Mother calls his "vitamins." Joe has not been told anything about his condition. Mother justifies her actions on the basis that she doesn't want Joe to become "odd." All discussion of the disorder with the doctor is done out of Joe's presence. She reminds him daily that he must eat only what she gives him so that the "vitamins" will work.

Mother's concern is understandable. When a child has an organic disability, we strive to keep him as normal as possible. However, evasions and lies seldom serve this purpose. Mother is overprotective. She wants to control this situation and to bear for him the responsibility for his food intake. Eventually, Joe will have to know of his condition, because he himself will have to deal with it. If Joe had the measles, Mother would tell him what was the matter and nurse him through it. One gets over the measles, so it doesn't seem as formidable as diabetes, which is likely to be a lifelong problem. The latter is much more difficult to explain to a child. However, at six, Joe is certainly old enough to understand that he needs medicine to help his body function. A casual attitude in the beginning will help the boy develop a healthy attitude of his own. "There is a gland in your body that doesn't work properly. We have to help it with this medicine called insulin. The insulin cannot help if you give it too much to do, so we have to be careful about how much you eat." Joe may gradually become aware that he has a distinctive disorder that he can manage and still live a normal life. It is Joe's problem. He needs help and encouragement to face it. The best encouragement is an acknowledgement that he can deal with it. As he grows older and learns more about body function, his knowledge of his disorder can be increased. The frequent urine tests can be explained. "This is how we can tell if the gland is getting enough help." If Mother doesn't feel overwhelmed by the problem, she can give Joe the necessary approach for meeting his problem. As long as she shields him from the problem, she denies him his right to learn how to cope with it.

There is nothing more frustrating than to be determined to do the impossible. We cannot arrange everything and control life, either for our children or for ourselves. The desperate attempt to do so accounts for a major part of the misery around us. Our children learn from us to fight the inevitable, especially if we try to protect them from all hardships and discomforts. Having accomplished it for a while, the child feels that we should continue to do so. The resulting disillusionment leads to anger and resentment—not only against the parent, but against life itself for not letting us arrange it according to our liking. The "spoiled brat" is the child who is in a constant fury because life is not amenable to his wishes. What a futile and pathetic demand! Unfortunately a child does not necessarily lose his "spoiled bratishness" as he grows into adulthood. It may become a fundamental attitude toward life. When we pamper and coddle our children and try to protect them from life, this is the gift we give them: a helpless fury against an outrageous world.

To avoid this grievous mistake we must realize that we are not omnipotent nor omniscient. But we have the obligation to instruct our children in ways, means, and attitudes with which to cope with life. The formula: let us first examine what it is that confronts us. Then we seek an answer to the question, "What can I do about it?" Even a very young child can be led into an analysis of a disturbing situation by the use of simple questions. Children have very active brains. Let us train them to use them.

"Mother! George tore my book," screamed Bruce in fierce anger at the action of his baby brother.

Bruce has stated his problem—and shown his reaction to it. He wants Mother to solve it for him and to do something about it. Preferably, punish George.

"Oh, darling, I'm awfully sorry the book is torn. There is nothing we can do about *that*. But what could you do so that George doesn't tear another book?" "I don't know," Bruce yelled in fury. "You have to do something to make him stop." Mother remained calm in the face of Bruce's anger. "You think about what *you* can do, Bruce, and we will talk about it later." "I want to do something now!" Mother left for the bathroom. Later, when Bruce was calm again, Mother brought up the subject. Bruce, remembering the "injustice," at first responded with renewed hostility, but Mother walked around it. "We can't *make* George stop tearing, you know, Bruce. What else could be done?" By continued adroitly placed questions, Mother finally enabled Bruce to see that he could keep his books out of reach.

It is our own sense of superiority over our children that makes us think they are too little to solve problems or to take frustration in their stride. This false impression must be acknowledged and replaced with trust and confidence in the child's abilities, and with our desire to provide guidance. Certainly we don't abandon a child to his fate, nor do we let him experience the full impact of life all at once. We use our heads! Instead of being a front behind which the child basks in innocence, we become a sieve, which filters life experience in amounts which the child can meet. We are constantly on the alert for opportunities to step back and allow our child to experience *his* strength. We stand ready to step in at the point at which the problem becomes too much for him. We can start this procedure at the day of his birth. Little by little, with care and guidance, we hand our child life and its problems, challenges, and satisfactions.

CHAPTER 23

STIMULATE INDEPENDENCE

Never do for a child what he can do for himself.

THIS rule is so important that it needs to be repeated many times.

Five-year-old Mary was the delight of her mother's heart. She was exceptionally pretty, and her mother kept her beautifully dressed and well groomed. She gave her her daily bath, put on her dresses, fastened her shoes for her, brushed and combed her hair. Mary was a regular doll; charming, delightful and winsome. She couldn't fasten buttons, pull on socks, tell the front from the back of her dress nor the left from the right shoe.

One night in a Mothers' Study Group meeting the point came up that we should never do for a child what he can do for himself. Mary's mother was incensed. "But I *want* to do everything for Mary. I just *love* taking care of her. She's everything I've got!"

If Mary's mother could realize what she is doing to her child she would be horrified. Actually, her love for her daughter is self-love. She sees herself as the utterly loving mother whose life is dedicated to the service of her child. Mary, on the other hand, is being taught that she is inferior, helpless, dependent, inadequate, useless. Mary probably feels that she has a place only as long as everything is done for her and Mother serves her. She has so little to contribute in terms of action; all she can offer is her charm, which she displays passively.

Within the next year Mary must go to school. Then Mother won't be there to do everything for her and Mary may flounder. Her courage may be undermined and her helplessness even greater. She may then face a crisis for which she is totally unprepared.

Whenever we do something for a child which he can do for himself, we are showing him that we are bigger than he: better, more capable, more deft, more experienced, and more important. We continually demonstrate our assumed superiority and his supposed inferiority. Then we wonder why he feels incapable and becomes deficient!

Doing for a child what he can do for himself is extremely discouraging, since it deprives him of the opportunity to experience his own strength. It shows our complete lack of faith in his ability, courage, and adequacy, robs him of his sense of security, which is based on the realization of his own capacity to meet and solve problems, and denies him his right to develop self-sufficiency—all in order to keep our own image of our indispensability. Thus, we show an immense lack of respect for the child as a person.

Mother, Jean, four, and Wendy, almost three, were putting on wraps to go out and play in the snow. This was always a highlight for the girls since Mother really enjoyed the romp and took pleasure in building snow figures with them. Jean put on all of her wraps, including her boots, with no trouble. Wendy dawdled and pouted. She merely stood looking at her self-help snow suit, making no attempt to put it on. "Come on, Wendy, put your suit on," Mother admonished as she fastened her own boots. Wendy put her thumb in her mouth and stood helpless. "Oh, for heaven's sake, Wendy! What is the matter with you? Sit down and do as I taught you." "I can't," the child whimpered. "You do it." "Oh, all right. Come here." Mother impatiently dressed Wendy. Jean watched all of this very contentedly.

Wendy is the baby, who has learned that being incapable and helpless brings Mother's attention and service. Her older sister's ability adds to her discouragement. Jean is content for Wendy to remain helpless because it keeps her own superior position safe. Mother, in her hasty impatience, reinforces the schemes of both girls. She succumbs to Wendy's helplessness and does for her what she could do for herself. Wendy has no chance to develop independence as long as Mother is impatient, in a hurry, and takes the easy way out.

Wendy needs a great deal of encouragement; she needs a new idea about herself and a new way to find her place. What she does not need is the service she gets. It may take time and patience to encourage her. Since Mother has shown Wendy how to get into her suit, she can assume that Wendy knows how. Now she must step back and allow Wendy room to move for herself. It might be wise to give Wendy more time to put her wraps on, let her start earlier. Then encourage her patiently—no hurrying. "You can do it, Wendy. You are a big girl." When Wendy claims that she can't, Mother just refuses to accept Wendy's self-evaluation and turns away with words of support: "Sure you can. Keep trying. When you are ready, come on out with us." It is possible that Wendy may play the situation to the hilt. She may cry pitifully and make no further attempt. This time she may never join Mother and Jean. Mother must avoid her impulse to feel pity and give in to Wendy's helplessness by eventually going back in to dress her and bring her outside to join them. When Wendy finds that she misses out on the fun and that no one is impressed with her pitiful situation, she may change her mind and decide to solve her problem for herself.

Three-year-old Beth Ann was playing at Mother's feet while she was ironing. "Mother, I want you to stop ironing now." "I have two more shirts to finish, honey, and then I'll be through." "But I have to go to the bathroom," Beth Ann whimpered. "You can go by yourself," Mother replied gently. "No, I can't, Mother. I want you to go with me." "I'm sorry. I'm ironing now." "But I can't go by myself." Mother smiled at her daughter and said nothing more. The child threw herself on the floor to start a temper tantrum, seemed to consider for a moment, got up and went to the bathroom alone.

Mother had received counseling at one of the Guidance Centers. Beth Ann, being an only child, had Mother completely in her service. Mother is extricating herself from her daughter's undue demands and letting her become independent. Previous experience had shown Beth Ann that she no longer could get what she wanted with a temper tantrum —which is why she started, then reconsidered. When Mother refused to stop ironing at the girl's demand, Beth Ann tried helplessness as a means of putting Mother back in her service again. Mother quietly and gently refused to do for Beth Ann what she could do for herself. She also refused to engage in a contest of words. Beth Ann is responding with growing independence and a sense of self-sufficiency.

Mother and Kitty, three and a half, entered the elevator of the apartment building. Kitty reached up as far as she could and pressed button number five. Another passenger laughed dryly. "We will be stopping at all floors!" "Oh, no. She pressed the right one," Mother defended. "She did?" the man asked, amazed. "Yes, she knows." Kitty beamed.

Although Kitty is still young enough so that Mother must go with her to the play area of the large apartment building,

Mother is teaching Kitty independence by allowing her to do as much as she can. Kitty takes great pride in being big enough to reach the proper button. She knows that she can do things for herself. And what a thrill it must be for her to realize that she can make that big elevator go and stop!

From earliest infancy, our children show us that they want to do things for themselves. The baby reaches for the spoon because he wants to try to feed himself. All too often we dissuade these early attempts in order to avoid the mess, thereby promoting discouragement and a false self-concept in the child. What a pity! It is so much easier to clean up the baby than to restore his lost courage. As soon as a child demonstrates a desire to do things for himself, we must take advantage of it and let him go ahead whenever possible—and there are so many more opportunities for a child to help himself and others than we usually imagine. He may need help, supervision, encouragement, and training. These we must supply. We do not have the right to do everything for him nor to stop him from making useful contributions that he is eager to make.

The littleness of children is very appealing. It is always a first impulse reaction to reach out and help a child when we see him having a little trouble with what he is trying to do. But we must watch that first impulse. Without realizing what goes on, we so frequently allow ourselves to continue to help our children long after it is necessary because we are so used to doing so. Children find pleasure in having things done for them. There is a certain feeling of power in being able to command services. But children also enjoy their ability if they have a chance to be helpful. As a child grows, his natural inclination leads him to try to do more things for himself and for others. However, this inclination may be smothered by the fear, protection, and service of parents. In such a case, the child gets discouraged and quickly discovers the positive value of his weakness. He assumes that he is unable to do things for himself, assumes he is inadequate, and has a low opinion of his own ability; then he finds comfort in gaining service from others, and his already weakened self-reliance and self-confidence are further undermined. The alert parent can prevent such a development by following the rule at the opening of this chapter. This sounds simple enough. However, the practice becomes difficult when we are in a hurry to get things done or are in the habit of doing them ourselves. We may even be unaware that the child has become capable of taking over. Or, as is so often the case, we underestimate the child's faculties. We tend to minimize a child's abilities and to magnify his helplessness. We must be sensitive to the subtle difference between expecting too much of a child, which is a form of imposing our demands upon him, and having confidence in his abilities, which is a form of respect.

As part of a Girl Scout project, Joan was expected to interview a local veterinarian. "Mother, please. You call him for me." "Why should I call, honey?" "I don't know what to say," Joan replied. "Well, what is it that you want from him?" "I want to talk to him about horse health for my project." "Well, tell him so." "But I don't know how," Joan cried in distress. "I think you can figure that our for yourself, dear." "Mother, please call him for me," the girl begged. "But *I* don't want to know about horse health, Joan. It isn't my project. You can do it. Just try." Joan turned away in dismay and refused to make the call. Mother did nothing further. At the next Scout meeting, Joan's Leader asked how she had come out with her interview. She shamefacedly admitted that she hadn't made the call. "Why don't you get it done this next week, Joan? It is all you have to do to complete your project." That evening Joan again asked Mother to make the call for her. Again Mother refused. "But I don't know the phone number." Mother handed her daughter the phone book with a loving smile. "Go ahead, honey. You can do it." Joan took a long time to find the number, then stood even longer looking at the phone. As she got up the courage and started to dial, Mother left the room. A little later Joan came running with a beaming face. "Gee, he was nice, Mother. He told me so much. And now I can finish my project!" Mother's smile expressed her satisfaction. "I'm so glad you were willing to do it by yourself." And she gave Joan a hug.

Mother was aware of Joan's feeling of panic at facing an unknown person, making a request from a stranger, and dealing with a totally new situation. Her first impulse was to pave the way for Joan. But she quickly recognized her daughter's need to grow and took advantage of this opportunity to let Joan solve her own problem. She knew that the incentive of finishing her project and gaining her Scout award would prompt Joan to follow through. She also had confidence in Joan's ability, and she avoided pressing her into action. Stepping back gave Joan room to develop. She refused to do for Joan what the girl could do for herself. Joan's gain was her growing independence, while Mother's was her satisfaction at her effective stimulation.

This was a delicate situation which needed all of Mother's sensitivity. We must be alert not to ask too much, but, on the other hand, we must be able to recognize a child's ability. Mother provided support for Joan's courage by being firm in her belief that Joan could do it. When the girl finally started to dial, Mother left the room so that Joan would not have to be conscious of Mother's judgment as to how she managed and would be free to conduct the conversation on her own.

Very few parents would, with conscious intent, cripple a child's self-sufficiency. It is for this reason that we must become aware of the dangers of overprotection and be alert to the opportunities to stimulate independence.

Every mother remembers the thrill that accompanied her baby's first steps. Many home movies or pictures have recorded this exciting event. Opportunities for the same feeling of thrilled pride occur countless times through the life of a child if the parents are alert to the various phases of development. The process that led to the baby's first steps alone needs to be repeated in all other aspects of a child's growth. Mother moves back, away from the baby, and holds out her hands—just beyond his reach. She thus encourages him. She has given him *room* to move, independent of her support. He tries. When he succeeds in reaching Mother, he is flushed with triumph, and she is thrilled with his accomplishment. So it is in all other fields—we must step back, give the child room, deny our assistance, and give our encouragement.

CHAPTER 24

STAY OUT OF FIGHTS!

Most parents feel deep concern about the endless fighting that goes on among brothers and sisters. They love each child, and it hurts to see those one loves hate and hurt each other. A great deal of child-raising energy goes into settling fights and trying to "teach" the children to get along together. Many children eventually "outgrow" fighting and begin to appreciate and care for each other as they grow up. Others continue the hostility into adulthood and never make peace with their siblings. No amount of preaching seems to ease the friction. It keeps on popping up. Most parents have tried every known procedure for stopping fights —and still they continue. Fighting among siblings is so common that it has become accepted as a "normal" form of child behavior. It is *not* normal just because it occurs so regularly. Children do not *have* to fight. Homes where children do not fight *are* possible. When they fight, there is something wrong in the relationships. No one can honestly feel good while fighting. Therefore, if children continue to fight, they must be able to gain satisfaction, not so much in the fight as in the results.

This evaluation presupposes that we recognize behavior as

purposive. In this light we cannot be satisfied with the usual "explanations" for fighting—that it is "caused" by an aggressive nature or drive or by heredity and so on. From our point of view, we need to understand a child's behavior in terms of the field in which it occurs and the purpose which it serves.

Lucia, eight, and Calvin, five, were watching TV while Mother fixed dinner. Calvin shoved closer to Lucia. She moved over. Calvin laid his leg over Lucia's. She pushed him aside. Calvin leaned his full weight against Lucia. "Cut it out," Lucia said quietly, annoyed, but still deeply absorbed in the story. Calvin, still watching the show, but not as attentively as Lucia, began tracing the design of her blouse with his finger. She hit his hand away with her fist. "Cut it out, I said." Calvin giggled. He reached up and ran his finger around Lucia's ear. She grabbed his hand and planted her teeth into his arm. "Ow-w-w," Calvin screamed and started crying. Mother dashed into the room. "What on earth is the matter?" she asked in a frenzy. She quickly took in Calvin's anguished crying and the way he was rocking with his arm held against his body. She rushed over to him, took him up, and pulled him to her. He held out his arm. The teeth marks were very evident. "Lucia!" "Well, he kept bothering me." "I don't care what he was doing. You have no right to inflict this sort of thing on your brother."

What was the purpose of this fight? What were the results?

Calvin, the baby, wants Mother's protection. So he behaves in such a manner as to precipitate a situation where he will get it. Lucia feels abused because Mother *does* protect Calvin and wants to use Mother's intervention to promote this feeling of abuse. Therefore, she does the thing that Mother hates most, knowing that Mother will then support Calvin and give her the dickens. Since Calvin was provocative, naturally she suffered abuse, first from Calvin, then from Mother, who took his side against her when she already had put up with so much annoyance from her brother. Without Lucia's form of retaliation, Mother might not have sided with her son and might have even recognized that it was *he* who disturbed.

What should Mother do? First, she should deny herself that first impulse to run at the scream. Now that is a big demand to make of any mother. But stop and think a minute. The scream gets Mother's attention—dramatically. It indicates that something is violently wrong. However, it is, at the moment, the only danger sound. Then comes the crying. Oh. The house isn't caving in, the TV didn't explode, there is no sound except the crying. Well, it must be a fight and Calvin got hurt. Well—it is their fight. I shall just stay out of it.

For a mother to be able to take this action, she will need past experience in keeping herself out of fights. So let us say that she does obey her first impulse—dashes to see what happened. Now she must school herself again not to give in to that first impulse of being horrified at the teeth marks. Having discovered it is a fight that caused the scream, she can withdraw to the kitchen without saying a word. After all, if Calvin doesn't like to get bitten, he will have to stop provoking. This action of Mother's puts the responsibility for the relationship between Calvin and Lucia right into their laps, where it belongs. We have no "power" to arrange the relationships between our children. We can influence their interaction by what we do. If we act in such a way as to eliminate the satisfying results of the fight, we stimulate a new pattern in their relationship. But in order to do this, Mother must learn to recognize the purpose behind the behavior.

"For heaven's sake, stop that fighting. You're driving me crazy," Mother yelled from another room. "Well, Gail won't let me watch my program," Keith yelled back. "I've got a right to see *my* program," Gail answered stormily. With a sigh, Mother wearily went into the living room to settle the fight.

Mother gives the clue to the purpose in this fight situation. The children are bickering over TV. Mother is *annoyed*. "You're driving me crazy," she states. It may be hard to believe, but this is the purpose of the fighting—it drives Mother "crazy." This proves to be an effective means to keep her attention. She moves in as an arbitrator. The fighting annoys her, keeps her in a dither, makes her stop what she is doing and come to "settle matters"; actually, to provide undue attention and service.

Mother can stop being annoyed over the bickering as soon as she realizes that she doesn't *have* to do anything about it. So much of our exasperation results from our feeling overly responsible for our children and their welfare; consequently, we cannot step out of *their* problems. The dispute over the television is between Gail and Keith. Mother has no business to butt in. Once she is aware of this simple principle, she no longer feels compelled to be annoyed. Therefore, she merely goes on with what she is doing and lets Gail and Keith work out their problem. The chances are that when Mother fails to come running, one of the children will. Mother answers, "I'm sorry you are having trouble, but I'm sure you can work it out between you." She turns the responsibility over to the children, where it belongs, and refuses to be involved in what is not her business. She also deprives the children of the expected results that render the bickering useful.

Whatever the reason behind the children's fights, parents only make matters worse when they interfere, try to solve the quarrel, or separate the children. Whenever a parent interferes in a fight he is depriving children of the opportunity for learning how to resolve their own conflicts. We all experience situations in which there are conflicts of interests, and all of us have to develop skills in dealing with conflict situations. We have to learn the give and take of life.

Every time Mother decides who shall see which program, she sets herself up as an authority, and the children learn nothing about co-operation, adjustment, or fair play. As long as we do things for our children, they cannot learn how to manage for themselves. This applies equally to fighting and to developing independence. A child who has all his fights settled for him may never know how to resolve difficult situations and will resort to fighting aimlessly every time he is crossed or can't have his own way.

It is extremely difficult for parents to see why fights between children are none of their business. They consider it their duty to "teach" children not to fight. And they are right. We *should* teach our children not to fight. The trick is to succeed in doing so. Unfortunately, interference and arbitration do not bring this result. While it may stop the children from fighting momentarily, it fails to teach them how to avoid the next fight or how to settle a conflict in another way. If our interference in the fight satisfies the children, why should they stop fighting? If a fight yields no result other than a bruise or even a bloody nose (which will mend), won't the child be more inclined to resolve his conflict in another manner? If the hurt of a fight is not mitigated by electrifying side results, the child may exert much more care in avoiding another hurt. In this way each child may even develop a sense of responsibility for his sibling. (Naturally, Mother may assist in getting the bloody nose taken care of, but without taking sides, without comment as to who is right or wrong. "I'm sorry you got hurt in your fight" is quite sufficient.)

The following is a report made by a mother in one of our Study Groups.

"My husband and I started ignoring the two children's battles. Ordinarily, one child would come running to tattle on the other, and we would jump into the fray and choose a culprit. It was a most nerve-wracking ordeal, with me yelling and spanking. I should feel tense from one of these sessions for the rest of the day. Then I started saying to them, 'I think you can solve your problem yourself,' and kept absolutely quiet no matter what else was said. Very quickly I was able to ignore anything that happened, and, just as quickly, the children stopped coming to enlist our aid. One day I heard the younger one say, 'I'm going to tell Mommie what you did.' The older one said, 'There is no use in telling her. She'll just say you can settle it yourself.' That was the last I heard. I can't tell you what a difference this has made—not having to take sides any more, not to feel myself boiling with rage when one child took advantage of the other. I certainly learned that most of the fighting was to get my attention and that a younger child can take care of himself much better than you'd think. I just so *firmly* believe now that parents should stay completely out of their children's battles; not only for the good of the children, but also because it takes away about ninety per cent of the tension that child-raising entails."

Mother sat on the patio talking to neighbors. Margie, four, started into the house, followed by her younger brother, Bobby. It took him a bit longer to climb the steps so that Margie was already through the door by the time he got there. She carefully closed the door as Bobby started in, a solemn, closed, tight expression on her face. Bobby screamed. Mother dashed up the steps, yanked the door open, grabbed Margie, and swatted her. "What do you mean, treating your brother like that? You could have pinched his fingers. Now you stay inside until you are ready to behave." Mother picked Bobby up, returned to her chair, and held him on her lap. Soon he climbed down and went on with his play. Meanwhile, muted sobs could be heard from the house. Several moments passed. Finally Mother went to Margie. "Are you ready to be a good girl now?" More sobs. Mother picked the child up. Margie nestled her head on Mother's shoulder. Mother carried her outside and sat down with her on her lap. "There, now. There, now. You are Mother's good girl again. I know you won't be bad any more."

Not all fights between children are on the verbal level. Baby Bobby gets lots of protective attention. Capable Margie harbors a natural resentment about being dethroned. This is augmented every time Mother "protects" Bobby. Every once in a while, Margie's sentiments spill over. Margie craves Mother's attention as a sign of her love. She found out that after punishment comes love. Had Mother really seen what happened, she would have noticed that Margie was careful to shut the door without pinching Bobbie's fingers. This indicates a desire for attention, rather than revenge. Had it been the latter, Margie would have actually pinched the boy's fingers. It was not her intention to hurt her brother, but to involve Mother—to provoke her first, and to experience Mother's love after she had been "bad." And the scheme worked beautifully!

Most of the time when the quarreling leads to abuse of the youngest, parents can be sure that the older children are creating a big commotion rather than actually doing harm. One mother gave the following report at a Guidance Center.

She passed the door of the playroom just in time to see Kerry, four, holding a truck over the head of Lindy, eleven months. He seemed to be getting ready to hit her over the head. Lindy started to scream. Mindful of the many admonitions to stay out of fights that she had received at the Center, Mother took her courage in hand and went on past the door. However, she peeked through the crack. What she saw totally amazed her. Kerry was watching the door that she had just passed, and, at the same time, he gently lowered and raised the truck over Lindy's head, barely touching her with it.

Now Mother could really believe what she had been told. Kerry and Lindy were co-operating to involve Mother. Even at eleven months, Lindy knew that if she screamed, Mother ran, and things would happen to Kerry. And Kerry knew that if he made Lindy scream, Mother would come running. The children worked as a team to make Mother run!

As a rule, when one child threatens another with a dangerous object, Mother can quietly come and remove it. The main point is to do it quietly, without excitement, words, and all the fuss which children know only too well how to produce.

At the dinner table, the parents had no chance to converse without constant interruptions. The family consisted of Rose and Billy, aged four and six, Mother's children by a former marriage, and Carl and Marilyn, five and seven, who were Daddy's children by his late wife. Rose swung her feet, kicking Carl's leg. "Daddy, Rose is kicking me," Carl complained. Mother intervened. "Rose, keep your feet quiet and mind your manners." Rose settled down to eating. "Daddy, Billy won't let me have the salt," Marilyn whimpered. "Pass the salt, Billy," Mother demanded. Billy passed the salt. "Mother, Carl keeps bumping my elbow," was Billy's complaint. This time Daddy pitched in. "Keep your elbows where they belong, Carl." The boy tucked his elbows in. "Mother, Marilyn took my napkin," Rose whined. "Give Rose her napkin, Marilyn," Daddy commanded. One after the other, the children annoyed each other, and the victim immediately called for justice. Finally, Daddy blew up. "When will you kids stop this constant fighting? Can't we have *one* meal in peace? I'm sick and tired of all this hullabaloo. Now the next one who steps out of line is going to get thrashed." The children finished the meal without further incident, but everyone was tense and unhappy.

The children's bickering kept their parents busy—not without intention. For this they gladly renounced happiness. It will be noticed that each child complained to his natural parent and that the parent of the offender tried to correct the situation. Each child annoyed a child of the other parent because it was the surest way to provoke action. Parents are far too prone to consider children as being "insecure" and feeling compelled to maintain fair procedure. Therefore, each child is now engaged in trying to provoke the child of the step-parent and to keep his own parent busy with him. It works admirably.

In some families, the parents protect their step-children, in others, their own. But in each case, the children will provoke whoever responds most effectively.

The fact that the children stopped their bickering when threatened with a thrashing shows that the purpose was attention-getting; otherwise such a threat would have led to increased disturbance. They had reached the maximum to be achieved for the moment and were willing to let it ride. Also, each child conformed after he had succeeded in getting the attention of the parents. This, too, shows that the fighting was a bid for attention.

Both parents can help their children only if they discontinue this undue attention and let the children work out their problem. If the behavior of the children at the table disturbs the peace of the family, the parents can refuse to eat with them until they are willing to make dinnertime pleasant. As soon as discord arises, all four children as a group can be excused and asked to leave the table. In this way the children can learn to get along at the table. In removing them, the parents do not enter the conflict, do not take part in the quarreling, and demonstrate firmness.

Six-year-old Susan was sitting beside her brother Harry, nine, who was building with his Erector set. Allen, seven and a half, helped him. All was quiet and serene until Susan slyly dug her heel into Harry. "Cut it out, Susan," Harry yelled at her second thrust. "What?" Susan asked in pretended innocence. After all, she had merely been moving her foot about. Could she help it if Harry was in the way? It happened again. Harry struck Susan with his fist. She jumped up whimpering and ran to the window to look out. Then she ran to look out from a window on the side of the house, and from there she ran to the back bedroom. Here, from the window, she saw Mother working in the rose bed. At this point she let out a piercing scream and burst into tears. "Mother," she screamed out the window, "Harry hit me—hard." Mother stopped her work and came into the house. She looked at the red spot on Susan's arm, comforted her, and went to the boys' room. "Harry, why did you hit Susan?" "She started it," the boy defended himself. "I did not. You just hit me," Susan screamed. "I didn't do a thing." "You did too!" Harry yelled. "You kicked me. Several times." "Mother, I didn't kick him. I just moved a little bit and my foot touched him. I didn't kick him." "You big baby!" Harry exploded. "I didn't hit you all that hard." Mother interrupted, "You ought to be ashamed of yourself. Susan's the littlest one of the family and you're the biggest. You should set a good example. You're just a big bully when you hit someone smaller than you are. Now apologize to your sister. And don't ever hit her again." While Mother was scolding Harry, Allen sat taking in the whole situation. "I don't hit her, Mother," he reminded. "I know, dear. You are a good boy. Harry, you do try me so! Why can't you behave yourself? Now apologize." Susan had dried her tears and stood watching Harry with absorbed interest. Her chin was tucked almost to her chest and she watched from under her eyebrows. A smirking smile played about her lips. "Sorry," Harry grumbled, looking at the floor. "Now play nicely together," Mother admonished. "You should all love each other because you are brother and sister. You shouldn't fight each other." Mother left the room. Harry returned to his building. "Snitch," he hissed between clenched teeth. "Mother said you're supposed to be nice to me because I'm the littlest," Susan sniffed. "Nuts! Get away from this stuff. It's mine and I don't want you around." Susan flipped around and started out of the room. "Go snitch again, Baby," Harry jeered after her. Susan found Mother in the kitchen. "Mother, Harry won't let me play with him. He's teasing me," she whined. Mother returned to the boys' room. "For heaven's sake, Harry. What's got into you, anyway? Why don't you let Susan play with you?" "She keeps messing my stuff up," Harry glowered. "Harry, you are just being too naughty. You come sit in the kitchen chair until you feel like playing with your sister." Mother grabbed Harry's arm as Susan watched with a righteous indignation. Mother led Harry to the kitchen and shoved him into the chair. He kept his eyes down and puckered his mouth into lines of complete rebellion. Satisfied, Susan turned to Allen. "Let's go play outside, Allen, huh?" "Okay, let's play in the tent." The two dashed from the house, slamming the screen door as they left.

So many times we feel that we need eyes in the back of our heads. In this case, Mother could have profited had she really looked at what the children were saying with their faces. Harry, belabored on all sides with a heavy burden of responsibility for being the oldest, is having a tough time adjusting himself to his "good" younger brother and his "baby" sister. The relationships between the children are intensely competitive and highly explosive. Mother, in her sincere efforts to settle fights by separating the fighters, and preaching against fighting and for brotherly love, only makes matters worse. She takes sides with the provocative baby by defending her against the older and bigger child. Her overprotection reinforces Susan's concept of herself as the "baby," who can demand special consideration. At six, Susan is well able to take care of herself and no longer needs protection. Even if the older and bigger children really should go after her, she is quite capable of defending herself. In making Harry the culprit, Mother falls right into Susan's scheme to put Harry down and herself up. This teeter-totter is always kept in motion when parents take sides in the fights between children. The child who is defeated gets even with his more successful sibling. Thus, as soon as this fight seems to be settled, another is brewing. Whenever parents take sides, one child becomes victor and the other vanquished. One can be pretty sure that the victor, the one who manages to convince the parent of his innocence, usually started the fight—by overt or subtle provocation of his rival. The effort to win favor and have the parent on one's side makes it highly profitable to provoke even a beating from the brother. Sibling rivalry, then, lies behind the fighting. With this in mind, how could any words or moralizing about brotherly love have any effect? Particularly if these words support the culprit who poses as victim. Moralizing only increases the difficulty because it poses an "ought" which one can't meet and adds to the tension.

Had Mother looked at Susan for just a second, she might have gained a new insight into the relationships between the children. There is always a look of satisfaction on the face of the child who is not scolded. The one being scolded is out of favor—again! Susan deliberately provoked this fight (although she had no idea why!) to get Harry into trouble. It provided excitement and again reinforced her role. The fact that Susan ran to find out where Mother was before crying was a dead giveaway. Allen took advantage of the situation to remind everyone of how "good" he is in order to reinforce his position. Harry again finds himself in the role of the "naughty" one. Since he already considers himself hopelessly condemned to this role, he does not even attempt to keep himself out of trouble with Susan. He knows it will come,

anyway. When Mother interferes in their quarrels, she reinforces each child's self-concept, his mistaken opinion of his
own value, and, rather than teaching the children to stop
fighting, she shows them how profitable it is to fight.

If Mother were to ignore the whole situation, express
confidence in Susan's ability to take care of herself, and
leave it to the children to work out their differences, the
fighting would soon lose its glamor. Susan's piercing scream
is a technique, not the result of the blow. If Mother is no
longer impressed every time that Susan screams, Susan
might decide to give up a useless technique.

Naturally, if Mother and Daddy fight, the children may
imitate them. They see this technique used by adults as a
means of settling differences and so may use it themselves.
In this case, fighting as a means of solving problems can
become a family value, although a rebellious child may move
in an opposite direction and develop values contrary to those
of his parents.

There is always a power contest involved in a fight. Equals
don't need to use conflicts as an opportunity to gain superiority. They can resolve the difference without victory or
defeat. But when one's feeling of status is threatened by the
move of another, the conflict becomes a contest. Hostility is
aroused to justify disregard for politeness and consideration,
and one seeks to restore his supposed loss of status at the
expense of his opponent. When we side with the baby, protect the youngest against the oldest, stand up for the seemingly "abused" one, we reinforce his feeling of inferiority
and teach the victim how to use deficiency and weakness to
gain special consideration, thus augmenting the very predicament we want to eliminate. When left to their own
devices, children establish far more equal and just relationships than we can provide for them. They learn by the
impact of reality to develop diplomacy, equality, fair play,

justice, consideration, and respect for each other. These are what we want our children to learn. We can best help them by stepping out of the situation and giving them room.

One can, and should, have a friendly discussion about fighting, without the least hint of finger-pointing or of moralizing, and work out with the children the ways and means of settling difficulties. However, this cannot be done while the fight is taking place; for at this point, words do not "teach" or "help"—they merely become additional weapons in the fight already in progress.

CHAPTER 25

BE UNIMPRESSED BY FEARS

"Oh, but I absolutely must be home by five," Mother told her friend. "How come?" "Because I told Betty that I would be. She will be watching at the window. If I don't get home on time she gets absolutely terrified. She cries so hard that she gets hysterical."

Betty has Mother thoroughly trained. The girl holds the hoop and Mother jumps through. Fear is used to control Mother. Betty's fear is real—and devastating. Her life is miserable because of it, and Mother, naturally, doesn't want to add to Betty's misery. How in the world did such a situation develop?

We all have emotions. They are the fuel with which we fire the furnace of action. Without them we would be indecisive, weak, without direction. Without being aware of it, we create those emotions that fortify our intentions. We have the choice of fuel, which we use to give us the necessary push. Betty is not "possessed" by fear—as if fear were some kind of ghost that reached out and grabbed her! Betty possesses fear, and she uses it to control her mother. The fact that she creates it for herself does not make it any less real. It is no pretense, but *very* real, indeed.

The possibility of using fear as a technique was probably discovered by Betty accidentally. When she realized the benefits she could attain in this way, naturally, she capitalized on it. Now she is enmeshed in a web of her own making. Mother has her share of responsibility because it was she who, being impressed by Betty's fears, provided the experience of success in the use of fear.

All of us have experienced fear, and all of us recognize that we cannot function when we are frightened. Therefore it would seem that fear is a luxury we can ill afford. Actually, it has been demonstrated that one does not experience fear at the time of life-danger, but only before or afterward, when our perceptions and imagination run wild with "what will be," or "what might have been." If one is involved in a traffic hazard, one is much too busy dealing with the situation to experience fear. It is only after the crisis is over that the trembling and palpitations start. This, then, would indicate that we do not naturally need fear to avoid danger. On the contrary, fear usually increases it. Fear implies the assumption that we are unable to control a situation. And when we are afraid that we cannot do something, we paralyze ourselves so that we can't.

We must make a distinction between shock reaction and fear. A loud noise or a fall may "frighten" a young child. But this is only a short, temporary reaction. The emotion of fear as a continuation of a first "frightening" experience develops only when parents also become "frightened" and therefore are susceptible to the child's continuous fears.

A small child, suddenly faced with a new and surprising situation that seems threatening, has several choices open to him. He can stop and wait to see what the adults do, or he can withdraw and escape. He also can try fear.

Mark, sixteen months, saw a dog for the first time when Mother took him to visit friends. Faced with this strange moving object, he hung onto Mother. All adults around him made a big fuss. "He won't hurt you, Mark. See? Come on, pet him. He likes you. Don't be afraid." And so on.

Mark evaluated the situation rapidly. Uncertain as to what he should do, and given the clue of people's reaction to his fear, he chose to use it to cover up his confusion and to keep the fuss going. And this may have started his use of fear. The tone of voice and the behavior of most adults at such incidents is particularly conducive to the development of fear. There is an overanxious, strident tone in their voices and a hectic busy-ness in their behavior. It really is quite sensational to be able to produce all that activity among adults just by being afraid. This is usually only a beginning. More intense fear brings further exaggerated assurances and even *very* special attention, such as being picked up and soothed. A natural reluctance has now been converted into fear, and fear has become useful as a means of stirring up adult activity.

Children are natural hams. They constantly play to the gallery. They have no inhibitions, because they are as yet ignorant of the consequences of their behavior. Gradual experience with the results of certain actions leads children to develop a "front" and finally the sophistication of adulthood. We all have intentions we wouldn't dare admit, even to ourselves, because they are not socially acceptable. Young children are not so much concerned with what is socially acceptable and so respond freely. Their feelings are on the surface. When they meet an unexpected situation, new to them, they hold back, size up the occasion, and look for clues as to how adults would respond. The adults indicated to Mark that they expected him to be afraid. He met their expectations by putting them into his service.

Mother could have confidence in Mark's ability to meet

a new experience. She can move back and give him room to cope with it. Above all, she can stop assuming how Mark will respond and stop trying to arrange his reactions for him. Let Mark meet and solve the problem. If he shows fear, Mother can remain completely unimpressed. As it is, Mother was afraid that Mark would be afraid and so actually precipitated what she wanted to avoid. However, if Mark cannot impress Mother with his fear, the emotion ceases to be useful.

Sometimes fear can be used for its dramatic shock value.

At five, Martha had no fear of grasshoppers. However, one day a very large one jumped on her and surprised her. She gave a small startled yelp and brushed at the grasshopper in such a way that it went inside her dress. The sensation was unpleasant, so she yelled again—but mostly because her cry had made her brother, nine, laugh in ridicule. Her attempts to get rid of the grasshopper appeared to him more and more hilarious. She, in turn, screamed louder and louder, because she was so mad at him. Mother came tearing out of the house, white-faced and shaken by the screams.

That evening, brother came up to her with his hands closed. "Got something for you." "What?" He opened his hands and a grasshopper jumped out. Martha let out a blood-curdling scream, and both parents responded in haste. They sternly reprimanded brother and scolded Martha for her silliness. From now on, Martha screamed in terror at grasshoppers. But she knew, just underneath, that she wasn't really *that* scared of them! It was just that her fear had such shock value.

The most useless thing Martha's parents can do is to tell her that she is silly. This is a challenge to uphold her position of being terror-stricken. If Mother and Daddy can be unimpressed by her screams, they eliminate the purpose of the fear.

Four-year-old Benny was playing with the electric train under the Christmas tree. Suddenly he jerked back and screamed. A loose connection had caused a shock. Mother, sitting nearby, realized what had happened and picked him up to soothe and comfort him. "You're all right, darling. You just got a shock— that's all. Something is wrong with the train set. When Daddy comes home, he will fix it."

That evening Daddy found the trouble and repaired it, but Benny refused to play with the train. He hung back, acting terrified. He buried his head in Mother's lap every time Daddy tried to get him to come over and operate the controls. Finally, over Benny's buried head, Mother and Daddy exchanged glances. Mother shook her head ever so slightly. Daddy nodded his agreement, left the train, and sat down with the evening paper. Nothing further was said. Benny still made no move toward the train, and two days later, Daddy dismantled it along with the rest of the Christmas decorations and put it carefully away in the box. Benny watched the process solemnly without comment. However, at bedtime he pouted, "Daddy, I want to play with my train!" "We will get it out soon again, Benny. What story would you like me to read tonight?"

Benny's reluctance to play with the train was only natural after such an unpleasant experience. His parents understood this. But when Benny continued to resist, refused to accept on faith that Daddy had fixed the train, and when he began to get them involved with his fearful apprehensions, Mother and Daddy dropped the whole thing and "took their sails out of his wind." They realized that Benny was still too young to understand the principles of electricity. They made no attempt to get Benny to overcome his fear by explaining something beyond his skill to understand. Thus, Benny failed to gain any more advantage. The train was put away, and then he discovered that he would like to play with it again: his fear had no chance to become a useful tool. Daddy avoided any sermons on foolishness, nor did he rebuke. He accepted his son's reaction and put the train away. When Benny asked for the train, Daddy promised to get it out again soon and changed the subject.

Mother was trying to help Marcia, three, overcome her fear of the dark. She tucked the child into bed, turned on the hall light, and then turned off the bedroom light. "Mommie, Mommie," Marcia screamed in terror. "That's all right, honey," Mother soothed. "I won't leave you. Come, now. There really isn't anything to be afraid of. See? Mother is right here." "But I want the light on. I'm afraid in the dark." "The hall light is on, baby. And Mother is right here." "You won't leave?" "No, I'll sit right here until you are asleep." It took Marcia a long time to fall asleep. She roused frequently to see if Mother was still there.

Mother thought she could gradually get Marcia used to the dark by moving the light further away. She failed to see how Marcia used her fear to keep Mother near her, to keep her in her service.

Children who express terror are very persuasive. They seem to us to be so little and helpless, and life probably does appear frightening to them. However, if we can understand what is in back of the child's behavior, we can become aware that, with our response, we do not help the child, but train him further in the use of fear as a means to control.

Mother can put out the bedroom light, leave the hall light on, tuck Marcia in, fail to respond to her fears, and leave her with a word of encouragement. "You will learn not to be afraid." When Marcia screams, Mother acts as if her daughter were asleep.

This will be impossible to do unless Mother can discard the common assumption that she is cruel if she ignores the child's suffering. We feel so impelled to comfort a suffering child. However, when we realize that by so doing we merely increase the suffering because the child gains the premium of our full attention and sympathy, we can see the sense of discontinuing such a practice.

Our children cannot solve life's difficulties if they are full of fears. Fear does not increase the ability to cope with problems; it diminishes it. The more afraid one is, the more he courts danger. But fears serve beautifully as a means to gain attention and put others into one's service.

It is necessary to teach children caution in potentially dangerous situations. But caution and fear are distinctly different. The first is a reasonable and courageous recognition of possible dangers, while the second is a discouraged and paralyzing withdrawal. Naturally we must teach our children to use caution in crossing the streets, never to accept attention from strangers, that guns are lethal weapons and not toys, that swimming must be done only in depths comparable to skill. All this can be taught without instilling fear. It is a matter of learning limitations, learning how to take care of situations which appear difficult or dangerous. Fear saps courage. Fear is dangerous. For children, it serves a purpose. If parents do not respond to fears, their children will not develop them, and parents and children alike will be free from the resulting torture and suffering.

As far back as Manfred can remember, he had heard Mother tell stories of the agonies of childbirth and the pain and suffering of operations. Three months ago it was discovered that Manfred had a bone tumor in his leg that required surgery. When he was told that he must have the surgery, he screamed and cried in abject terror. For three months he pleaded, begged, and made hysterical scenes. He would rather die of the tumor than have the operation. Mother tried to console him, but without avail. The day of surgery arrived, and strenuous measures had to be taken to control the boy. His fear was so great that the usual dose of preoperative sedation did little to calm him.

Pain is part of life. There is no way to escape its existence. Mother's tales to the children and to her friends may have been her attempt to show what a heroine she was in having suffered through so much. But Manfred had little experience with real pain, and in his imagination he had built up ideas about operations that were far beyond reality. And, contrary to his mother, he had no desire to be a hero! Faced with an actual threat of pain, he had no training to accept it courageously. And Mother was extremely sympathetic to his fright because she herself knew all about the "horrors" of surgery. Far from helping her son to face a difficult and inevitable situation, she unconsciously aided and abetted his fear in her attempts to console him.

No parent wants to see his child suffer. However, there are times when pain is inevitable. The child who is courageous *actually suffers less.* Fear of pain magnifies it out of proportion. It makes the sufferer tighten up in resistance and actually increases the pain. We must help our children to accept pain and distress. Only if we are impressed with the child's fear does he become timid and fearful.

A cowboy father of three "rough riders" had his own method of reinforcing native courage. Whenever a bump, bruise, or skinned spot was presented to him for inspection, he remarked, "Well, shucks. Guess it hurts a bit, doesn't it? But don't worry. It will mend." One day his six-year-old was bucked off a green colt that was being trained. Stunned for a second, the child sat shaking his head. Dad slid off the fence and casually strode over to inspect the damage. The boy started to get up, but winced in pain and held out his arm to look at it. It was obviously broken. "Looks like you got a broken arm there, boy." "Don't worry, Dad, it will mend. It sure hurts, though." He started crying as the stunning effect of the fall wore off and the pain increased. " 'Spect it does, son. 'Spect it hurts even enough to cry about. Let's put that arm in a sling and take a trip down to Doc's." Dad made a sling with his scarf and tenderly placed the injured arm in it. The boy screamed when Dad moved his arm. "Yep, guess that arm hurts mighty much." He helped the boy to his feet, but after a few steps the child swayed. Dad lifted him as he fainted. A few minutes later, coming out of the faint, the boy whimpered, "It hurts, Dad. But it will mend, won't it?" "Sure thing, son. And the pain won't last forever—just for a while. You really are a 'rough rider' now, aren't you, boy?"

CHAPTER 26

MIND YOUR OWN BUSINESS

Arthur, crying violently, came running into the kitchen. "Mother, Daddy slapped me," he said between sobs. Mother dropped what she was doing, put her arms around her son, and comforted him. "What on earth for?" "He said I was sassy and then he slapped me." "All right, darling, I'll take care of it. There now, don't cry any more." As soon as Arthur quieted down, Mother went to the garage, where Daddy was working. A quarrel between the parents ensued in which Mother made it plain (for the hundredth time) that she didn't believe in physical punishment and Daddy made it equally plain that Arthur was his son, too, and that when he told him to put his bike away he didn't expect sass. Arthur stood on the sidelines taking it all in.

INDIVIDUAL relationships between two people belong to the two involved. Arthur's relationship with his father belongs to them, and Mother has no business trying to control this relationship. At the most, when the boy comes to her to "tattle" on Daddy, Mother can say, "I'm sorry, Arthur. If you don't like Daddy to slap you, perhaps you can figure out a way to prevent it." At a later time, when the immediate conflict has subsided, Mother could have a discussion with Arthur to help him see how a person could avoid being slapped. Mother cannot afford to take sides if she wishes to be an educator. As things stand at the moment, however, Arthur is quite happy with the relationship. All three members in this family are actually co-operating together beautifully. Let us examine the action and see how it justifies such a statement.

Arthur is adept at keeping things stirred up between his parents. Mother obviously is the dominant member of the family, and she and her son are united in an attempt to subdue Daddy. Arthur is clever in utilizing the point of disagreement between them for his own ends. He makes sure that Mother is still his champion, will protect him, will assist him in defeating the demands of his father. While Arthur is skilled in manipulating his parents to these ends, his development is lopsided. He seeks protection from adverse situations rather than skill in dealing with them. Without recognizing Arthur's game or the harm done to his self-concept, Mother falls into his trap. Father, determined to cancel out Mother's indulgence, continues to slap Arthur whenever the boy provokes him. Mother, determined to control her son's whole environment and to force Daddy to comply with her system, berates Daddy. Arthur wins in all directions. Son and Mother co-operate to keep Daddy in the doghouse, and Daddy and Arthur co-operate in getting Mother involved. Mother and Daddy co-operate in an attempt to show each other who is boss.

But this is not harmonious family living, nor is Arthur induced to respect others, especially his father. Naturally he doesn't like to be slapped. But he is willing to bear this in order to compromise his Daddy and win Mother's championship. Mother, feeling as she does about physical punishment, doesn't like to have Arthur slapped. So she uses such occasions to impose controls on her husband. Mother should mind her own business and stop trying to control everything. She has the right to follow her own convictions by not slapping her son, but she has no right to tell her husband how to treat him. It is not her business to control the relationship between Arthur and his father: that belongs to them.

This is a difficult point for most of us to understand. Are we not supposed to see to it that a child is treated properly? Yes, in a way, we are. But, what, exactly, *is* "proper" treatment? It takes an "authority" to decide this question, and in a democratic family, we have no such authority. In addition, since we recognize the child's creativity and his right to make decisions, we can see that each child, in his own way, stimulates much of the treatment he receives. It therefore becomes our duty to understand the total situation, the goals of the child, the interaction of relationships. With this knowledge, we can and must train the child toward acceptance of order and stimulate him to co-operate with the needs of the situation. This is the only way we can promote proper behavior.

It is only natural that both parents, as distinctive individuals, have different ideas about many things. It is nice if they can agree about the way children should be raised. But such an agreement *is not necessary*. The child makes up his own mind about what he will accept and what he will reject from each person within his environment. And because of the child's own active part in any relationship, even if the parents *do* agree in general principles, they treat each child differently. This is why the child is not confused by different treatment he receives from Mother, Father, grandparents, or other relatives. He usually knows very well how to gain the greatest benefits for himself from each relationship.

Furthermore, we find a peculiar correlation between a mother's confidence in her ability to deal with the child and her resentment of the treatment he receives from others. The less she feels able to cope with the problems her child

presents, the more sure she is about how others should manage him. When she becomes effective in stimulating proper
behavior, she is much less concerned about what others do.
They merely become part of the reality of the total situation
with which she has to deal.

Esther, seven, is an only grandchild. Daddy's mother dotes on
her and showers her with many gifts on every possible occasion.
Mother and Daddy limit their gifts to what they consider reasonable and fitting. Esther received six gifts from Granny at
Easter, five on her birthday, and ten at Christmas. She opened
the gifts from Mother and Daddy, thanked them, and enjoyed
the presents in a natural manner. But after she had opened the
last gift from Granny, she complained, "Is that *all?*" A few days
later Mother discovered that Esther had all possible gift days
marked on her calendar in heavy red crayon. Very disturbed by
such a gold-digging attitude, Mother talked it over with Daddy
and begged him to ask his mother if she would limit her gifts for
each occasion. Daddy refused. He thought Mother's request was
unreasonable. A heated in-law argument ensued. Mother felt sure
that Granny was spoiling Esther beyond all hope.

Poor Mother. She has absolutely no confidence in her own
influence over her child and sees danger out of proportion
to reality. Since Mother and Daddy maintain a normal balance in gift-giving, Esther does not display a greedy attitude
toward them—only toward Granny. Mother cannot control
what Granny does. It is none of her business. The relationship Granny develops with Esther belongs to them. In this
situation, Mother can feel confident that the home atmosphere of normal exchange of gifts sets a pattern which coun-
teracts Granny's lavishness. However, it is essential that the
child learn not only to receive but also to give presents. She
must remember Granny's birthday, give—and even better,
make—presents for her at Christmas and for Valentine's Day.

For the rest, Mother should keep her hands off and let Esther establish her own relationship with Granny.

Every child lives in an environment that includes adults other than his parents. Grandparents and other relatives are usually the first and closest contacts, followed by neighbors, parents' friends, teachers, and then an ever widening circle of people in the community. It is quite impossible for the parent to control the influence these people exert on the child. However, when the child encounters unfavorable influences, we are prone to take a stand against the adult concerned, hoping to diminish or altogether eliminate his influence upon the child. This is futile. The child does not need to be protected from his environment, nor does he need to have it rearranged for him. What he does need is guidance in his responses. The stimulus to which a child is exposed is much less important than his response to it.

The child is an individual, and as such, develops his own individual relationships with every person with whom he comes in close contact. Our children need experience with a wide range of people so that they can learn to understand and to evaluate people. It is our obligation to watch for opportunities to support the child in correct evaluation.

The relationship with grandparents is the source of much strife in our homes today. This fact alone is an indication of the changes coming about in our culture and our break with tradition. Daughters and sons have entirely different ideas about how children should be raised and resent the interference of their parents. If they make the mistake of trying to force their parents to accept their ways, they merely upset all relationships. A parent can withdraw from the conflict situation with a grandparent by saying to him, "You may be right. I will have to think about it." And then proceed to do what he feels is right. Grandparents enjoy their grandchildren. They are in the position of being able to have all the privileges and none of the responsibilities of raising their grandchildren. The mother or father who becomes upset over the "spoiling" of the grandparents reveals his own pessimism and doubt in his own ability to influence his child. Any energy spent in trying to "correct" the grandparents is misdirected, futile, and only adds to the tension and strife. The relationship between the child and his grandparents is the business of the child and his grandparents. However, we must help the child in his response to them. A spoiling grandparent may give the child the impression that he has the right to get whatever he wants, and that whoever opposes his desire is an enemy. In such a case we must help the child to change his mind. Through aiding the *child's* response, Mother is able to stop the grandparent from giving the child a wrong impression about life and his own rights.

Bobby, six, had been visiting his father, divorced from Mother and remarried. When he arrived back home he had crusted blood about his nose. Mother, quite concerned, asked what had happened. "She slapped me and made my nose bleed." "What on earth for? What were you doing?" "Reading my book to her." "Well, why did she slap you?" " 'Cause I couldn't read a hard word." Mother was furious. What right did that other woman have to slap her child! That evening she called her former husband in a rage, and the following day she called her lawyer. A big fuss ensued, but nothing concrete came of it.

In the complexity of today's interrelationships such incidents are not uncommon. Divorce and remarriage create complicated situations for children as well as for adults. Old hostilities that caused the divorce are reinforced, and the children so many times are not mere innocent bystanders. They take a stand in the confusion, often playing one against the other. One can well imagine that a child could provoke further disturbances in order to get sympathy and special "consolation." It is most essential that Mother not fall for such incidents and that she not exaggerate them. If Bobby can no longer create a disturbance in this complex situation, if Mother fails to respond to what happens when he visits the other home, Bobby may develop a better relationship with his father's second wife. Mother can help Bobby best by suggesting that perhaps he could behave so as not to get slapped. "It is your choice, Bobby. I'm sure you will find a way to keep out of trouble with her."

A neighbor called on Daddy to complain that Pat had run his bike into his son's bike and caused Eddie to fall and be hurt. (Both boys were nine years old.) The neighbor was obviously angry and wanted Daddy to punish Pat and make him stop "... this constant fighting. Pat always starts these fights!" "I'm sorry you are so distressed over this. But don't you think that the fights between the boys are *their* problem?" Startled, the neighbor stared for an instant and then asked, "Just what do you mean by that?" "I mean that I don't make it my business to control Pat's relationships with his friends. I feel sure that the two boys will work things out if we let them alone." "But Eddie is always getting hurt. Pat is always doing something to hurt him. And I'm getting tired of it." Daddy had to repress a smile, since Eddie was taller and heavier than Pat. "Pat comes home hurt many times, too. I just feel that if you and I mind our own business the *boys* may get tired of being hurt and do something about it themselves." "I think it is about time you exerted some control over that boy of yours." "I have no idea how to *make* Pat stop doing anything unless I bodily restrain him and stay with him every minute. I don't feel such action would help him to get along with other kids or to settle the problems that arise between them. Of course, I'll talk to Pat and see if I can help him to understand the situation. But that is all I can do."

After the neighbor left, Pat, who had heard the conversation from another room, came in, his manner half swagger and half hesitation. Each studied the other for a moment. Father remained silent. "Well, he was riding on the curb side and—" "I don't want to hear the details, Pat. I just wonder if you and Eddie don't enjoy these fights. It seems to make his folks awful mad." A grin and a stifled chuckle were Pat's only answer. "Perhaps you and Eddie can discover other ways of having fun. It is your choice. Let's see what you will do about it."

Contacts with other people are part of the reality of life. It is our business to help the child to develop proper attitudes and effective approaches to reality. Eddie's father attempts to control or modify reality. He is not helping Eddie, but is giving him the false impression that Daddy will always be there to "fix things up." Eddie does not need to make any effort on his own part toward developing the art of social participation. Pat, on the other hand, has been given the responsibility for his own relationships. Without preaching, Daddy has suggested that Pat re-evaluate his approach and then has suggested his interest by his last sentence.

Madalen complained to Mother, "I hate Miss Case. She's just a dumb teacher! And so unfair." "What happened, Madalen?" "Oh, she's always making fun of me in front of the class. She's always making nasty remarks about how I can't spell, and she never calls on me when I have my hand up. Today she took my spelling paper and read all the wrong spelling to the class. I could just kill her!" Madalen's anger and humiliation engulfed her and she burst into tears. Mother was incensed. "I'm going to talk to your teacher, Madalen. That simply is no way to treat a child."

Mother is right. Children do not learn by being humiliated. However, Mother will not be able to do much about retraining the teacher. Her indignation, thoroughly expressed to the teacher, will only add fuel to the fire. If the whole truth were known, Madalen undoubtedly had a share in provoking the teacher's attitude. A certain twist to her shoulders and a manner of lowering her eyes showed her scorn of "such a dumb teacher."

No doubt, the relationship between Madalen and her teacher is poor. But it is not Mother's business to change the teacher. It is her business to help her daughter to see how she contributes to the poor relationship and to suggest a course of action that Madalen might take to make herself more comfortable in the school situation. Getting Madalen to see her share must be done in an indirect manner. A direct approach will only make matters worse. "Do you suppose a teacher feels happy when a student dislikes her?" Or "What would you do if you were a teacher and one of your students hated you?" Then, further, "Miss Case may be dumb, as you say. I don't know. Unfortunately, no one can have the best of everything all the time. We have to make the best of what we have. I'm sure you are very uncomfortable as things are now. So suppose we try to figure out what you could do to be more comfortable."

Mother does not challenge Madalen's evaluation because this would increase the child's antagonism and induce her only to defend her attitude. If Mother sides with the teacher, she incurs her daughter's antagonism; and if she sides with Madalen, she supports her provocative behavior in school. Pointing up Madalen's discomfort and frankly discussing the problem aids Madalen to seek more co-operative forms of behavior in order to relieve her discomfort.

Harry, an only child, was doing poorly in school and had to be forced to do his homework. Every evening after dinner Daddy sat down with him to see to it that he got it done. Daddy questioned and drilled the boy in every lesson. Many of these sessions ended in stormy crying from Harry and angry frustration on the part of Daddy. Still the boy's work did not improve.

Actually, Daddy is getting the education and Harry proves every night that no one is going to *make* him learn. Just as long as Daddy is determined that his son do well in school and continues to "help" him with his homework, so long will Harry continue to do poorly.

Oddly enough, Daddy should mind his own business. It is Harry's job to study—not Daddy's.

Traditionally many teachers still ask parents to see to it that the children do their home assignments. However, if we approach the problem head-on, we invite a power contest. If, however, we consult with the children and establish together with them the time when they will study and then help maintain this order, we may provide the stimulus required.

If the child is having unusual difficulties, we should supply a tutor. It is a questionable practice for parents to attempt this role, even if one happens to be a teacher, because the child's unwillingness to study, to assume responsibility, or to perform a task which he finds unpleasant usually manifests a poor relationhip with his parents to begin with. More than likely he is resisting pressure from a parent who is personally involved and cannot stand it that he does not study; either because the parent fears for his future or wishes to show the child that he *must* assume obligations. Under these circumstances, further parental pressure only adds to the power contest. We can best help such a child by extricating ourselves from the contest, providing a tutor, and making it clear to the child that if he does not want to study, no one can make him do so. "It is up to you. You will make the choice as to whether or not you want to study and to learn."

A similar problem arises with the child who neglects to practice his music. So many children want to play an instrument, but hope to do so without the necessary work! Parental interference and pressure turn the anticipated enjoyment of music into a detested chore. Here again we should mind our own business. It is up to the music teacher to stimulate the child to work.

To mind our own business does not mean that we abandon the child to his instrument and teacher. We can offer encouragement—not through pressure or criticism, but by providing situations where he can play for a small audience of either adults or peers. We can even arrange opportunities for him to play music with others. Thus, music becomes functional and not mere detested practice.

In these situations we need to be aware of exactly what is the business of the child and then leave that responsibility to him.

Mother and Nancy worked out an allowance program for the girl. Mother was widowed and had to support them. Nancy's needs were taken into account; she was given enough allowance to cover her lunches, bus fare, school supplies, occasional movies, and after-school treats. One day Nancy came home with her closest friend, and Mother noticed that both girls wore new identification bracelets. She asked Nancy where she got hers. "I saved up for it out of my allowance." Mother said nothing more until Nancy's friend left. Then she berated her, pointing out that she worked hard to support them, denied herself many things so that Nancy could have ample allowance, and she was deeply hurt that Nancy had spent her money on something that was not stipulated in the original agreement.

Mother wants to control everything Nancy does, even the way she spends her allowance. When parents give children an allowance, the money then belongs to them. What they do with it is not the parent's business. Undoubtedly Nancy got along without something specified in the agreement in order to save for the bracelet and had made a sacrifice in order to have something she wanted. Mother would certainly be outraged if a friend attempted to force her to spend her money as the friend saw fit. Mother would feel that the friend was butting into something that was none of her business. By the same token and out of the same feeling of respect, Mother should mind her own business and let Nancy spend her money as she sees fit. Mother's only responsibility is to remain firm as to the amount of the allowance and never to cover up for Nancy if she should be indiscreet in the spending of her allowance.

Of course, if we see our child developing mistaken values, we can always have a friendly discussion. However, this must be done in such a way that no criticism is presented, for this would only make the child cling tighter to his evaluation. "I wonder if you have considered . . ." "Had you thought about . . . ?" "How do you suppose it would work if everyone thought this?" provide an opening for discussion without prompting the child to immediate rebellious rejection. It is important to present all possible aspects, even though many may not be acceptable to us, for objectivity is essential to any true evaluation. Thus, together with our child we can discover those values that will be of greatest benefit now and in the future.

CHAPTER 27

DON'T FEEL SORRY

Pɪᴛʏ is damaging, even when justifiable and understandable.

Claude, seven, was highly excited over plans for his birthday party picnic and hayride at a suburban farm. Such excursions into the country were relatively rare. Mother talked all the plans over with him. A guest list of eighteen included two other mothers to aid in transportation. As the day came closer, the anticipation of Claude and his friends mounted. When he awoke on his birthday the sky was heavily overcast. Alarmed, he raced to Mother. "It won't rain, will it? We can still go, can't we? Can't we, huh?" Mother had dreaded this possible difficulty and was very worried about the results of such a disappointment. True, she had "raincheck" arrangements with the farm, but another day wouldn't be his birthday—and things like this were *so* important to children. She tried to pacify the boy. "Oh, I think it will clear up, son. Let's wait a bit and see." Claude ate little breakfast and spent the morning at the window. The party was scheduled to leave the city at two o'clock. At noon a soft rain started—at twelve thirty, it became a heavy downpour. It was obvious that the arrangements for the day would have to be canceled. Claude was sobbing, heartbroken. Poor kid, thought Mother. What a horrible disappointment for him. Tenderly she took him into her arms. "Darling, I know how you feel. I'm sorry.

It's a horrible disappointment for you. I'd give anything to make it stop raining. But I can't. We can still go tomorrow. The people at the farm said we could." "But tomorrow isn't my birthday! Today is. And I want my party today!" "I know, dear. It's a shame it had to rain today." "It isn't fair, it isn't fair. Things never go right for me!" "Honey, please stop crying so hard. There really isn't anything I can do to make it stop raining." Claude was inconsolable. Mother herself was almost in tears because she felt so sorry for Claude in this terrible disappointment.

A large part of Claude's bitter suffering was unnecessary. Children are extremely sensitive to adult attitudes even if they are not openly expressed. Therefore, if we pity a child, he thinks he has the right to pity himself. His misery becomes more intense if he feels sorry for himself. Instead of facing his predicament and doing what can be done, he relies more and more on the pity of others, waiting for them to console him, and in the process he loses more and more of his courage and willingness to accept what is. Such an attitude can prevail throughout life. He can become convinced that the world owes him something in recompense for what he misses. Instead of doing what he can, he counts on what others will do for him.

Claude feels abused when things don't go as he desires. He may become an "abuse gatherer." Mother's assumption that disappointments are extremely hard on him because he is so little leaves the door wide open for the boy to prove just that. Far from being consoled that he could have the party on the following day, he feels that his whole life is ruined by this one rainstorm.

When Mother assumes that disappointments are much too difficult for Claude to bear, she shows her disrespect for her son. She considers him too weak and helpless to be able to meet life. Her approach stimulates Claude to make this false assumption.

Our children will learn to take disappointments if we avoid pity.

Mother could have prevented this bitter disappointment from the beginning had she not expected it. Discussing the plans with Claude, she could immediately bring up the possibility that rain might interfere; in that case they would merely move to the next day. A casual acceptance in her own mind of the need to adjust to weather conditions could quickly be conveyed to Claude, and this would reinforce him against deep disappointment. It is natural that he is distressed when it rains on his birthday. Mother can help her son face this by remaining casual. She cannot help if she feels sorry for him.

Ruth, nine, arrived home after months in the hospital with polio. She wore braces and got about with the aid of crutches. Much time and effort had been spent in the physiotherapy department teaching her how to do things for herself and to walk with the aid of appliances. The personnel at the hospital had given Mother instructions for Ruth's care and had been firm in insisting that Mother help Ruth to help herself. However, Mother's heart was so deeply wrenched by this tragedy her child had suffered that she felt she just couldn't do enough for her. Ruth quickly responded to the deep concern of her mother. When she whimpered, "It's too hard, I can't," Mother jumped to her assistance. Because walking was so difficult, Mother helped Ruth more and more. Ruth sat in her wheel chair and did less and less walking. Her hands were awkward. Mother wanted to make things easier for her, so she fed her. Mother devoted her entire time to her child, doing things for her. She felt she wanted to make up to Ruth for the savage blow that life had dealt her. She begged Ruth to try to walk; but when the girl whimpered, "It hurts," Mother gave in, saying, "Poor baby. What a shame." Daddy tried to encourage Ruth but was intimidated by Mother, who scolded him for "asking too much" of the child. Daddy and Mother quarreled about this in front of Ruth. She withdrew from Daddy and leaned more and more on Mother. In a month's time Ruth had changed from the laughing, courageous, self-helping child who had come home from the hospital to a petulant, demanding, helpless invalid. When Mother took Ruth for her scheduled visit to the clinic, it was found that her condition had regressed. The doctors advised readmission to the hospital. Brokenhearted, and furious with the apparent "hardness" of the physiotherapist who had found Ruth un-co-operative, Mother refused. At this point, Daddy stepped in; and, after consulting with the doctors, Ruth was readmitted over Mother's protests. It took concerted effort, understanding, and firmness to overcome the debilitating effect of Mother's pity and to put Ruth back on the road to progress. Only after Mother had seen a psychiatrist was she able to understand how her attitude of pity had actually done damage to Ruth and caused the regression. Both Mother and Ruth made admirable progress and learned how to turn tragedy into useful endeavors.

A child who is physically handicapped as the result of a birth injury, or who is blind, deaf, or crippled, easily becomes the object of pity. It is almost beyond human nature to avoid feeling sorry for such children. But in so doing, we only add to their handicap. Nurses and therapists who work with handicapped children marvel at the courage they often display and the cleverness with which they can overcome or sidestep a handicap. Therapists are also very much aware of the danger of pity. They have seen children who had made progress crumble under the undue sympathy and loving pity showered on them by misguided parents and relatives. Nurses, doctors, and therapists are frequently subjected to tirades from parents who misjudge their firmness of approach as harshness, cruelty, or lack of sympathy. True, it is much easier for therapists to avoid pity since they are not so emotionally involved. However, whenever they have a child under their care for a long time, they, too, learn to love him and yet don't react with pity to his predicament. Instead, they stimulate the child to be proud of each accomplishment under difficulties.

Peggy, five, developed a high fever and symptoms that were not immediately recognized. She was a very ill child and was placed in the hospital for study. Besides being worried, Mother felt a tinge of rebellion that such a thing should happen to her baby. Medication had to be given by injection and blood samples taken from the vein. Peggy, although semidelirious, cried out whenever she was stuck. Mother remonstrated because she felt it was cruel to do this to a sick child. Her pity for Peggy mounted. After diagnosis was made and suitable treatment instituted, Peggy slowly recovered and was finally allowed to go home. Convalescence was slow. Mother waited on Peggy hand and foot. She just couldn't do enough to make up for this long and severe illness. As Peggy got better, she became more and more demanding. Mother, exhausted by the long seige and interrupted sleep, began to lose composure. Finally, one day she gave way to temper. Shocked and bewildered, Peggy burst into tears. "How can you be so mean to me when I've been so sick?" Repentant, Mother again tried even harder to be patient with her child.

Peggy has absorbed Mother's pity and now pities herself. Mother feels guilty at having lost her temper and again submits to undue demands. A vicious circle has been established.

We most frequently feel sorry for the child when he is sick. Naturally, an ill child needs our attention and understanding. He isn't able to care for himself. We must help him. But it must be done with a wary eye to our attitude. We must beware of succumbing to the temptation to pity the poor little thing who suffers. Unfortunately, we cannot protect the child from suffering. This is a part of life. At best, we can only meet his needs while he is sick, help him to tolerate suffering, and show him how to manage under difficulties. The sick child, more than the well one, needs our moral support, our faith in his courage, our understanding and sympathy. Illness has a demoralizing influence—it impresses the child with his smallness and helplessness. Pity at this point adds to his demoralization, lowers his resistance, and saps his courage. Pity implies a patronizing attitude: it does not support courage. The skillful mother shows the greatest kindness to her child when she firmly refuses to treat her as more helpless than the condition warrants. The period of convalescence is the most difficult for both mother and child. It can be made much easier for both if sympathy and courage replace pity and undue service.

Sandra, three, was happily enjoying her new swing set. Mellie, five, a neighbor's child who was adopted in infancy, came running from her house next door, dumped Sandra out of the swing, and took over. Sandra picked herself up, slapped Mellie, and went to the other swing. Mother was watching from the kitchen window. As soon as Sandra was settled in the other swing, Mellie left hers and demanded Sandra's. Voices were raised. Mellie's mother came running over and talked to both girls. She encouraged Mellie to choose which swing she wanted, got her into it, and started pushing her. Mellie changed her mind. She wanted the other swing. Her mother persuaded Sandra to change; then she pushed Mellie and afterward wanted to push Sandra. "I can pump myself," Sandra said. As soon as Sandra got going, Mellie again demanded to change swings. Her mother again prevailed in the switch. Curious, Sandra's mother joined her neighbor. "Why do you let Mellie have her own way all the time?" "Why, the poor child! I *never* cross her. I'll never be able to make up to her for the rotten start she got in life." "What do you mean —rotten start?" Mellie's mother turned aside and whispered, "Oh, she was born out of wedlock, you know."

Mellie's mother sees herself as the bountiful heroine who came to the rescue of a poor unfortunate illegitimate waif. However, in her mind, all the love and indulgence in the world cannot make up for the hideous blight that marks this child.

Mellie's mother has a completely unrealistic outlook. Her sense of pity, far from helping the child, produces a totally different result. The infant was not blighted—but her adoptive mother's concept *has* blighted her and continues to do so. Mellie is so spoiled that it is impossible for her to make any constructive contribution. Without conscious awareness, she, too, has absorbed the attitude, "I am unfortunate. The world must make it up to me."

Pity is an easy trap for adoptive parents. It is equally disastrous. An adopted child has no more obstacles to overcome than any other child, unless the adoptive parents provide these obstacles through erroneous pity. The child, in his first years, is incapable of distinguishing between his membership in a family through birth or adoption. His growing awareness of those around him is identical to that of a child born into the family. For the sake of his future adaptation to life, he should never have a "special" position. Children who consider themselves "special" in any way acquire mistaken values and develop false expectations. The adopted child needs the same respect and care as a natural child.

One mother of two adopted children allowed them to grow up knowing they were adopted by occasionally mentioning it casually and naturally within their hearing. When the day arrived when they wanted to know exactly what this meant, she explained that sometimes people were unable to provide for a baby; on the other hand, sometimes there were people who could provide for a baby, but were unable to have one. So wasn't it fortunate that it was possible for the baby to change places?

This casual discussion of the rather happy solution of a difficult problem eliminates warped impressions. Adopted children make an issue of being adopted only if their parents do.

Bonnie, nine, Jackie, seven, and Clyde, six, were living with Aunt Marian and their two cousins, Frieda and Beulah, eight, and five, because Mother was in the hospital. Daddy ate dinner with them every night and then went to the hospital to be with Mother. Sometimes Aunt Marian went, too, and then Uncle Henry made it fun for everyone with his games and stories. Aunt Marian found herself under considerable emotional stress, partly as a consequence of the sudden addition of three lively children, and also due to her deep concern for her sister, who was very close to her. The adults knew that Mother was in critical condition; she had cancer. They carefully avoided letting the children know of the seriousness of the situation. A year and a half ago, Mother had been in the hospital and had returned home to them. Whenever the children asked when Mother would be home, they were cheerfully told, "Soon, now." They sensed the falsity of these cheerful assertions and were keenly aware of the worried glances and whispered conversations between Daddy and Aunt Marian. Unable to understand, they were nonetheless upset by it, became unruly, cranky, and ill at ease. Bonnie missed Mother's care more than the others did and had a greater realization of the situation. Since she was the eldest of the group, Aunt Marian asked her to help with the younger ones and impressed her with the obligations of being the eldest. Bonnie readily assumed much responsibility, but developed a very bossy attitude, which the younger children resented. This added to the confusion under which they all lived.

Then Mother died, and the grief of the adults could no longer be hidden. The children had to be told. Daddy asked that he be left alone with his three for a while and that Marian tell her two. Marian's grief was near the point of hysteria. Daddy gathered his three and, fighting his own grief, said, "Children, I have something very serious to tell you." The children were already subdued, being aware of the changed atmosphere in the house. "Is something wrong with Mother?" Bonnie asked. "Mother went to heaven today to be with Jesus. She will be very happy there. We must all be very brave, now, and take care of each other." It took a few seconds for the impact of what Daddy had said to be felt. Shocked, Bonnie burst into tears. "Why did she leave us, Daddy? Why did she have to go to heaven now? *We* want her." "We can't do anything about it, Bonnie. God called her to Him and we can't question what He does." "You mean Mommie isn't coming home any more?" Jackie asked. "That's right, son," Daddy replied gently. "But I want my mother," sobbed Clyde. Daddy comforted them quietly, realizing that their grief needed expression, too. When the children had somewhat quieted, Daddy said, "It will be hard without Mother. We will need a little time to get used to it, and we must all work together and help each other. Soon we will have to make plans as to what is to be done next."

At this point, Marian and the cousins entered the room. Beulah and Frieda were crying, more because everyone else was than because they were directly involved in the tragedy. Marian swept the children into her arms, muttering over and over between sobs, "Poor little lambs, poor little motherless lambs." Daddy shook his head at Aunt Marian, but she failed to understand. The children burst into renewed sobs, which quickly mounted toward hysteria. Daddy signaled to Uncle Henry, who quietly asked his girls to go to their room for a while. The three children jerked away from Aunt Marian and returned to their Daddy. Uncle Henry finally persuaded Aunt Marian to lie down for a while. Then Daddy, with his arms around his children, spoke with a small measure of firmness in his voice. "Now, children, we all feel this grief. Remember, we must honor Mother's memory with courage, not with despair. That is how she would wish it, and I am sure you will want to do as she would wish. Come now, gather yourselves together." He waited quietly for the children to adjust. When they had become somewhat composed, he said, "It is time for supper. Aunt Marian needs our help. Suppose we all see about getting some supper on the table." "Daddy, I just couldn't eat now," Bonnie uttered between subduing sobs. "Life goes on, Bonnie. It is all right if you don't want to eat tonight, but perhaps by the time supper is ready, you will find that you can." And with further words of encouragement, Daddy won the children over and suggested a job for each one.

The children were demoralized by the pity which Aunt Marian had displayed. Daddy showed the courage and sensitivity needed in the situation, and by looking forward to the next thing to be done, started his children onto the path of recovery.

At one time or another, tragedies occur in the lives of all of us. As adults, we are expected to "take it" and to make the best of the situation. Our natural inclination is to feel sorry for the innocent child in a tragic situation. However, our well-meaning pity can bring about more damaging effects than the tragedy. If adults feel pity for a child, no matter how legitimate the reason, he feels justified in pitying himself. He can easily spend a lifetime feeling sorry for himself; he is then unable to accept his responsibilities in dealing with life's tasks and searches fruitlessly for someone to make up to him for the deprivation that life has imposed upon him. It will be hard for him to become a productive member of society because his attention is completely centered upon himself and on what he should get as his rightful due.

One of the most serious predicaments for a child is the loss of a parent. The reconstruction period following such a loss may color the child's whole life. If it is the mother who has died, the situation is doubly difficult. Such children need all the sympathetic support possible from everyone around them. The very last thing they need is pity. Pity is a negative emotion—it belittles the individual, weakens his self-reliance, and destroys his faith in life. Death is part of life. It must be accepted as such. Without death, life would be impossible. Naturally, we hate to see children hurt by the passing of a parent. But our distress and sorrow do not restore life to the dead. While death occurs, life goes on. And, difficult as it is, children need to be aware of their obligation to go on building their lives courageously, even under these extreme difficulties. Pity at such a time saps the very courage which the child urgently needs.

We cannot protect our children from life. The strength and courage with which we meet the blows of life in adulthood are built during childhood. It is then that we learn how to "take it in our stride" and to go on. If we hope to lead our children into the courageous acceptance of life, if we hope to teach them the satisfaction that comes from overcoming handicaps and to strengthen their ability to do what has to be done next, we must forego the indulgence of pity. We need to recognize first the pitfalls of pity to which we are culturally inclined, to avoid our first impulse, and then to show our sympathy and understanding by supporting the child in his grief as well as in his courageous search for a way forward. This in no way means that we abandon the child to his trouble. On the contrary—we rally to support him just as we do to an adult in trouble.

Everyone has at one time or another encountered an adult who resents pity, who withdrew from anyone who offered pity as a form of sympathy, because he was too proud to be pitied. In such a case, one has to be careful to express sentiments of understanding without implying doubt in that person's ability to face the ordeal courageously. So it must be with our children. Our respect for the child demands that we support his sense of dignity, not lower it by stimulating his self-pity. In times of crisis, children look to adults for a clue as to how to deal with the unfamiliar situation. They sense our attitude and use it as a guideline.

It is not difficult to distinguish between sympathy and pity. Sympathy implies, "I understand how you feel, how much it hurts, or how difficult it is for you. I am sorry about it and will help you to overcome the hardships of your situa-

tion." Pity implies a rather subtle, patronizing, superior attitude toward the one pitied. "You poor thing. I feel so sorry
for you. I'll do all I can to make up for what you suffer."
Feeling sorry about the *"it"* which happened is sympathy.
Feeling sorry for the *"you"* to whom it happened is pity. We
are inclined to doubt the ability of all those whom we consider small or weak, and as a result, we diminish the resource-
fulness that they could display if our pity did not induce
them to retreat into sad passivity, full of complaints—and
demands.

CHAPTER 28

MAKE REQUESTS REASONABLE AND SPARSE

Tommy and his parents were visiting friends. As they sat on the front porch talking, Tommy wandered off. "Tommy, come back here," Mother demanded. Then she turned to her friend and continued her conversation. The boy turned the corner of the house and slowly walked to the swing in the back yard. Here he paused and continued to lick his popsicle. Mother appeared at the back walk. "Tommy, come here," she demanded with a downward thrust of her finger to indicate the spot to which he must come. Tommy turned his back, lifted his chin, squinted his eyes and twisted his mouth into a derisive grin, sat down in the swing, and took another lick of his popsicle. "Tommy, I said to come here this minute," Mother called angrily. Tommy continued to ease the swing back and forth. "I'm going to tell your daddy," Mother called out as she walked away. Tommy finished his popsicle, flung the stick into the flower bed, and started swinging in earnest. Nothing more happened. He continued to swing. Finally, in boredom, he languidly walked back to the front porch.

Tommy showed complete lack of respect for Mother's wishes. In this situation, Mother got what she deserved. She had made an unreasonable request. Tommy responded with open defiance to her "order." At this particular moment there was a contest of power between Mother and son. Tommy won. There was no real reason why he couldn't play on the swing. Mother attempted to show her authority, and Tommy stood his ground against it. Then Mother failed to act, but continued to use words as weapons. Finally she threatened to tattle to Father. Tommy apparently knew that his father would do nothing, as subsequent events proved. A threat to "tell Daddy" is always ill-advised. Daddy should never be put in the role of having to exert superior authority, since the authority role no longer works for either parent.

Reasonable requests are characterized by respect for the child and a recognition for order. A parent who becomes frantic because a child won't "do as I say" probably makes unreasonable requests and merely attempts to "control" the child. This usually provokes a power struggle. The parent fails to recognize his attempt to establish a superior-inferior relationship. However, adult superiority is no longer accepted; therefore, the child is determined to be disobedient as a matter of principle, to escape domination. A child who feels imposed upon or "bossed" will retaliate with disobedience. We can avoid these conflicts if we make only reasonable and necessary requests in a nonauthoritative manner.

Linda, ten, was playing about a half block from her home. Mother wanted to send her to the store, so she called from the front door. Linda kept right on playing, acting as if she could not hear Mother. When Linda failed to respond, Mother gave up. A few minutes later she called again. Linda still gave no sign that she heard. Finally one of the children said, "Linda, your mother is calling you." "Oh, I know—but she hasn't yelled, yet!" Mother meant business, but instead of yelling, she came out carrying a small strap. She descended upon Linda, who looked up in some surprise. "Didn't you hear me call you, young lady? You get home!" She emphasized the words with a crack at the girl's legs with the strap. Linda jumped up, began to cry, and hurried toward home. Mother followed, hitting her at each step. A few minutes later Linda started off toward the store.

Linda has become "mother-deaf"—an affliction that occurs in most homes.

Children should perform certain duties that contribute to the family welfare. Going to the store can well be one of these chores. However, the task must be one that is agreed upon by the child and should be consistently performed.

Mother and Linda should work out together a program that meets the needs of the family and reflects recognition for Linda's right to play with her friends. At lunchtime Mother could say, "We need some things from the store before five o'clock today. What time would you like to go?" When Linda makes her choice, Mother can ask, "Shall I call you then?" Now Linda knows what is expected of her and has the opportunity to choose the time. Since the request is now reasonable, Linda will be more likely to respond with a sense of pride in her responsibility.

Mother was sitting in the living room mending. Polly, eight, was watching television. "Polly, will you please bring me my cigarettes?" The child jumped up and got the cigarettes. A few minutes later Mother said, "Honey, will you get the white darning cotton for me?" Polly got the thread. Somewhat later Mother requested, "Darling, go turn the fire down under the potatoes." The girl willingly did as requested.

Mother treats Polly as a servant. The child complies even to unreasonable requests because she wants to please. She is not learning to function as a self-determined individual.

Mother and Daddy sat in the back yard talking to friends who had dropped by unexpectedly. Hazel, nine, was playing nearby with the two girls from next door. David, eighteen months, was very fretful because it was his bedtime. Mother held him for a while, but his restlessness was distracting. "Hazel," she called, "come take David for a ride in his stroller." "Aw, Mother." "Hazel!" The child sighed, left her friends, and did as she was asked.

Mother has made a most unreasonable request. We should never ask a child to do what we would not like to be asked to do. Mother wanted to visit with her friends, so she asked Hazel to leave hers and take care of the distracting baby. This implies gross disrespect for Hazel's rights. Mother should have excused herself and put David to bed.

When we want to make a request of a child, we must be sensitive to the situation and to the capacities of the child. Many children enjoy the responsibility of taking care of younger children. However, there should be an agreement beforehand as to when this responsibility is to be assumed. Naturally, if Mother is in a spot where she really needs extra help, she may call on the older child.

We can always be suspicious of a situation in which we "demand" that a child do something "right now." This is an authoritative approach and is usually an unreasonable request. The child's response, "Aw, she's always hollering at me to do something," indicates a poor relationship lacking in harmony and co-operation. When we make our requests few and far between, and enlist the child's help rather then command his service or obedience, we promote friendliness and a satisfactory interrelationship.

CHAPTER 29

FOLLOW THROUGH—BE CONSISTENT

The shoe salesman brought several pairs of shoes for Winifred to try on. "You decide which ones you want, honey," Mother said. The navy ones seemed satisfactory, but Winifred said rather wistfully, "I want red shoes, Mother." The salesman brought the red shoes, and the child was delighted with them. "But, Winifred, the navy shoes are more practical. They will go with everything. Are you *sure* you want the red ones?" "Yes, Mother," she answered as she posed before the mirror. "Come, try the navy ones on again." Winifred examined the appearance of the dark shoes in the mirror. "We'll take the navy ones," Mother told the clerk. "No, Mother. I want the red ones." "Oh, Winifred! The red ones are too impractical. You will get tired of them. Come on now, be a good girl and take the navy ones." Pouting, the child accepted Mother's decision.

First Mother told Winifred that she could choose, and then she made the choice herself and even argued Winifred into agreement. Mother is not consistent, nor does she keep her word.

If we want to teach children how to choose wisely, we must give them opportunities to choose and, if necessary, to make mistakes. They learn through experience, not from our sermons. Winifred sees Mother as the big boss who won't let her have what she wants. Unable to see beyond her resentment, she cannot understand whether the choice is practical or not. Had Mother followed through on her promise and let her daughter get the red shoes, Winifred might have discovered for herself that red shoes did not go with all of her clothes. Since no more shoes can be bought until the red ones are worn out, Winifred must live with her decision and might, of her own accord, give greater consideration to the problem the next time. Mother would then have acted as an educator rather than as a boss.

Holly, three, had been playing in her sandbox in the sun on the first hot day of summer. Mother felt that she had been exposed to the sun long enough. "Put your sun hat on, Holly," she called as she continued to weed the flower bed. Holly appeared not to hear Mother and continued to pour sand into her bucket. "Holly! I said to put your hat on." The child jumped out of the sandbox and ran to the swing. "Holly, come back here. I want you to put your hat on." The girl turned her back on her mother and sat on the swing. Mother shrugged her shoulders and let the matter drop.

It is obvious that Holly is being trained in disobedience. Mother talks too much and doesn't act. She makes a request and doesn't follow through. Holly has discovered that she can disregard what her mother says.

Mother might feel that her reqeust was prompted by concern for Holly and a desire to avoid sunburn—a respect for order. However, her procedure showed disrespect for Holly and for herself, as well as for the rays of the sun. Holly knows nothing about sunburn and feels that the demand is merely tyrannical—especially when it is made in the form of a command, which prompts instant rebellion. Mother's "request" was an invitation to a power contest. If Mother really felt that Holly should be protected by the sun hat, but her child ignored the first request, Mother should follow through and personally put Holly's hat on her head. If the child puts up further resistance, Mother's decision that her daughter must be out of the sun requires that she remove Holly indoors. Mother must learn to *think* before demanding compliance and then follow through with firmness of action.

"Mother." Six-year-old Paula tugged at Mother's skirt as they walked past the dime store in the shopping center. "Yes, what is it?" "Can I have a dime?" "What for?" "I want to ride on the horse." "No, Paula. Not today." "Please, Mother," the child whined. "I said 'no,' Paula. Come on, now. I still have a lot to do." Paula started to cry piteously. "Oh, for heaven's sake! All right, I'll let you have *one* ride. But remember, that's all." Mother helped Paula onto the mechanical horse, inserted the dime, and waited while the girl enjoyed the ride.

First Mother said "no" and then she gave in. She lacked the courage to say no and to be firm about it because she pitied the poor child who cried when threatened with not having what she wanted.

Mother is training Paula to disrespect her word and to feel that if she uses "water power" she can get what she wants. There is a very simple solution to this problem. Paula should have an allowance. When she asks Mother for the dime, Mother can reply, "Use your allowance money, Paula." If the girl has none left, that is the end of the matter. Mother neither answers, reasons, responds with pity, gives in, nor allows borrowing against the next allowance. If Paula has a dime to spend for the mechanical ride, fine. If she doesn't, that is her affair. Mother must remain consistent in her "No" and follow through by withdrawing from the child's provocation.

Mother was completely fed up with the struggle to get Alex and Harry out of bed in the morning. She had attended a Guidance Center where she received an idea that she decided to put into practice. She bought an alarm clock and told the boys that it would be up to them to set their alarm and get themselves up. The next morning she heard the alarm go off and then stop ringing. She listened and waited. Nothing further happened. Finally, a half hour later, she realized that the boys had fallen asleep again. She wakened them. "I told you that you would have to get yourselves up and I meant it. Your alarm went off a half hour ago. Now come on. Get up!"

Mother started out splendidly, but failed to follow through because she didn't really mean that the boys would have to get themselves up! She has been inconsistent. She still wants to "make" them get up. It is still *her* business to awaken them.

If Mother wants the boys to get up by themselves, she must give them the responsibility and withdraw completely. If they shut off the alarm and continue to sleep, it is their affair. When they finally awaken, they must go on to school, regardless of how late it is—and face the consequences. Day after day, with no leniency, Mother must be consistent and follow through with her decision. When the boys find that they can no longer engage Mother in a struggle to get them up, they may become willing to accept the responsibility.

Michael, eleven, and Robbie, nine, had begged for a dog for a long time. Finally Mother and Daddy decided to get one, but only upon the condition that the boys assume the responsibility for feeding and grooming the pet. They promised emphatically. A dog was selected, and they were totally delighted. At first the boys conscientiously cared for the dog, but, as the newness wore off, they gradually neglected him. Mother found herself feeding the dog more and more frequently. She prodded, reminded, and preached, but the boys still forgot. Finally one day she threatened to get rid of the dog if the boys didn't do their part. Michael and Robbie responded to the threat for two days. A week later

Mother resigned herself to the situation. After all, she just couldn't deny the boys the joy they had in playing with the dog.

Poor Mother. She has all the responsibilities and the children have all the fun.

The evening of the first instance of neglect, Mother can ask, "What is to be done if you forget to feed the dog?" A friendly discussion can follow in which Mother makes it clear that she will not assume the responsibility for it. Neglecting the animal would be cruel. "How many times can neglect be permitted?" The boys name a figure. "Then you agree that after n times of neglect, we will have to get rid of him?" After the nth instance of neglect, Mother must follow through and place the dog elsewhere: not as punishment, not in anger, but simply as the logical result of neglect.

Consistency is really a part of order, and as such helps to establish boundaries and limitations that provide the child with a sense of security. We cannot possibly expect our training methods to be effective if we apply them haphazardly. This only bewilders the child. On the other hand, the child will feel certain and secure if we are consistent and if we follow through with our training program. He learns respect for order and knows exactly where he stands.

CHAPTER 30

PUT THEM ALL IN THE SAME BOAT

Daddy discovered that one of his three daughters had decorated the new brick fireplace with crayons. He summoned the three and asked each in turn who had done it. Each one denied having committed the crime. "One of you is lying. I want to know who did this. And I won't tolerate a liar. Now who did it?" None answered. "All right, then, I'll punish all three of you." He took each girl in turn and spanked her. Then he again demanded, "Now, who used the crayons on the fireplace?" Finally the eldest admitted the misdeed. "That's more like it. Now clean it off." Daddy got a bucket, water, scrub brush, and detergent and stood over her until she had cleaned the bricks.

I⊤ is a popular concept that we should deal with each child individually and award praise or condemnation as the child's behavior warrants. It may be difficult to see how often all the children in one family team up against the adults, either to defeat them or to keep them busy. It is common knowledge that members of a peer group have a code which abhors "squealing." In our example, the three girls were in an alliance. They all three bore the punishment rather than squeal.

When we deal with each child individually after some misbehavior, we tend to promote a teeter-totter action in which one or the other child seeks parental approval and elevation at the expense of another, who in turn is pushed down. Thus, our action intensifies competition among the children, since we play one child against the other. We thereby stimulate each child to seek the satisfaction of approval rather than that of contributing. Since it is impossible for anyone to win constant approval, getting approval must be recognized as a false goal. However, we can *always* contribute, under any circumstances; therefore, this is a realistic and obtainable goal, which leads to unity. When we stimulate competition among our children we fortify their mistaken goals. The "good" child is good, not because he likes to be good, but because he wants to be *better* and to keep ahead of the child who gets less approval. His interest is centered upon himself, not upon the needs of the common welfare. The "bad" or deficient child remains so because he can get recognition in this way, too—but on the useless side of life.

We can overcome the existing intense competition and its damaging effects if we treat all the children as a group— by putting them all in the same boat, so to speak. This is perhaps the most revolutionary step Mother can take. Treating all children as a unit violates the spirit of competitiveness, of moral judgment, of personal preferences. It can accomplish something that had been a Biblical ideal but has lost its impact on modern society: Man is his brother's keeper and not necessarily his mortal competitive enemy.

In our foregoing example, Daddy could call all three girls together, asking all to clean up the bricks with no effort to find out who made the marks. This prevents the "good" child from proving his goodness or the "bad" child from promoting a power contest or seeking revenge.

"But," you say, "is it not unfair to make the innocent clean up something they did not do?" The children may voice the same objection. Our children get their ideas of what is fair or unfair from us and use it to our disadvantage. If we can overcome our assumption or conviction that such a procedure is unfair, the children may discover its justification. They may become aware of how they work together as a team against us anyhow—one by being good, another by being aggressive, a third by being helpless, and so on. Their competition is for our benefit. If we eliminate the competition for parental recognition, the three girls have a chance to develop respect for each other.

Considering the broader aspects of what is fair, it would seem to be unfair to each child to reinforce his false goals, his mistaken concept of his role and value, which disrupts harmony and co-operation. All depends upon what we want for our children. If we put them all in the same boat and make them responsible as a group for what each one does, we take our sails out of their wind. They have no desire to impress each other; so the wind of their misbehavior becomes meaningless.

The same is true of jealousy among children. It is so extremely useful because it makes such an impression upon the parents. It evokes all kinds of parental antics to try to rectify the situation. Jealousy becomes useless if the parents fail to be impressed. But how many parents can remain unimpressed? And so the pain of jealousy grows by what it feeds on!

The recommendation to put all the children in the same boat usually works even better than expected. A mother attended a lecture in which this treatment was suggested. She tried it out and later reported the following:

She had three children, nine, seven, and three. The older two have little influence upon the baby and usually complain about the special privileges granted to him. One night shortly after she had heard the lecture, the baby was playing with his food and making an awful mess. Mother told all three of the children to leave the table, since they didn't know how to eat properly. The older ones expressed mild resentment, but all three left. From this time on, the baby never again played with his food. Mother was amazed at the dramatic results of her action, but failed to understand why it worked.

The baby's misbehavior gained him special attention. He was continually reminded to eat properly. Mother's procedure not only deprived him of this special attention, but now the older children shared the attention which he stimulated. Now there is no fun in misbehaving if the older children share the special attention!

This effect of mutual responsibility becomes even more obvious in another example.

Charles, eight, was in the middle between an effective and capable older brother and a "good" younger sister. He was a holy terror. He lied, stole, and had twice set fire to the basement. His main enjoyment was to paint the walls with crayon. Mother could do nothing to stop him. When she came for help, she was advised to treat all three children as a unit and to make all of them responsible for Charles's behavior. This was in sharp contrast to her procedure of blaming Charles and praising the others.

Two weeks later Mother and Charles returned for another interview. Mother was utterly amazed. She reported that Charles had dropped all offensive behavior. He had used crayons on the walls once, and Mother had stated that it was up to the children to clean it up. Charles did not participate in the clean-up job, but neither did he again use crayons on the walls. When he was asked why he had stopped marking the walls, he replied, "It's not fun any more. The others have to clean it up."

Charles figured there wasn't any sense in bad behavior if it didn't provoke a fight and engage Mother in long negotiations with him. He certainly didn't want the others to get what *he* was after!

In a fight it is difficult to establish who is guilty. It is not the result of the misbehavior of one child—they all contribute equally to the disturbance, which is the result of their combined effort. The good one may egg on the bad one, may dare him, may push him, or provoke transgressions in hundreds of ways for the desired result of involving Mother. The children are responsible for each other, co-ordinating their efforts whether for the welfare of the family or for furtherance of its tensions and antagonisms. Usually when the "bad" one gets better the "good" one becomes worse; so closely are all children co-ordinating their behavior in their united front, in dealing with us. If Mother can see this and treat all of her children as a group, she may get dramatic results, and they will see their interdependence and take care of each other.

CHAPTER 31

LISTEN!

MOST of us are familiar with the joke about the child who asked, "Mother, where do I come from?" Mother gave a lengthy explanation about the birds and bees. "I know all that, Mother. What I want to know is where *I* come from." So Mother explained further about the birth of babies. Still the boy was not satisfied. "Mother, Roy comes from Chicago and Pete comes from Miami. Where do *I* come from?"

It is part of our general prejudice against children that we are inclined to assume that we know what they mean without really listening to them. We keep our own mouths so busy that we fail to hear what comes out of theirs. And yet many of us thoroughly enjoy a popular book and television program based upon the unsophisticated wisdom of the children of other parents. It is not necessary to go abroad for this fun; it is right in our own home. All we have to do is to *listen*.

Al, six, was helping Daddy pack suitcases into the trunk of the car preparatory to the family vacation trip. One small overnight case simply would not fit into the trunk. "Daddy, take Mother's seat cushion out and put it in the back seat." Daddy ignored Al's suggestion, rearranged the suitcases, and tried again, but in vain.

When Daddy went back into the house, Al took the seat cushion out. When Daddy returned he was surprised to find that the overnight case could be put into the trunk.

Daddy had failed to listen when the child's suggestion had so clearly been correct. Our children are very adept at sizing up situations. They *do* have intelligent solutions to offer. They even have a different perspective which we could use to our advantage.

A father of five children came for professional help. After he had explained his problems, an analysis of the situation led to concrete recommendations to solve the dilemma. Then the father was asked to leave the room and the five children were invited to come in. The counselor inquired what they thought was the reason for the conflict, and they explained it very clearly. Then they were asked what should be done to resolve the conflict, and they made exactly the same recommendations which the counselor had made!

Father could have saved the cost of a consultation if he had only thought about listening to his children.

So many times our children know what we do wrong. And yet we feel so sure that only *we* have the right to tell *them* what they are doing wrong. Our pride prevents us from listening to them. How much we could profit from their sensitivity if we would treat them as our equals and really listen!

Kelly, Mabel, and Rose were fighting over who got to see what program on TV. Kelly held out for the cowboy show, while the girls wanted a comedy. Finally Mother became exasperated. "Kelly, I'm sick and tired of this squabbling. Go to your room." "Why the heck do you always pick on me?" Kelly growled. "No back talk, Kelly. Leave the room."

Mother should listen to Kelly. He asked a very good question. Why *does* she always pick on him? Because she falls for the trap laid by the two girls to keep Kelly in trouble. If Mother were to listen to Kelly, she might discover how she herself helps to keep the fights going.

Nine-year-old Johnny was romping with his dog in the living room, although this was strictly forbidden. Boy and dog rolled against a table, knocked over a lamp, and broke the bulb. Mother rushed angrily into the room, gave Johnny a tongue-lashing, and ended with, "Now for this, you can't go swimming this afternoon." "I don't care," the boy sullenly retorted.

Johnny does care—very much. But his pride won't let him admit it. His reply is an extension of the defiance already displayed and further defeats Mother.

Many times we need to listen to the meaning behind the words the child uses. Johnny's "I don't care" really says, "Even punishment won't subdue me." When a child screams, "I hate you," he means, "I don't like it when I can't have my own way." When he asks a series of "whys" he is saying, "Pay attention to me."

George, ten, sat beside his friend, Pete, in the school bus. The driver overheard the following conversation. "Why weren't you in school yesterday, George?" "I just didn't want to come to school, so I put it in my mind to be sick, and I was." "How were you sick?" questioned Pete. "Sick to my stomach." "Why?" "I didn't want to come out in all this cold. This morning I felt the same, but Mother had the house so hot I didn't want to spend another day in that place. First I put it in my mind to be sick, but then I changed my mind. I sure had to hurry to catch the bus, though. And I didn't have any breakfast because I still felt sick."

Children are amazingly frank with each other. However, they seldom give us an opportunity to overhear them. We usually make such an issue of anything we overhear that they are more than cautious. The bus driver listened, however. She learned that children can make themselves sick in order to escape what they dislike. She also learned something of the meaning of equality among children. Pete accepted George and what he had done as part of life. Nor did he moralize.

Every mother learns to distinguish the meaning of the tones in her baby's cry. With nothing more than the sound to go on, she knows when he is in distress and when he is angry. We have this talent, but seem to put it away when the children are older. We hear a scream from a child and dash madly to see what the trouble is. So many times our dash is the purpose of the scream. If we were to stop and listen for a minute, we could avoid a response that serves the child's mistaken goal.

How much we have to gain if only we will listen!

CHAPTER 32

WATCH YOUR TONE OF VOICE

WHEN we speak to our children they frequently hear more in our tone of voice than in the words we use. It would pay us to listen to ourselves. Sometime when you are in the store, or the park, or at a gathering where parents and children are together, make it a point to listen. Listen to the tone of voice used by the adults. They seldom talk to children in the normal tone they use to talk to each other. Then when you are home again, listen to your own tone of voice. What do you express with it? What does your child hear?

We ourselves so many times instigate misbehavior on the part of the child because of the tone we use.

Billy announced that he was going to water the lawn. "Oh, no you aren't, young man," Mother said firmly. "You are going to stay right in this house." Billy eyed his mother for a few minutes and then slipped away. Presently Mother was aware of the sound of running water. Billy was watering the lawn.

Mother's tone of dictatorial firmness, by which she meant to express determination, precipitated the contest for power that Billy started. A sixteen-year-old who had been present at the time was asked what she had heard in the tone of voice used by Billy's mother. "She's frightened. It is a tone of false bravado." (See what we mean?)

Daddy was helping Jody, ten, with his homework. Jody seemed not to understand very much of what he was supposed to do. "Well, surely you understand *this* much," Daddy said with heavy scorn. Jody hunched closer to his book and looked more perplexed.

Daddy's tone indicated that even he didn't have much hope of Jody learning. Therefore he added to the boy's discouragement.

In the store, Mother met a friend whom she hadn't seen since Cynthia was born. "How old is she now?" "Eleven months." "Oh, isn't um dust the sweetest ittle sing?" The friend chucked the baby under the chin and clucked at her.

The simpering "baby talk" and the condescending "simple talk" which we use with young children indicate our feeling that children are inferior. We speak to them in a manner and with a tone of voice that we would *never* use with a friend. If we make it a practice to listen to ourselves we can soon discover the amount of disrespect we show our children. We are prone to talk down to them, to splash false gaity and exude excitement to stimulate interest, or speak with saccharine sweetness to win co-operation. Once we become aware of errors in our tone of voice we are in a position to change. If we speak to our children as friends on equal footing with us, we keep the doors of communication open.

CHAPTER 33

TAKE IT EASY

Cheryl, five, and Cathy, seven, stood at the kitchen counter watching very intently as Mother put two chocolates on the scales, noted the weight, and then put two more on. "Cheryl's weighed more, Mother. That's not fair. I won't get as much," Cathy whimpered. "It's the same, it's the same," chanted her sister. "No, Cheryl. Cathy is right. I'll try again." Mother continued to weigh the chocolates until each girl got exactly the same by weight.

Mother is straining to the utmost in her efforts to be fair. Her overconcern, contrary to her intentions, is damaging. She has created a tense atmosphere and has intensified the competition between the girls. Each is determined to get her full share and to be certain that the other doesn't get more. At the same time, the girls are in an alliance to keep Mother involved in anxiety over what is fair. How in the world did Mother get into this mess?

She has a mistaken conviction that she must be "fair" to the children and show absolutely no favoritism. But who can always be completely fair? How can Mother possibly arrange everything in life so that both Cheryl and Cathy receive even amounts? Mother's overconcern has put the accent on "getting" rather than upon contributing. Neither Cheryl nor Cathy can be happy as long as they operate upon this false basis.

Mother needs to relax, to take it easy, to give up her concern over fairness. If she has decided that the girls may each have two chocolates, give them each two and let it go at that. If they fuss over who has the larger amount, Mother can withdraw from the scene—to the bathroom, if necessary. Let the girls solve it.

Mother is quite worried because Raymond, three, seems to have developed a chronic case of constipation. Ever since he was six months old, when she started toilet training, she has had some trouble getting him to be "regular." While he was still an infant, he occasionally got an enema. Now she finds it necessary to give him one almost every day.

Mother is too concerned about Raymond's bowel movements. Her overconcern for his health really masks her determination that her son will move his bowels when she thinks he should. Mother and son are actually in a power struggle. He refuses to move his bowels, so Mother has to do it for him! Mother is right to be worried. As long as she takes the responsibility for Raymond, he will never assume it for himself. He is being well trained to let his bowels speak for him. He may continue this pattern all of his life.

Mother should relax and let Raymond move his bowels when he is ready. It should be his concern. When he no longer needs to use his bowels as a form of protest, nature may restore normal function.

Mother took Dorothy, five, with her on a shopping tour in a large department store. Dorothy lagged behind constantly. She stopped at every display case to admire its contents. When Mother stopped to make a purchase, Dorothy wandered away.

Mother spent half of her time keeping track of Dorothy and running after her. Finally she missed her daughter altogether and became frantic. When she finally found her, she said, "Oh, Dorothy. You scared me to death. Now, for heaven's sake, stay near me. I don't want to lose you in this big store." The child looked at Mother with solemn round eyes.

Dorothy plays a game of hide and seek whenever she goes out with Mother. It is so much fun to see Mother get frantic. Dorothy isn't lost. She knows exactly where she is. It is up to Mother to stay with her.

Mother can give up her anxiety that Dorothy will get lost and take time for training. Two can play this game! When Mother notices that Dorothy is no longer with her, she can quietly remain out of sight. The child will soon become aware that Mother isn't looking for her and will return to where she left Mother. Mother is gone! Now Dorothy will become a little anxious and start her own seeking. Mother continues to remain out of sight until the girl is really concerned. Then she quietly steps into sight, but in such a manner that she appears to be going on about her shopping. When Dorothy runs up, frightened and crying, Mother can fail to be impressed with the fear and quietly say, "Sorry that we lost each other." This strategy should be repeated every time that the child wanders away. If Mother refuses to play the game of hide and seek, takes it easy, and does not worry about Dorothy getting lost, the child will soon make sure that she keeps track of Mother.

A friend was talking with Mother in the living room. Every few minutes Mother would get up and look out of the window to check on her six- and four-year-olds, who were playing with neighborhood children in the side yard. Finally the friend asked, "What is going on out there that seems so interesting?" "Nothing, really. I just want to be sure that the children are all right."

Take it easy, Mother. If everything is not all right, you will know about it soon enough!

Danny, ten, kept Mother in a constant state of uneasiness. He frequently failed to obey her order to come home directly from school. One day it was five thirty and Danny still had not come home. Mother was frantic. Since the boy rode his bicycle to school she was absolutely sure that he had been struck by a car. She had just decided to call the local hospital when Danny came in, his pants and shoes soaked and muddy. He carried a jar of filthy-looking water. "Danny! Where in the world have you been? It's five thirty! I've been absolutely frantic. Where were you?" "I went down to that pond we saw on the highway. Look, I got some tadpoles." "How many times have I told you to come home after school and to let me know where you are?" Mother demanded angrily. "You have no right to worry me like this!" Danny's face remained impassive as Mother continued her tirade. The following day Mother attended a Guidance Center with a friend. A similar problem came up in the discussion. Mother received an idea. She was cheerful whenever Danny came home. But once, when he was late, *she* was gone!

So much of our worry and concern over our children is needless. Worse, they are aware of it and use it as a tool to get our attention, to promote a power contest, or to get even. Our worry about possible disaster in no way prevents it. We can only deal with trouble *after* it happens. Our best refuge is to have confidence in our children and to take it easy until such time as our talents for coping with disaster are really called upon.

Mother had had her problems. When Billy was sixteen months old, she had been forced to place him in a foster home because of the turmoil of a divorce and her need to go to work. Then, when he was two, she remarried and took him back with her. When he was three, she again placed him temporarily in the foster home while she had her second child. Now, at five, Billy seems dreadfully unhappy. No matter how much Mother tries to show her love, the boy isn't convinced. Whenever Mother has to say "no" or denies Billy something he wants, he cries piteously and sobs, "You don't love me." Mother is frantic. Billy seems to want so many things that are beyond their means or that would really not be good for him. She is at her wits' end trying to console him.

The trouble lies in Mother's guilt feelings about having put Billy in a foster home. Although it was the only sensible thing to do under the circumstances, she feels that she has failed him. Now she is dreadfully overconcerned about the effect this experience had upon him. She assumes that Billy felt abandoned.

Billy responds to Mother's attitude and even uses it for his purposes. He knows her vulnerable spot and uses it as a club over her head to keep her deeply concerned with him. This provides him with a never ending source of control. As long as he expresses his doubts in her love, she will bend over backward trying to prove it.

Mother knows that she loves Billy. (He knows it too!) She can stop falling for his "doubts." She is a good mother as long as she fulfills every present necessity. Mother has to learn not to be afraid of Billy. Becoming aware of the purpose of his behavior, she can render it ineffective. When Billy sobs, Mother can casually respond by saying that she is sorry he feels that way.

A child who displays jealousy presents a similar problem. Most of us are on the lookout for the first signs of envy of the new baby, and we soon find what we are looking for! Our efforts to dissipate this miserable feeling in the child help him to discover how useful it can be. Unknowingly, we *teach* him to be jealous! As long as we are impressed by jealousy, the child will find it useful. Our best defense against this bitter emotion is to remain casual and to avoid pity. We can feel confident that the child can learn to take even unpleasant situations in his stride. Naturally Mother cannot spend as much time exclusively with him after the new baby is born. But he will adjust himself to his new role if she refrains from feeling sorry for him and does not try to make up for what he has "lost." It is possible that some children at times get more advantages than others; but this, too, is part of life and must be taken in stride without undue fuss. The child will use jealousy only if it pays.

It is amazing how many things we find to be concerned about in our children. We watch over them for signs of bad habits, question them to find if they have bad thoughts, worry about their moral attitudes, fret about their health, and superimpose upon them our own interpretations of whatever happens to them. Instead of finding out how a given situation appears to them, we assume that we know how they feel about it. We prod and press them to do well in school so that they will be a credit to us and shove and push them into activities that will "develop" them. We are suspicious and want to know exactly "what they are up to" every minute. We behave almost as if we believed that children were born bad and had to be forced to be good. We spend a tremendous amount of time and energy trying to live our childrens' lives for them. How much better it would be for all concerned if we would relax, have confidence in our children, and give them a chance to live for themselves.

So much of our concern is based upon our feeling that we don't really know what to do. However, it is not necessary for us to "deal with" every little problem that comes up. So many of them will disappear if we take it easy, for the simple reason that the children promote many problems just to keep us concerned. Striving to make life perfect is futile. We won't succeed!

If we know what to do and what not to do when our children misbehave, our confidence that we *can* be effective makes it possible for us to take it easy. It *is* possible to relax and enjoy our children.

CHAPTER 34

DOWNGRADE "BAD" HABITS

Four-year-old Mark's mother was hanging up clothes when she noticed him and two of his playmates standing together, partially hidden in the weeds of the vacant lot next door. Looking more closely, she discovered that they had their pants down and were urinating. She rushed over to them, sent the other two boys home, and hauled Mark into the house. Mark started to cry. "I'll teach you to do such an awful thing," Mother screamed as she spanked him soundly. "Don't you ever, ever do such a thing again. You come into this house and go to the bathroom. Now go to your room. And you can't go outside to play for three days." Then Mother called the mothers of the other boys and told them what had happened.

A few days later, when Mark was again allowed outside to play, his mother received a phone call from an indignant neighbor. Mark was urinating on the front sidewalk while a group of children, including two girls, stood by and watched. Mother dashed out and pulled Mark into the house. Again she spanked him, more fiercely than before. That evening she told her husband about the incident. Daddy scolded Mark and threatened, "If I ever hear of you doing such a thing again, I'll give you a thrashing you won't forget." Incidents of this nature continued at intervals all summer. Each time Mark was spanked and kept at home for a few days.

I<small>T</small> is obvious that punishment did not deter Mark. On the contrary, it made the act more interesting, and it was fun to see if he could do it and not get caught.

We cannot meet a problem of this nature head on. If we do, we only make it worse.

The wisest course for Mother to follow is to quietly call Mark in and, without emotional upheaval or moralistic preaching, tell him that since he doesn't know how to behave outside, he will have to stay in. This procedure should be followed every time that Mark is discovered urinating outside. He knows that he is misbehaving. This is a time for action, not for explanations.

The more fuss we make over "bad" habits, the worse they get. Included in this classification are all forms of sex play, bed-wetting, thumb-sucking, and nail-biting. We put the word "bad" into quotes deliberately. None of these acts are any "badder" than other forms of misbehavior. They serve the child's unconscious purpose just as any other act does. It is only in the adult mind that these particular habits take on more severe connotations. Our first step in dealing with these problems, then, is to downgrade them in importance. Once the child discovers that he has done something which bothers the parent even more than usual, he has at his disposal an even stronger weapon with which to hit his parents. Here, again, we take our sails out of his wind if we fail to be impressed.

Every psychiatrist knows that most sex play among children fortunately never comes to the attention of adults, and therefore no harm results. If we do become aware that our child is masturbating or involved in sex play with others, our wisest course is to act as if we were unaware of it. No harm can come from masturbation unless we create conflicts. This and thumb sucking are forms of easy pleasure, which indicate that the child has not found satisfaction on the useful side of life. If we try to stop him we only succeed in making the pleasure more gratifying. The child will then increase his determination to keep his pleasure and resist having it taken away from him. The habit now becomes fixed in its second purpose—the defeat of the oppressive adult. We can best ignore the matter completely and approach the problem obliquely by providing experience of satisfaction on the useful side of life by widening the child's interests and activities.

Marie, three, sucked her thumb, but with a difference. She also held her other hand in front of her face as if to hide what she was doing.

Marie withdraws from her environment and develops pleasure as a private affair. She doesn't need anyone else.

After dinner, Mother watched Jack, six, closely to be sure that he drank very little water. Every night around midnight, before going to bed, either Mother or Daddy awakened the boy and took him to the bathroom. Even then, Jack's bed was frequently wet by morning when Mother awakened him. She pleaded with him to try harder to keep his bed dry. Sometimes she was angry because of all the extra washing. She and Daddy had tried every kind of punishment and persuasion that they could think of. Nothing seemed to help. Jack was a chronic bed-wetter.

The child who wets his bed is usually a child who does everything when he feels like it. He is convinced that he cannot control himself. Actually, he is unwilling to accept the needs of a given situation. All the extra attention that Mother and Daddy give him serve to confirm his conviction that he can't help wetting the bed. Scoldings, punishments, and pleas merely serve to increase his discouragement. It seems to him that here he is, unable to control himself, and on top of it, he gets punished and humiliated.

Jack needs to learn to respond to what has to be done. Mother and Daddy can help him by handing the problem over to him. It is *his* business. They can say, but only if they sincerely believe it, that they are no longer concerned about his bed. "We are not going to get you up any more. You may do as you decide. If you are uncomfortable in a wet bed, you may get up and change it yourself." Then Mother and Daddy must follow through with genuine unconcern. This discomfort is a natural consequence. It takes time to change a child's opinion of himself and his confidence in his ability to take care of himself. Don't expect miracles.

A nail-biting child usually expresses anger, resentment, or defiance of order. Here again, the habit is a symptom, not a problem in itself. It is futile to scold, humiliate, or apply preventive remedies. We cannot force the child to stop. We can only seek to remedy the cause.

A child who lies or steals usually tries to "put something over." If the child arranges the situation so that we discover his transgression, we can be sure that the purpose is to gain our attention. If, however, he tries to deny it, then we will probably be right in concluding that he tries to show his power. The child may feel that he has a right to get whatever he wants, regardless of method. Or he may feel tremendous delight in getting by with something and not getting caught. The acts of lying or stealing are symptoms of deeper underlying rebellion. Naturally, a stolen article must be returned or restitution made. But we must "downgrade" the seriousness—be casual and remain very little impressed. This may be hard for parents who think that they have an obligation to "teach" the child not to do such things. But their scorn, criticism, and punishment do not teach him not to lie or steal; on the contrary, they provide him with further ammunition and increased desire to do wrong for the sake of power and defeating his parents. The child does not need any "instruction"; he knows very well that lying and stealing are wrong. Unconsciously, he prefers to do wrong because it yields results.

Five-year-old Susan played with a neighborhood child who had a sidewalk bike. She begged for one of her own. Mother and Daddy explained that they could not afford it just now. One day Mother discovered the neighbor child's bike concealed behind the furnace. She was uncommonly wise. "Well!" she thought. "I think I'll just wait a day or two and see what happens." She noticed that Susan seemed troubled. The bike stayed half-hidden, and Mother refrained from making any comment. Late the second afternoon Mother asked Susan, "Why don't you take Lucy's bike out and ride it?" Dismayed, Susan replied, "Because then she will see it and I'll have to give it back." "Then it didn't do much good to take it, did it?" Susan broke into tears. "Why not take it back to her? Then at least you both can ride it again." Mother won the co-operation of Lucy's mother so that the issue was played down. Susan had learned her lesson.

The real problem lay in the fact that Susan felt she had a right to have whatever she wanted. Mother helped her to discover that stealing just didn't work.

When a child swears or uses a "bad" word, he depends on its shock value. If we respond as he wishes and are shocked or make an issue of the matter, we encourage his further use of these words. We can take our sails out of his wind by playing dumb. "What is that word you used? I don't understand. What does it mean?" The child is likely to abandon a tactic which puts him in this position.

The child who presents a "bad" habit needs help and understanding. The habit is a symptom. We cannot accomplish anything by attacking the symptom. What are the underlying causes? Many times we can arrive at an understanding through friendly and casual talks. At bedtime, perhaps, when Mother and child are in a happy mood, Mother may make a sort of game and ask, "What did you like about today?" After the child has answered, Mother tells what she liked. Then she may ask, "What did you not like?" Here she may be able to discover what it is that the child resents. Mother can use the information she has gained as a basis for action, never for words. She makes no comment—does not try to explain away what the child disliked. But she may ask him what he feels could be done about it. This is an opportunity to *listen.* If the child has nothing to offer, Mother may continue the game by telling what she disliked—but mostly things which did not involve the child; otherwise it ceases to be a game and becomes criticism. We must be very careful not to probe. This makes the child clam up and closes the door to further efforts of this kind. The game can be repeated from time to time and may become a means of indirect communication.

We cannot expect a child to lay aside a bad habit overnight. At the same time, we are liable to become discouraged ourselves if, after a few days of corrective effort on our part, we see him continuing in his course. We as well as he seem to be convinced that he will never be able to stop his bad habit. Stop and think a moment. Really, now—will he still suck his thumb or wet his bed when he is in high school? Of course not! Our pessimism is unwarranted. We know he will stop. And after such a shot in the arm to our own courage, we subtly convey our faith to him. It will be a long-term project and will need the supplemental encouragement of increased activities on the positive side. But eventually, we can be sure, he may be willing to respond. Once we extricate ourselves from our own discouragement, our faith and confidence in the child can provide additional stimulus for him. Above all, if we don't mind too much, if we take it easy, if we are willing to let a few things go along imperfectly, we will find that the tension disolves and the bad habit becomes less paramount in importance, for the child as well as for us.

CHAPTER 35

HAVE FUN TOGETHER

In the "old days" with its large families, children were forced by circumstances to depend upon each other for fun. This custom was handed down from one generation to the next and prevailed until the introduction of mass entertainment through radio and later television. We all thoroughly enjoy stories which depict the solidarity of the family through the things they did together. One of the most appealing scenes in the "Nutcracker" ballet is the one in which both children and adults join in a folk dance around the Christmas tree. It is tragic to see so many of today's families so split that the children have their fun apart from the parents, with the latter supplying the means, but no participation. This state of affairs is partly due to cultural changes that pit children against adults, and partly due to our lack of skill in living together democratically. Parents are so deeply concerned with providing the best for their children that they neglect to join them.

Another factor is the loss of common interests between parents and children, which springs from the child's rejection of the adult world and the parents' inability to enter the child's world as an equal. In many homes the children don't want the parents to play with them! When a state of undeclared warfare exists in the home, it is impossible to have fun together. And yet when parents and children enjoy a game, the hostility is reduced and harmony has a chance.

It is up to the parents to foster an atmosphere of solidarity through play. In this manner we may be able to change the picture of big adults always picking on and fighting with little children to one of a group of people with common purposes and interests.

It is easy to play with a baby, but when the child is older we seem to lose the knack of playing with him. However, the child desperately needs this form of participation. The play hour can become the focal point for harmony and understanding between parents and children. Games at home can be a source of fun rather than bitter competition. Here, the child can learn that one doesn't *have* to win: that one can just have fun playing the game. This is a difficult lesson indeed, since most adults fail to realize that many children are accustomed to winning in whatever they do. Every home should have games geared to the level of the child's age. A definite time for family play can become part of the daily routine. The time taken for training of the little tot can easily slide into playtime with him when he is older. Naturally, the hour is changed so that the other family members may join.

A father of five children (three boys and two girls) was an avid baseball fan and played with a local amateur team. Every spring, as soon as weather permitted, he started "training" with his children. Even the three-year-old had a bat sized to his measure. Daddy pitched balls in a manner to permit success in batting. As the children grew older he pitched to meet their increasing skills. The older children picked up the attitude of tolerance for the younger and less skilled ones and played the game so that all were included. They were just as pleased with the growing skill of the youngest as Daddy was. He never criticized a bad play or a missed ball. He constantly shouted encouragement. And he obviously had a whale of a time. So did the children.

Hugh, eight, was fanatic about baseball. If there was a game going on within walking distance, he was there. Daddy and Mother insisted that he get permission to go so that they would know where he was. One evening Hugh was nowhere to be found. It got dark, and Daddy was on the verge of calling the police when Hugh walked in, totally unconcerned. Anxiety gave way to anger, and Daddy lit into him. "Wait a minute, Dad," Hugh pleaded. "Let me tell you what happened." He explained that he had gone with a group of older boys to a game about ten miles away. "Daddy, you never take me to a ball game. I've asked you hundreds of times. But you always say you're busy or have something else to do."

This was a revelation to Daddy. Hugh wanted his father to share his interest! Daddy acted upon this insight; and both parents now have a genuine interest in the local games and players, and all three attend games together.

All children love to "put on a play." Parents don't always have to be the audience. They can be in the play, too! Children particularly enjoy taking the adult roles when parents take the role of the children in a story. Any fairy tale or legend which is known to all can become an impromptu play. No need for an audience. Just "let's pretend."

There are all sorts of projects that can become a family affair. Shortly before Christmas, one family spends their evenings together making paper ornaments for the tree. The night before May Day, lovely paper baskets are made for the dinner table. Every occasion upon which paper ornaments could be used prompts a family creative session.

Another family took "pretend" trips around the world. They all helped to collect data and travel folders and information which was made into a scrapbook for each country.

Each summer's vacation trip was the subject of prior study by the whole family.

Such projects depend upon the interests of the family. The enthusiasm of the parents is contagious, and the children so many times display marked ingenuity. They themselves many times indicate what may interest them. One family developed a "museum" after the children had been on a school field trip. Any article which suggested something from the Old West was labeled and placed on a shelf in the museum. Everyone in the family kept his eyes open for bits and pieces that could be used. A bit of broken colored glass became a relic from a ruined church window. A feather found on a walk through the woods became a bit remaining from an Indian bonnet. One child made a corn-husk doll. And so on.

Singing together always brings wonderful family unity. The evening chore of dishwashing in a family of eight turned out to be an hour of real fun for the whole family because it was the "singing hour" with everyone participating. The children learned songs at home and taught songs which they brought home from school. As they grew older, they began to harmonize, and eventually created madrigal effects by dividing the group and singing two different songs together.

If parents listen and are alert, they will discover all sorts of things that interest the children, and with imagination, these can be developed into a family project.

What people enjoy together brings them together. Through games and projects in which all enjoy the fun, a feeling of group solidarity develops. Solidarity is essential for the equality it promotes and for the relaxed and harmonious atmosphere that can become a part of family living.

CHAPTER 36

MEET THE CHALLENGE OF TV

IN ALMOST EVERY HOME, the television set creates many problems. There are quarrels about what to watch. Mother and Daddy worry about wrong impressions the children may receive. They are concerned about such passive entertainment, with so much time spent on "trash." Homework is neglected when children watch the "really good" evening programs. Bedtime is ignored because the "best" programs come on late. Mealtime is regulated by television programs. Many homes have even changed their dining habits and now eat in front of the set, each member isolated in his absorption in the program. Parents fret because mealtime is no longer a common activity, promoting family unity. How many mothers frequently feel like putting their foot right through the picture tube! Instead, they try to "put their foot down" and to regulate television viewing. Fights and dissension ensue. Some parents even refuse to have television in the house, with the result that the children either go to the neighbors' to watch or keep up running complaints that they must be denied what "the other kids" have.

Television is here to stay. It presents problems that we must learn to solve rather than to resent. When children quarrel over who gets to see what program, parents may either keep out of fights or turn the set off until the children have reached an agreement. When the quarrel involves both parents and children, the situation becomes more complicated. But it is not a question of whether Mother and Daddy have the right to see the evening programs or whether they should give in to the children's rights to see what they want. This is a *family* problem and must be solved by the family all together. The question becomes, "What are *we* going to do about it?" not Mother or Daddy saying, "What must *I* do to regulate watching television?" All members of the family must come to an agreement together. This is usually a subject for the Family Council. If the dissension is very severe, the parent can remove a tube from the set, and no one, including the parents, sees any program until an agreement is reached. (Rather like an industrial strike, during which no work is done until the argument is settled.)

As far as the neglected homework is concerned, we can reach an understanding with the child through discussion. He may choose for himself what time he will do his homework and what time he will watch television. Mother may then remain firm and hold him to his agreements—by action, not words. Or if he is older, the question becomes, "What is to be done now." Let the older child offer a solution.

If children want to watch television after their bedtime, parents must be firm in order to maintain routine. If the child is young, we take him to bed without any words. There is no power struggle involved if Mother does not have a personal stake in "making him mind." If she is firm in maintaining order and follows the demands of the situation, she merely takes him to bed. If the child is older, we must come to an agreement with him and then follow through on what he has agreed to. All this is not easy if we have failed to develop a relationship of trust and co-operation with our children. Actually, the TV set is not a problem in itself; it merely highlights the lack of co-operation between parents and children.

The quality and content of the television programs is the subject of national concern. However, we can hardly sit back passively and wait for the nation to solve the problem for us. It is in our homes, and it is here that we must act.

June, eleven, Mona, eight, and Robert, seven, particularly enjoyed a weird horror-mystery program. Mother and Daddy felt that it was "no program for children." The more they protested, the more the children insisted. "What's wrong with it? It's really a good show. All the other kids see it!" Every week there was a family fight over this program.

When we insist that a child is not to see a given program, we invite a power contest. The child wins. There is no more powerful argument than what "all the other kids" do. And if we still deny the program, the child seeks revenge in other ways. What solution is there? To begin with, we cannot protect our children from television nor from the impressions that they receive. However, we can help the child to develop resistance against bad taste and poor judgment. This cannot be done by preaching to him! Words in today's culture are used much more as weapons than as a means of communication: the child becomes deaf as soon as the parents start sermons. However, a discussion in which the parent asks questions and then *listens* can be very profitable. The parents can watch the program with the children and then share their impressions in a gamelike atmosphere. "What did you think of this? Was what the man did wise? How do you suppose the others felt? Why? What else do you think they could have done?" In such a manner the parent helps the child really to think for himself and to take a critical look at the program on his own. If the parent *listens*, the child discovers his ability to offer ideas—a most gratifying discovery. The parent must not spoil the "game" by trying to "correct" the impressions that the child expresses. We can accept what the child says as he says it. Then watch the progress as time passes and the child himself develops a critical eye! If the parent occasionally wishes to contribute his own thoughts, he may do so in the form of a provocative question. "I wonder how it would have been if . . ." or "What do you suppose would have happened if . . ." After a cowboy story, we may ask, "Do you know any 'good guys'? Are they always 'good'? Is it really fun to beat and torture somebody? How does the victim feel?" In such discussions, where we avoid imposing our own ideas and tease the child into thinking for himself, we develop a rapport with the child. Children never learn to think for themselves if we do it all for them and hand it down ready-made. If a good relationship exists, the child will be candid in his replies, will tell us what he thinks—that is, if it brings no reprisals upon his head. And we may be completely amazed at the astute judgment and knowledge of right and fair play that children display.

Following the above course of action, we will also discover that most children take television in their stride. If it is not a source for a power struggle, the interest often wanes. Our concern for too much passive entertainment can be offset if we make sure that we have other forms of fun together as a family. We cannot take something away from a child. This is a form of imposing our will. We need to offer something of greater interest to stimulate and influence the child so that he voluntarily leaves the less desirable thing.

Television need not be a source of worry when we know what to do and have confidence in our ability to cope with the problems which it poses.

CHAPTER 37

USE RELIGION WISELY

No matter what our religious faith, it has a significant place in our homes. For most people, religion serves as an inspiration in striving for a Good Life. Our ideals, our moral values, our highest aspirations spring from and are upheld in our religion. It is difficult to see, therefore, how the use of religion could be detrimental to a child. But religion can be misused.

Vincent, five, had been in a cross mood all morning. Nothing that Mother suggested seemed to please him. Her patience was wearing thin. She finally gave him a magazine and a pair of scissors and suggested that he sit in the den and cut out pictures. She returned to her housework. Later she discovered that Vincent had pulled all the books within reach off the shelves and strewn them around the room. The desk drawers were open and the contents dumped on the floor. Furious, she yanked the boy to her, shook him, and cried, "Whatever ails you? You've been a naughty boy all morning. Now you're going to sit on the kitchen chair until lunchtime if I have to tie you to it. Don't you know that God will punish you if you don't learn to be good? He doesn't like bad boys."

Vincent is not a happy boy. He is angry. He seeks revenge. The more Mother punishes, the more he feels he has to avenge. He doesn't want to be bad. He wants to be good. He has no idea why he does these things.

Whenever a parent threatens a child with "God will punish you," he is in effect admitting defeat and throwing the whole problem into the lap of a higher authority. The child senses this and is somewhat proud that no one can do anything with him. Since no punishment from God is immediately forthcoming, he scoffs at such a threat. Therefore, it is completely useless as a training technique.

Mother caught her daughter in a bald-faced lie. "Donna, you know it is very wrong to lie. People who tell lies get to the point where they can't be honest and straightforward. Their souls become miserable and mean. Do you think that God and all His Saints have any use for such people? God wants us to be honest and truthful. There is no place in Heaven for wrongdoers. You must always tell the truth. Truth is goodness. When you lie, you are not good."

It is so much easier for a child to be good that he has no need to be bad unless he has met obstacles in his environment that have caused him to become discouraged and turn to misbehavior as a way out of his difficulty. Since the child has a purpose in his misbehavior, moralizing does not change it nor remove the obstacle. It adds to his discouragement. When we hold up the ideal for which we all strive and point out to him how far short he falls, we are only adding to the discouragement that made him fall short to begin with. Far from needing the condemnation implied in moralizing, the child needs encouragement and help out of his difficulty.

The child knows he must be good. Having no idea why he is "bad" (since the purpose of his behavior is unknown to him) he despairs of ever reaching his ideals. A conflict develops between what he knows he should do and what he finds himself doing. Since he cannot go in two directions at once, he must learn to pretend. He learns to hide behind good intentions when his real purpose may be quite the opposite. Wherever moralizing is used to stimulate good behavior, we find children with false fronts. They attempt under all circumstances to appear in the best moral light. They develop a horrible fear that their true worthlessness (their false self-concept is very real to them!) will show through the front. The more energy they spend on "appearances" and upon fear, the less they have for true growth and development.

The parents who insist that the child go to Sunday school while they remain home present a peculiar picture to the child. It is as if there were two moral standards—one for the child and another for the adults! The children must go to Sunday school to learn how to be good while the parents already know how and no longer need this training. But the child frequently feels that the parent does bad and unjust things to him and can't see why they are privileged to get by without attending religious services. His sense of equality is outraged. This adds to his sense of oppression by adults. It also makes Sunday school a disagreeable chore and defeats the very purpose of religious training.

If the child is old enough to have a concept of time after death, and threats of punishment in the hereafter are used, he may develop a morbid fear of death, of the future, of the unseen. Such fear, rather than "straightening him out," cramps his style, denies him freedom of growth and the strength to assume responsibility. He is already in trouble or he wouldn't misbehave. Now, in addition, he must face this unseen ogre who will punish him for his unhappiness. He may even develop an unspoken or unacknowledged hatred for this God who punishes. Since such a feeling is beyond expression, the child adds more to his false front. This kind of conflict between his real intentions and his pretense can lead only to further maladjustment or even to neurosis.

Religious teaching can be used to show a child how it was discovered long ago that certain types of behavior were found to be wrong because they spoiled a good, happy relationship between people. Parents and children can have discussions in story fashion (never using the children themselves as examples) and explore the possibilities of resolving conflicts so that friendship and harmony can be restored. We all get into difficulties! Children need to know that we are in the same boat, and that we, too, must seek ways of restoring harmony, which is the ultimate good, by whatever name it is called.

CHAPTER 38

TALK *WITH* THEM, NOT *TO* THEM

Several times throughout this book we have suggested that parents have a discussion with their children about their mutual problems. In the course of our work we have discovered that very few parents know how to talk with children. So often, it turns out that the parent talks *to* the child—in a friendly way, it is true; but nonetheless the child hears a sermon.

The tragic outstanding difficulty between teens and adults is the absence of communication. These doors can be kept open during adolescence if a sympathetic relationship has been established while the child is young. Much of this depends upon our ability to respect the child, even when we disagree with him. When we stop to think about it, we realize with awe the marvel involved in the development of a child's faculty for thinking. He, of his own accord, and often with unconscious awareness, observes, receives impressions, organizes them into a system, and then acts upon his conclusions. He has a mind of his own! Too often we use this expression disparagingly to indicate disobedience or rebellion. We hammer away at these "transgressions" and try to impress him with what *we* think. We want to "mold" his character, his mind, his personality; as if he were a bit of soft clay and our action should "shape" him. From the child's point of view, this is tyranny—and so it is. This does not mean that we cannot and should not influence and guide him. It merely means we cannot "force" him into our mold.

Each child has his own creativity: each child responds or reacts to what he encounters in his life. Each child has his own individual hand in the shaping of his personality.

Since our job as parents is to guide our children, it might be wise for us to discover what and how we are guiding. We can learn much by watching the behavior of our children and discovering its purpose; we can learn more if we are willing to find out what they think. This is not difficult to do, really, because young children are so very free in expressing themselves—darn it! However, if we rebuke them, criticize, admonish, or find fault with what they think, they soon take care not to expose themselves to such uncomfortable experiences. And slowly we close the doors to intercommunication.

If, on the other hand, we freely accept a child's ideas, examine them with him, explore with him the possible outcome, ask constant questions such as "Then what may happen?" "How will you feel then?" "How will the other person feel?" the child finds a sense of companionship in the business of solving life's problems. Asking leading questions is still one of the best methods of conveying ideas.

It is ridiculous to expect a child to have only "right" ideas. To tell him he is "wrong" and we are "right" merely makes him clam up. (It does the same thing to us, too.) This is talking *to* him.

"Billy! You know it is not right to hate your sister. Shame on you. You must love her. You are her big brother." This is talking *to* the child. On the other hand—"I wonder why a boy would hate his sister? Do you have any ideas?" " 'Cause she gets in my way!" "What else could a boy do besides hate her?" Now this is a discussion. We acknowledge the idea of Billy's hatred of his sister, without moral implications of good or bad. It exists. What and why—from the child's viewpoint —is what we want to bring into focus.

As parents, we are too much inclined to presume that we know how a child feels. "I remember how I felt when my sister got *all* Gramma's attention because she was so cute! I'm not going to let that happen to my child." Actually, my daughter may not let her cute baby sister get all of the attention. Instead of resenting her, as I did my sister, she may outdo her, in an unpleasant way. My child may have a totally different viewpoint. Perhaps I had better find out how she feels—not presume that she feels as I did, trying to be good and superior.

We ourselves must be willing to admit that there is more than one point of view—that our way of seeing things is not the *only* way.

We must use extreme care when we discover that our child sees things differently. If we say anything which causes him to lose face or feel disgraced, we immediately close the door to further confidences. We need to be ever ready to acknowledge and accept a viewpoint different from ours as having merits. "You may be quite right. We will have to think about it and see what else happens." We can admit to the child, "I don't agree with you." However, we should always continue, "But you have the right to think so if you wish. Let's watch and see how it works out." In a situation of equals, each must be willing to re-evaluate his own thinking—not according to a rigid idea of "right" and "wrong," but in keeping with practical results. If we want our children to change their opinions, we must lead them to see that another way would work better. We need to accept our children as partners in the business of creating family harmony. Their ideas and viewpoints are important, particularly since they act in accordance with them! These ideas form the child's "private logic"—his unconscious reasons for his behavior. To tell a child not to do what he already knows is wrong is futile, since the wrongdoing is his means of attaining a false goal. Such admonitions merely increase his determination. He feels he has a right to his own opinions. These cannot be disproved by logic. One has to see the *psycho*-logic by which even unpleasantness is desirable if it brings attention or power or reinforces a false self-concept. To listen to our child means to discover his logic. Helping him means guiding him to a different viewpoint from which he can see advantages not seen before. A child who wants power may also want to be liked. Here we can discuss the difficulties of getting both. He can begin to see that he won't be liked if he wants to be the bully, and he will have to make up his mind which he prefers. To tell him straight on—"You won't be liked if you are a bully," will only incite his further hostility. "How do people feel toward a bully? If a bully wants to be liked, what can he do? Does he have a choice?" Questions such as these lead the child to discover what is going on and the part he plays in it. He even has to admit that it is up to him!

Suppose Mother overhears her two boys fighting because one cheated in a card game. She decides to remain out of the fight. But later, at a time of quiet friendliness, she feels like having a discussion about cheating. "You both know that cheating is wrong. It also spoils the fun you can have when you play nicely. Why not decide to play by the rules of the game and not cheat?" Nicely said, in a friendly way. But this is not a discussion. It is a sermon. It is logical, but not psychological.

Suppose, however, that a day or two later Mother says to her boys, "I'm wondering about something." Now both children will be curious. What is it that Mother wonders about? She has their attention. She now proceeds obliquely. "Suppose two people are playing a game and one cheats. What happens?" "They get in a fight." "Why do you suppose one of them cheats?" From here on the answers will give evidence of how each child thinks. One speaks up, "Because he wants to win." Or "Because he wants to be big." Or the other may say, "Because I don't like to be always left behind." Each time Mother asks the other child what he thinks about his brother's answer. She is searching for information and at the same time wants to let the boys recognize what goes on in their minds. Finally, she may ask, "What happened to the fun of the game? How does a cheater feel toward the one he cheats? Do you think these two people could learn to play the game fairly? How? What could each do? How can they keep it all fun and not spoil it?" After the questions and answers, after Mother has obtained an insight into the competition, she can say, "I'm so glad to know what you think. This helps me a lot."

Mother has planted seeds for thought. She need not say anything at all about what she thinks should be done. The children have been led to see for themselves what may be the problem and what the possible solutions are. Let them mull it over and see what happens.

No one, child or adult, likes to face a problem in which he may be at fault, if it is presented as an accusation to start with. If we speak of the difficulty in generalities—speak of "people" rather than two boys or two girls, or a direct "you and he"—we create a distance which promotes objectivity. We are all so much more willing to look at the problems of others! When discussing difficulties with our children it is frequently so much easier if we talk as if it were someone else.

On the other hand, there are times when it helps to be very direct. "I have a problem. I wonder what you think about it? When I am trying to get dinner on the table and you want me to help you with your homework, I get all shook trying to do two things at a time. What do you think we should do?"

Whatever information we are able to elicit in a discussion can become the basis for future action on our part. We won't get any information if we attempt to correct an obviously faulty idea by moralizing; this only defeats us. Our children cannot be open with us if we impress them with how wrong they are. If they present an idea which is obviously unacceptable, we still must accept it for the moment. "You may have a point there; but I wonder how it would work if *everyone* did the same thing?" If the child shows reluctance to continue the discussion because we imply that his idea won't work, put it aside for the time being. "Let's think about it and talk again in a few days. Maybe we will have some other ideas by then."

Talking *to* our children means telling them how we want things done, expresses a demand for obedience, requires an image of our own thinking.

Talking *with* our children, we and they search together for ideas as to what can be done to solve a problem or improve a situation. Thus they have a creative part in the construction of family harmony and realize that they, too, contribute to the whole. This does not mean that they have the right to run the family according to their ideas. A discussion is a process by which we try to come to the best possible solution of any problem that confronts us for the benefit of all concerned. Many think that the "new psychological approach" means yielding to the children, giving up any adult leadership. The opposite is true. When we fail to sit down with our children to talk over the current problems, when we fail to let them express their opinions and listen to them, then they really do what they want and we lose every

influence over their behavior. Co-operation has to be won—
it cannot be demanded: and the best way to gain co-operation is to talk freely about what each one thinks and feels
and to explore together better ways of dealing with each
other.

CHAPTER 39

THE FAMILY COUNCIL

THE FAMILY COUNCIL is one of the most important means of dealing with troublesome problems in a democratic manner. It is just what its name implies—a meeting of all members of the family in which problems are discussed and solutions sought. A definite hour on a definite day of each week should be set aside for this purpose; it should become a part of family routine. The meeting hour should not be changed without the consent of the whole family. Every member is expected to be present. Should one member not wish to come, he must still abide by the decision of the group. Therefore, it pays for him to be present so that he can voice his opinion.

Each family can work out the details of the Family Council to suit its own needs; but the basic principles remain the same. Each member has the right to bring up a problem. Each one has the right to be heard. Together, all seek for a solution to the problem, and the majority opinion is upheld. In the Family Council, the parents' voices are no higher or stronger than that of each child. The decision made at a given meeting holds for a week. After the meeting, the course of action decided upon takes place and *no further discussion* is permitted until the following meeting. If at that time it is discovered that the solution of last week did not work out so well, a new solution is sought, always with the question, "What are we going to do about it?" And again, it is up to the whole group to decide!

At a Family Council meeting, a mother of eight children, ranging in ages from sixteen to four, brought up the problem of the distressing situation of the dinner hour. The children arrived late to the table. Daddy fretted and fumed over their tardiness and general bad manners. Hostility and bickering created a most uncongenial atmosphere. One of the children suggested that each one eat in his own room and that the dinner table be abandoned. The other children picked up the idea, thinking that this would be quite a lark. Mother accepted the idea while Daddy roared his disapproval. Mother asked how the serving of the meal was to be accomplished. "We'll each serve our own." "And what about the dishes?" "We'll bring them back." "I'm willing to wash the dishes that are in the kitchen," Mother stated. Daddy had to agree to the program since it was a vote of nine to one. That evening when dinner was ready, Mother and Daddy took their meal to their bedroom and ignored the rest of the family. An hour later Mother did the dishes which she found in the kitchen sink.

Four days later the children began to complain. There weren't enough dishes brought back so that they could all have clean plates. One complained about the spoiling food left by his room-mate, who failed to return the dishes. To each complaint Mother replied, "Bring it up at the next Council meeting." At the next meeting the idea was hastily scrapped. It hadn't worked. They all wanted to return to the table again. The children were induced to make recommendations of procedures to be followed at the table for the following week.

Even the very young children can participate in the Family Council. Chairmanship should be rotated so that no one "bosses" the meetings; and the chairman must be sure that each family member has a chance to be heard. If the parents see that a course of action is going to be uncomfortable, they still must abide by the decision, bear the discomfort, and allow the natural result to take place. The children learn more from these experiences than they will ever learn from words or from parental impositions.

Mother presented the problem created by the after-school guests of Jeanne, ten, and Jerry, seven. When both children had guests on the same day, bedlam ensued. The children ran in and out of the house, chased up and down the stairs, raced after the dog, made popcorn, drank Cokes, played "Chopsticks" on the piano, and left the television on full volume. After Mother had presented her grievance, she said, "I think you should take turns in bringing friends home. How about it?" Jeanne agreed and said that she wanted Monday and Friday. Jerry sat slumped in his chair, tracing designs with his fingers. He offered nothing. Mother asked him if Tuesday and Wednesday were all right with him. Jerry nodded indifferently. "What will you do about all the roughhouse racing around?" Daddy spoke up. "Their friends need to be taught some manners!" "I think you should speak to your friends about our rules, don't you?" Mother interposed. Jeanne agreed; Jerry remained sullen.

The following Monday Jeanne brought a friend home and they played quietly. Jerry also brought a friend home. "I'm sorry, Jerry. This is not your day to have a guest." "Can we play in the yard?" "Yes." Jerry came to the door four times within the next half hour to find out if they could come in to watch television, have some milk and cookies, have some money. Each request met with a "no." Mother happened to look out of the window a few minutes later and there was Jerry standing on top of the fence urinating. Mother called out, "I'm sorry, Jerry. Your friend will have to go home now and you will have to come in." Jerry yelled back, "It's all your fault for not letting me in the house to go to the bathroom."

Jerry feels overwhelmed by the alliance between his "good" sister and Mother. He had offered nothing at the

Council meeting since he thought he didn't have a chance anyway. However, he *had* agreed, although sullenly, and then chose misbehavior to show his resentment.

It would be better if Mother had presented her problem and asked the children what they thought could be done. The first time this is tried, the children may be nonplussed and be unable to think of a solution. After waiting a bit, Mother may then present her suggestion. It is always good to propose an idea as a question. "Do you suppose it would help if you alternated days?" or "What would happen if . . . ?"

Now that Jerry has shown how he feels, this should be discussed at the next meeting. Mother can possibly induce Jerry to participate if she shows her understanding. "I'm wondering if Jerry feels that he doesn't have a chance. He didn't seem to like the arrangement very much. What do you think, Jerry?" Further discussion about what is to be done ensues, and, perhaps, for a while, Jerry should be the first to be asked to suggest solutions. He may not be willing to comply at first; but if Mother continues her genuine interest in what he thinks, he may overcome his conviction and begin to participate.

It is not a Family Council meeting if the parents are the only ones who present problems and offer solutions. The children must be stimulated into contributing their full share.

A family of college-educated parents and three girls had a Council meeting. The girls had decided that the family should buy a new house. The oldest offered fifteen dollars toward the purchase, the next offered ten dollars, and the youngest offered five dollars. This completely stumped the parents. What could they do? Perplexed and confused, they sought help.

The parents assumed that the girls had no idea as to what the cost of the house would be. When the children were asked, they estimated that it would be around thirty thousand dollars. The parents were greatly surprised, because this was an accurate guess. Now what could be done? Daddy was advised to subscribe fifty dollars and have the girls buy the house.

Daddy followed through and this ended the matter.

However, if the girls had insisted that he give the full balance, he could have appealed to their sense of fairness. "Why? I'm only one of five. Why should I give practically all of the money?" Daddy could even agree in the desire for a new house and ask the girls to raise the money.

We may be able to reduce our feeling of being stumped by such problems if we use our imagination and consider what we would do if the children were adult friends who presented such ideas. The parent can always state how far he is willing to go in a plan and throw the problem back on the table for further discussion by the others.

The secret of the success of the Family Council lies in the willingness of all members of the family to approach a problem as being a *family* problem. After all, if Mother has trouble monitoring television viewing, Daddy and the children have a problem trying to get their own way with Mother. It *is* a family problem, since living together means multiple interactions. The solution must be as much a family procedure as the difficulty is. This approach develops mutual respect, mutual responsibility, and promotes equality. Democratic family living rests upon a foundation of equality.

THE NEW PRINCIPLES OF
CHILD-RAISING

1. Encourage the child (Chapter 3)
2. Avoid punishment and reward (Chapter 5)
3. Use natural and logical consequences (Chapter 6)
4. Be firm without dominating (Chapter 7)
5. Respect the child (Chapter 8)
6. Induce respect for order (Chapter 9)
7. Induce respect for the rights of others (Chapter 10)
8. Eliminate criticism and minimize mistakes
    (Chapter 11)
9. Maintain routine (Chapter 12)
10. Take time for training (Chapter 13)
11. Win co-operation (Chapter 14)
12. Avoid giving undue attention (Chapter 15)
13. Sidestep the struggle for power (Chapter 16)
14. Withdraw from the conflict (Chapter 17)
15. Act! Keep your mouth shut (Chapter 18)
16. Don't shoo flies (Chapter 19)
17. Use care in pleasing—have the courage to say "No."
    (Chapter 20)
18. Avoid that first impulse—do the unexpected
    (Chapter 21)
19. Refrain from overprotection (Chapter 22)
20. Stimulate independence (Chapter 23)
21. Stay out of fights (Chapter 24)

22. Be unimpressed by fears (Chapter 25)
23. Mind your own business (Chapter 26)
24. Avoid the pitfalls of pity (Chapter 27)
25. Make requests reasonable and sparse (Chapter 28)
26. Follow through—be consistent (Chapter 29)
27. Put them all in the same boat (Chapter 30)
28. Listen! (Chapter 31)
29. Watch your tone of voice (Chapter 32)
30. Take it easy (Chapter 33)
31. Downgrade "bad" habits (Chapter 34)
32. Have fun together (Chapter 35)
33. Talk with *them,* not *to* them (Chapter 38)
34. Establish a Family Council (Chapter 39)

APPLY YOUR NEW SKILLS

We suggest that you read the following incidents one at a time, study them and figure out what goes on, what principle has been violated or observed, and what could be done to improve the situation. Do not attempt to analyze the child, but rather the interplay. Our purpose is to help parents to be more effective in raising their children—to know what to do and what not to do at the moment when the child misbehaves. The examples permit a variety of interpretations, and one can cope with the problems in several ways. There is no one "right" answer. Our comments follow each example.

Example #1

Three-year-old Ann spilled her salad onto the table. "Clean it up, Ann," Mother said. The child pouted and did not move. "Come on. You made the mess, you clean it up." Mother waited. Ann pouted. Mother cleaned up the salad and said no more.

Comment

When Mother demanded, "Clean it up, Ann," she invited a power contest. When she gave in, she shooed flies and finally rendered undue service.

Mother should avoid that first impulse to make an authoritative demand (18, 5).* "What can we do now?" will probably elicit some kind of response. Ann may possibly suggest that she should clean it

---

* The numbers in parentheses indicate the principles involved. These are listed on pages 306–307.

up. If Ann indicates that she intends to do nothing, Mother can be firm, and perhaps take Ann's hand to clean it up. If Ann still resists, she may be asked to leave the table (11, 3, 6, 4).

Example #2

Ralph, eight, left his good clothes strewn all around the room. Mother had been trying for a long time to get him to pick up his things. Exasperated, she took all clothes that were lying around and put them away. The following Sunday he couldn't find his clothes. "Hey, where's my Sunday suit?" he yelled. When told that it had been put away and that he would have to go to Sunday school in his school clothes, he burst into a temper tantrum. "I've told you and told you to hang your things up, Ralph. Now let this be a lesson to you." "Then I won't go to Sunday school," Ralph screamed. "Oh, yes you will. Now get dressed. You haven't much time." "I won't, I won't, I won't." Mother finally gave up the fight with Ralph, who refused to dress. "Well, will you promise to hang them up when you get home, if I give your clothes back to you?" "Sure." Mother returned the clothes and Ralph rushed into them. When he got back, he left them strewn around as usual.

Comment

First Mother acted correctly, arranging logical consequences. But then she got involved in a power struggle and eventually gave in, losing the battle.

Mother could have a discussion with Ralph in which they come to an agreement about caring for clothes, and what will happen if they are neglected (33, 6, 11). Let Ralph have his temper tantrum without saying anything: go to the bathroom if necessary (14, 15). Later, either take him to Sunday school as he is or leave him alone for this one time (3).

Example #3

Ruth, three, dawdled and dawdled getting ready for the customary evening ride before bedtime. Finally Mother and Daddy got into the car and said to her, "Apparently you don't really want to go for a ride, but we do. Goodbye, dear. We'll be back after a bit." They drove around for a short while. When they returned, there was no comment made. The next evening Ruth was ready ahead of time.

Comment

Mother and Daddy are extricating themselves from Ruth's undue demands.

They made no effort to force Ruth in any way (13), but assumed responsibility for their own behavior (4). They maintained established routine and used logical consequences (3, 9).

Example #4

Mother bundled Marilyn, three, up to go out to play in the snow. Very shortly after going outside, Marilyn stood crying at the back door. Mother investigated and found that she had taken off her mittens and her hands were red and cold. Mother put her mittens back on, explaining, "Your hands won't get cold, darling, if you keep your mittens on. That is what they are for. Now is that better? Sure it is. Go play, now." A few minutes later Mother looked out to find that Marilyn had her mittens off again. This time Daddy went out to put the mittens on again. The process was repeated several times until Daddy got mad. "Leave her out there and let her hands get really cold," Daddy said. "It will teach her a lesson." "What a horrible idea!" Mother protested. "Why, her hands might freeze!" Mother again put the mittens on until she, too, was exasperated, brought Marilyn in, and spanked her.

Comment

Marilyn uses helplessness to gain service and to prompt pity.

Both parents can avoid giving Marilyn undue attention (12). It is not necessary to tell her what she already knows: that mittens will keep her hands warm! Both parents can avoid showing their concern (30), and allow the natural consequence to follow (3). When Marilyn cries—a bid for pity for her helplessness—they can avoid this pitfall (24) and respond, "I'm sorry your hands are cold. I am sure you know what to do about it" (20). If the disturbing behavior is repeated, Marilyn will have to stay inside (3).

Example #5

After swimming at the beach, Nancy, four, and her mother went into the shower room. Nancy declared that she was not going to shower. Mother, who had finished her shower, replied, "All right, dear, but you really can't get into the car all sandy and wet." She turned the shower off and dried herself without any further comment. Nancy, too, remained silent. Then suddenly she was ready and took her shower.

Comment

Mother stimulated co-operative action. First, she established limits (6), then avoided a power struggle (13), and was firm (4). She won co-operation and compliance with order through logical consequences (6, 11, 3).

Example #6

Nine-year-old Stan came to the dinner table with unwashed hands. "What do you mean, coming to the table looking like that?" Mother demanded. "You men! You always have filthy hands. Look at your hair. Don't you ever comb it? And your shirt—just filthy. And your towel looks just like it!" Stan's eyes filled with tears. "Can you find anything else the matter?"

Comment

Stan disregards order in a mistaken attempt to find his place. At least Mother notices him. Mother heaps discouragement upon the child with a flow of criticism.

When Stan arrives with dirty hands, Mother may simply say, "You are not presentable. You may not come to the table" (15, 6). When Stan is clean, Mother may say, "I'm glad to see that you know how to take care of yourself." Or "I'm glad you feel like being neat tonight" (1).

Example #7

"Stand right by me, Mary," Mother told her two-and-a-half-year-old as she filled out a bank form at the counter. Mary took a few steps away. "Come back here!" Mother called. Mary stood still, and Mother continued with what she was doing. Mary ran toward the open door. "Mary, come back here!" Mary, with a solemn face but dancing eyes, headed on into the doorway. "All right, a car will hit you," Mother threatened. She turned to the teller's window, leaving Mary standing in the doorway.

Comment

Mary is playing a game with Mother. She keeps Mother on tenter-hooks—keeps her busy. Mother talks too much and tries to control her child with a threat which she would never allow to happen.

Mother should take Mary by the hand and keep her at her side, but silently (12, 14, 15).

Example #8

Mother had paid for her groceries and was on her way out of the store when she noticed that Greg, five, was carrying an opened package of candy. "Where did you get that?" she demanded. Greg burst into tears. "Over there," he pointed. "You bad, bad boy! What do you mean by doing such a thing? Don't you know that that is stealing? Now I will have to pay for that, and we already have all kinds of candy at home." Mother spanked Greg as she spoke. Then she returned to the clerk and paid for the candy.

Comment

Greg takes what he wants and Mother takes the consequences.

Mother should avoid discouragement through criticism and name-calling (1), discard punishment as a training method (2), and talk less. (15) She can insist that Greg himself go up and pay the clerk (10) and take the money out of his allowance (3).

Example #9

Mother sat in the play area with several other mothers of infants. Mike, two, ran from one carriage to another, shaking them and pulling on the sides so that they threatened to tip. As he stopped at each carriage, Mother called out, "Mike, stop that," and then returned to her conversation. Mike continued, unheeding. Finally another mother got up, wheeled her baby and carriage over beside her, and held onto the side. Mike's mother finally got up, grabbed him and swatted his back side. "I said, stop that!" Mike sat down in the sand pile and started to play.

Comment

Mike keeps Mother busy with him, causing her to interrupt her conversation.

Mother can avoid giving undue attention and shooing flies (12, 16). She can shut up and act (15). As soon as he misbehaves, she can remove Mike to his stroller. When he screams his protest, she should withdraw from his provocation (14) and let him howl. When he is quiet again, he can be allowed his freedom. As soon as he misbehaves, he must be returned to his stroller (3, 10).

Example #10

It was a few minutes before bedtime, and Nancy's toys were strewn all over the living room. Mother said, "It's almost time for bed. Would you like for me to help you put away your toys or do you want to do it all by yourself?" This had always worked before. Tonight Nancy, three and a half, said, "I'm not going to pick them up. I'm too tired. You pick them up." "No, Nancy. I believe I'll just read now." Mother withdrew behind a book. A minute later, Nancy said, "I'd like to pick up my toys now. Will you help me?" "Yes, dear." As they worked together, Mother talked about what they would do the following day.

Comment

Nancy tested Mother.

Mother withdrew from the provocation (14), avoided a power struggle (13), won co-operation (11), and did not criticize (8). She offered to help Nancy but refused to pick up the toys for her.

Example #11

"Mother, I want some candy," Judy, five, whined as they stood in line at the grocery check-out station. A beautiful array of candy intrigued her. "No," said Mother. "We have plenty of candy at home." Mother's voice was forceful and determined. "But I want some candy now," Judy whined more loudly. Mother surreptitiously glanced at the other people waiting in line. "I don't have enough money," Mother responded a little desperately. "I want this candy *right now!*" Judy screamed as she selected a candy bar. "How much is it?" Mother asked. Then she stood puzzling over the price sign. Presently, with a sigh, she said, "All right, take it then." Judy gleefully opened the candy bar, took one bite, folded the wrapper around the candy, and deposited it in the shopping cart.

Comment

Judy feels that she has the right to get what she wants. She desires not only gifts but power over Mother.

Mother doesn't have to give Judy everything she wants, especially when the situation does not call for it. She should use care in pleasing and have the courage to say "No" once (17), then withdraw from Judy's provocation (14) and remain firm (4).

Example #12

Mother was "losing her mind" because of the bickering over chores between Ellen, twelve, Virginia, ten, and Mike, eight. Finally she and Daddy devised a system. Daddy put a bulletin board up in the kitchen. Each child was assigned specific duties and given a pay scale. A well-done job paid better than one passably done. If the job was poorly done or left undone, nothing was paid. Good behavior won a bonus. Bad behavior meant a dock, as did breaking a rule. Every evening after dinner, the family gathered at the bulletin board and scores were tallied. At the end of the week each child was paid according to the tallies. Much friction was reduced, and Mother felt that the situation had markedly improved.

Comment

The children keep their parents busy with them by bickering. Even the new arrangement provided them with the constant attention of their parents. In using reward and punishment to control, the parents teach their children to expect material compensation for services performed rather than to gain satisfaction from participation and co-operation.

The parents should stop the system of rewards (2). Let the children establish job responsibilities in Family Council (34), and then be firm that the children must finish the jobs they are responsible for (4, 9). At the first sign of bickering, Mother and Daddy should leave the scene (21).

Example #13

Donny, six, Patty, four, and the dog came dashing through the kitchen with muddy feet. "Oh, you brats!" Mother screamed. "I just got through scrubbing that floor. What do you think I am? Now look at what you have done. How many times have I told you to wipe your feet before you come into the house? Sit right down there and take those shoes off. Now I'll have to mop it all again!" Mother tossed the shoes outside to clean later and remopped the floor. The children ran around in their stocking feet.

Comment

The kids do as they please while Mother takes the consequences, accepts abuse, and punishes by scolding.

Mother should stop using words as weapons (15) and hand the mop to the children. She can structure a logical consequence (3). How will she be able to cook as long as the kitchen is muddy?

Example #14

Mother was trying to teach Kathy, one, to drink out of a glass rather than a bottle. With Kathy on her lap, she gave her a sip of milk. Kathy stiffened and pushed the glass away. "See the birdie over there," Mother distracted. Kathy sat up to see, and Mother slipped the glass to her lips again. Each time that Kathy stiffened, Mother found something else to talk about. Each time, Kathy drank a bit more milk before refusing.

Comment

Mother is trying too hard to be a "good" mother. Her lack of confidence in herself leads her to expect Kathy to resist a new experience.

Mother should put Kathy in her high chair and have confidence that she will want to learn (5). She can treat the training period more casually, without apprehension. She can present the milk in the glass along with other food at the same time every day without coaxing or distractions. The bottle should be withheld entirely for this one feeding (9, 10). In a short while, Kathy will take the milk from the glass rather than be hungry (3).

Example #15

Whenever George, six, was upset or had been frustrated, he curled up in a chair in the living room and sucked his thumb. Mother had worried about this problem for almost five years. She had tried bitter applications, adhesive, splints, and spankings. George's front teeth were beginning to show the effects of constant thumb-sucking. Whenever Mother saw George sitting like this she felt horrible because she knew that he was unhappy. "What is the matter, George?" she asked with marked sympathy. "Don't suck your thumb, honey. It really doesn't help. Now tell Mother what has made you unhappy." Sometimes George would answer. Other times he continued to suck his thumb until Mother removed it from his mouth. Then he sulked and refused to answer. Mother pleaded and begged to find out what was the matter. If he finally answered, Mother made every effort to "fix it up."

Comment

George seeks easy pleasure and comfort. In addition, he uses his "unhappiness" to make Mother feel horrible—to punish her. Mother falls for the bid for pity and tries to arrange life to keep her son happy.

Mother should ignore thumb-sucking altogether (31) and be sincerely unimpressed when George sits mournfully in the chair (12, 24). At a time when George is happy, Mother could chat with him to find out what he doesn't like (page 280). Through encouragement, she can help him to be active and useful (1).

Example #16

Sally, seven, the middle of three, wanted to help Mother carry the newly purchased glasses into the house. "No, Sally. I'll do it. You might drop them." "Please, Mother. I'll be careful." "Well, all right. But for heaven's sake, don't drop them." Mother picked up several packages and followed her daughter. While going up the steps, Sally stepped on her coat, lost her balance, and fell with the glasses. She burst into tears. Mother put her packages down in despair; opening the box of glasses, she found all but two broken. Furious, she broke into a tirade. "I told you you couldn't carry the glasses without breaking them! What makes you always want to do things that you can't do? Why are you so clumsy? Do you think we have money to buy glasses for you to break? Get in the house and go to your room. You can go without your supper. Maybe that will teach you not to be so careless."

Comment

Sally met Mother's expectation of failure. In doubting Sally's competence, Mother offered discouragement, then criticized.

Mother should have confidence in Sally to begin with and avoid fortifying the child's mistaken self-concept (1, 5). She should eliminate all criticism and accept mistakes casually (8). Sally is already miserable enough. If Sally slips and breaks the glasses, Mother should be more concerned about what happens to the child rather than to the glasses. Encouragement is needed. "I am sorry this happened. I know you did not do it deliberately."

Example #17

Daddy came home to find his tools lying on the lawn, where Billy, nine, had been making a "racer" out of his old wagon. Daddy was furious. He found Billy down the block and commanded him to come home. From the tone of Daddy's voice, Billy knew that he was in trouble. He approached Daddy shyly and hesitantly. "I want to know the reason for this," Daddy pointed to the tools. Billy was silent. "Time after time I have told you to put my tools away when you are through with them. Why is it that you refuse to mind me?" Billy still stood silently looking at the ground, all huddled into himself. "Well, young man, are you going to answer me?" "I don't know, Daddy." "O.K. I'll have to thrash you. Maybe next time you will remember to put my tools away." Daddy turned Billy and spanked him. Sobbing, Billy picked up the tools, took them into the house, and put them away.

Comment

Daddy used anger to intimidate Billy, who lacks respect for order and for the rights of others. Daddy mistakenly believes that words and punishment are effective training devices.

This situation clearly indicates the need for proper training. Daddy should have a series of discussions with Billy to arrive together at an understanding in the use and care of tools (6, 7, 33). Perhaps he could provide Billy with his own tools and let the boy be responsible for what happens to them (23). Then Daddy can be firm and not replace any of Billy's tools that become lost or damaged (4). If Billy wants to, he can replace them out of his allowance—or he may do without them (3).

Example #18

Mother and Daddy took Jack, two, to visit friends. "We are so proud of Jack," Mother announced. "He no longer needs to wear diapers. And he hasn't even had an accident in the past two weeks." During the next hour Mother asked Jack six times if he had to go to the bathroom. Finally he obliged by saying "yes." A great ceremony was made by Daddy, who hustled Jack up the stairs to the bathroom.

A week later the friends visited the family. During dinner Jack told his father three times that he had to go to the bathroom. Each time Daddy went with him and each time Jack produced results.

The following week, Daddy said to his friend, "We can't understand it. Jack has reverted to wetting and soiling his pants. He is wearing diapers again, and he won't even tell us when he needs changing."

Comment

Mother and Daddy made a "great production" about toilet training. They are much too concerned about a normal learning procedure and precipitated a power contest because their own pride was at stake.

Mother and Daddy should have confidence that Jack will learn (1, 5) and take a more casual attitude (30). The situation demands that Jack learn to use the toilet, not that Mother and Daddy should be proud of dry pants.

Example #19

Mother had a job in the mornings and employed a sitter for those hours. One day when she got home she discovered that Rita, three, had used her crayons on the doors, couch, and chairs. Mother had planned to take Rita to the beach that afternoon. After lunch, she said, "We will have to clean the crayon marks off the doors and the furniture before we can leave for the beach. You may help me, if you like." Rita eyed her mother for a moment and then took the cloth and rubbed as Mother showed her. Mother took her time with the work. Every little while the girl asked, "When are we going to the beach?" "As soon as we get this all cleaned up," Mother answered. Finally, Mother had to admit that when the marks were cleaned up it was too late to go to the beach. Rita accepted this without any comment.

Comment

Mother provided a training experience. She refrained from demanding that Rita clean up, thus avoiding a power contest (13). She was firm (4), but invited the child to help, thereby winning co-operation (11). Finally, she allowed logical consequences to follow (3) and showed Rita that they must meet the demands of the situation (6).

Example #20

"Lily, I said you couldn't go to the movies with Jane this week because you stayed out so late last time." Mother spoke quietly to her nine-year-old. The girl's eyes filled with tears. She turned away dejectedly without offering any argument. Mother felt horrible. Lily was taking it so hard. "What is on this week, Lily?" "It doesn't matter, Mother, since I can't go," she answered with tears in her voice. "I think you told me it was a Disney program, didn't you?" "Yes." Mother considered. "If I let you go this time will you come straight home?" Still tearful, Lily answered, "Yes, Mother." "Well, all right. But if you aren't home on time I won't let you go next week regardless of what is on. Do you understand?" "Yes, Mother."

Comment

Lily has discovered the value of "water power" and provokes pity to get what she wants. Mother stumbled into the pitfall. She lacked the courage to say "No," and was inconsistent.

Mother can be unimpressed by Lily's tears, hurt, and dejection (24). If Lily doesn't know how to keep her agreement to come home, the logical consequence is that next time she can't go (3). Mother can remain firm (4) and maintain order (6, 26).

Example #21

After cleaning him up, Mother and Timmy, four, came out to the back yard to relax in the early part of the evening. Friends had come to visit. "Don't get wet again, Timmy," Mother admonished as they sat down. There was a small wading pool in the back yard. Timmy busied himself for a short while with his toys. Presently he went to the pool to play with his boat. "Timmy, be careful not to get wet. You had better stay away from the pool." The boy pouted, stood at the side of the pool, and then, on his knees, put his boat in the water. "If you get wet, Daddy will spank you," Mother called. Timmy continued to play with his boat at the edge of the pool. Suddenly he reached too far and fell into the water, getting his clothes wet. Daddy rushed over and pulled him out. Timmy started to cry. Mother scolded, "I told you not to play near the water. Now you are all wet again." Daddy took the boy into the house for a change of clothing.

Comment

Timmy is mother-deaf and does as he pleases. "Don't get wet" invited a power contest. Mother made an undue demand when she expected Timmy to play near the water and not get wet. Then she threatened punishment but didn't follow through.

Mother should sidestep a power struggle by not deciding for Timmy what he is going to do (13). She can make up her mind whether or not the situation demands that he stay away from the water. If the evening is warm, it won't matter. Timmy won't fall in if Mother doesn't stimulate him to through her attempt to control. Mother should make reasonable demands, then act quietly to maintain order (25, 26, 6).

Example #22

John, seven, was outside, playing. Before long Mother heard the sound of fighting and determined to investigate. John had snatched all the toys from the neighbor children and was hoarding them. His delight in having the other children yell was obvious. Mother called the boy to her. He refused to leave his hoard. She went to him. "John, really, dear. You must share the toys with the rest of the children." John glared at the other children, who stood watching to see what would happen. Mother reached for a toy to take it away. John snarled, "Cut that out!" "John! What has gotten into you! That is absolutely no way to behave. You come into the house and go to bed." Mother dragged John into the house and put him into bed. He cried himself to sleep.

Comment

John keeps Mother busy by misbehaving. First, Mother got involved in a quarrel between John and the neighborhood children, then tried to teach by moralizing, and finally used punishment as a training device.

Mother should mind her own business (23) and let the other children handle John. They will! She can talk *with* him (33) about his dealings with his friends.

Example #23

"Martha! Will you get up!" Mother shook her eight-year-old. "You'll be late for school if you don't hurry. Come on, now. This is the third time I've called you." Martha rolled out of bed, and Mother returned to the kitchen. "Martha, come on!" Mother called a little later. "I'm warning you. I'm *not* going to drive you again this morning. You simply have to learn to get up and get moving." Martha eventually arrived at the table. She read a comic book as she ate. "Put that thing down and pay attention to your breakfast. It's getting late!" The phone rang and Mother became engaged in a long conversation with her sister. Suddenly Martha interrupted with, "Mother! I've only got ten minutes. Please. Come on, drive me to school." "No, Martha. Go on by yourself." "But Mother! I can't get there in time even if I run all the way. Please. Please, Mother, take me." "I said no, Martha." "But Mother, I haven't been tardy once this year. Please, just this once. I don't want to spoil my record. You wouldn't want me to spoil my record, either, would you?" "Oh, all right." Mother told her sister that she would call her back and then drove the girl to school.

Comment

Martha makes Mother assume all responsibilities and give undue service. Mother lacked the courage to be firm and allowed pride in a record to interfere with her training program.

Mother should provide Martha with an alarm clock and let *her* be responsible for getting up and off to school on time (20, 23). No matter what cajolery the child uses, Mother should be firm and consistent about not driving her to school (4, 26).

Example #24

Mother was in the laundry room. Rose, eight, Joyce, six, and Susan, two and a half, were playing in the bedroom. All at once Mother heard Susan screaming, but the sound was muffled. She ran to the bedroom. Rose and Joyce had closed Susan into the closet and were holding the door. Because of the screams, they didn't hear Mother come in. "Stop that this instant!" Mother yelled. The girls jumped back as Mother reached out to yank them. She grabbed the closet door open and took Susan in her arms. When Susan had quieted down enough so that Mother could be heard, she demanded, "What do you mean by doing such a thing? You know she's afraid of the dark!" "We were only playing, Mother." "What kind of a game is it to torment your sister?" Furious, Mother took Susan and left the room.

Comment

Rose and Joyce are in an alliance to keep Mother busy protecting Susan, who, in turn, controls through fear.

Mother could listen (28) and interpret the meaning of the screams. She can hear the terror, decide to mind her own business (23), and fail to be impressed by Susan's fear of the dark (22). She can avoid becoming involved in this subtle quarrel among the girls (21). Chances are that when Mother fails to come running to Susan's aid, the older girls will let her out of the closet. Or, if this is too much for Mother, she can calmly enter the room, let Susan out of the closet, and proceed about her own business immediately, without saying anything. In addition, at Family Council meetings, Mother can have a series of discussions about the sibling roles. "Why do you suppose Rose and Joyce get such a kick out of teasing Susan? What can we do about it?"

Example #25

Jean, six, was about halfway through dinner when her friend called her. She jumped up from the table and ran to the door. "Come back here, Jean. You aren't through with your dinner," Daddy commanded. The girl stood at the door still talking to her friend. Daddy went after her, carried her back to the table, sat her on her chair, and said, "You aren't excused yet. Finish your dinner." Jean slumped back in her chair and pouted. She didn't attempt to eat. Impatient, Daddy started a tongue-lashing. Jean sat. Finally Mother asked, "Are you through, Jean?" "Yes." "Then you may go out to play." Daddy broke in, "Since your Mother says it is all right, go ahead." Jean dashed from the table. Mother and Daddy finished their meal in grim silence.

Comment

Jean involved her parents in a power struggle and then used it to promote dissension between them. The demand, "Come back here," invited a power contest. Daddy also disregarded Jean's need to be courteous to her friend.

Since Daddy was "dealing with" Jean, Mother should mind her own business (23). An agreement must be reached among all three as to what behavior is expected at the table (9, 34). Even if it is established that no one leaves the table unless he is finished, Jean's right to be courteous takes precedence, and she may be excused to tell her friend that they are eating now but that she will join her later (5, 7).

Example #26

A sudden gust of wind had blown a curtain into the living room and upset a large vase of flowers. Mother was hurriedly mopping up the water, hoping that the carpet would not be marred. "Adele, please baste the roast for me, will you?" "I don't know how, Mother," the girl whimpered. "You've seen me do it hundred of times. Just do it like I do." Adele went to the kitchen. A few seconds later Mother heard a crash followed by a cry. She rushed to the kitchen. The roast, potatoes, pan, and juices lay on the floor and Adele was crying because she had burnt her hand. "Adele! You are absolutely impossible. I never saw anyone so helpless. Why is it you can't do even the most simple things? Now get out of here!" "But my hand. It's burned." "Put some ointment on it." "How can I? It's my right hand." In despair, Mother found the ointment, put a dressing on the burn, and then returned to the mess in the kitchen.

Comment

Helpless Adele really proved her helplessness.

Mother can refuse to accept Adele's mistaken self-evaluation and encourage her by providing experiences in which she succeeds (1). In general, she can eliminate all criticisms and overlook Adele's many mistakes (8). In this situation, since Mother could not be in two places at once, she should have decided which was the most necessary and taken care of it herself. She should avoid calling upon Adele to do something she has not had experience with (25). Mother can take time to teach Adele how to be useful (10) and let her learn by doing before demanding assistance with tasks which the girl feels are beyond her abilities.

Example #27

Two of Mother's friends dropped in. Patsy, four, stood watching eight-month-old Billy crawling along the floor. Mother and her friends were admiring Billy and his cleverness. Patsy dashed over and bit Billy on the arm. Mother jumped up, grabbed Patsy, spanked her, and yelled, "What do you mean, biting your baby brother? Now you go to your room until you are ready to behave." Swatting Patsy again, Mother pushed her out of the room and picked up Billy to comfort him.

Comment

Patsy is jealous of baby brother and gets even with her Mother. Then Mother responds to Patsy's act of revenge.

The bite is accomplished. Nothing can be done now. Any action on Mother's part reinforces Patsy's belief that she must get even for all the attention her brother gets. Mother can do the unexpected and hug Patsy, saying, "I understand, dear, and I'm sorry you feel so cross" (18).

Example #28

Lucy, one and a half, had just discovered the raised hearthstone and kept climbing up onto it. Every time she did, Mother took her down, saying, "No, no." As soon as Lucy was free she again toddled over to the hearth and climbed upon it. Again, Mother took her down, saying, "No, no. You'll get hurt." After five times, Mother finally spanked the child and took her from the room.

Comment

Lucy tests her strength and courage. In overprotecting her baby, Mother provides discouragement. First, with her "No, no," she shoos flies, then she uses spanking as a training device.

Mother should have confidence in Lucy's ability to develop skill in handling her body and let her alone (5). If Mother fails to make an issue of climbing on the hearthstone (12), Lucy will lose interest after she has discovered her skill. Or, if climbing on the hearthstone seems to be an infraction of order (6), Mother may quietly remove Lucy from the room every time she climbs up onto it (2, 15).

Example #29

Jerry, six, greeted his aunt as she entered the house, "Hi, ole prune face!" Mother gave his mouth a stinging slap. "Don't you ever let me hear you say anything like that again. You show respect to your aunt. Now apologize!" Jerry resentfully apologized through angry tears.

Comment

Smart-alec Jerry wanted to make a big impression. Mother followed her first impulse by slapping the boy.

Jerry was speaking to his aunt; therefore, Mother should mind her own business (23). Auntie can do the unexpected by responding as usual or making a game and answering in kind (18).

Example #30

Sandy, six, stood watching the men dig the holes for a storm fence. Presently he began to kick dirt back into the holes. The foreman called out, "Hey, buddy. That's enough of that." Sandy impishly kicked more dirt into the hole. Mother, hearing the disturbance, came to the door. Sandy continued to kick the dirt, despite reprimands from the foreman. Mother watched. Finally the man went to Mother. "How about stopping that kid?" "How can I stop him? I'm not going to stand out here all day just to keep him from playing in the dirt." Sandy kept right on. The foreman got so mad that he threatened to beat the daylights out of the boy. Sandy ran crying into the house. Presently he returned to harass the workers at each hole. This continued until Daddy came home and kept Sandy inside.

Comment

Sandy is a powerful "bad" boy. Mother accepts the misbehavior and lets him do as he pleases.

Mother can stop being helpless and afraid of Sandy. She must stimulate respect for the rights of others (7). If necessary, Mother can take the boy inside. No power struggle is involved if Mother's action implies the maintenance of order and respect, rather than her intention to "make" Sandy mind.

Example #31

Joan, five, is the only child, only grandchild, and only niece. She and Mother were invited to a patio supper next door. Since Joan played with the neighbor girls, Lucy and Mary, a separate table was set up for the children. When they sat down to eat, Joan started to cry. "I want to sit by Mother," she pleaded through her tears. "Now, honey. See how nice it is for you to sit with Lucy and Mary. Come on, eat your supper. Look how good everything is." Joan continued to sob and repeated again and again, "I want to sit by you." Mother became somewhat angry. "I'll take you home if you don't behave!" Joan continued to cry. Finally, Mother gave in, pulled Joan's chair from the children's table, and set it beside hers.

Comment

Spoiled Joan must be pleased, regardless of the needs of the situation. Mother "reasoned" with Joan, trying to win her co-operation, then threatened to take her home, but failed to follow through. Finally, she gave in to "water power."

Mother can maintain order by stating, "The children are sitting at the card table, Joan" (6). Then if Joan continues to cry, Mother can say, "Joan, do you want to eat with Mary and Lucy, or would you prefer to go home?" (11). Mother must follow through on Joan's decision (26).

Example #32

Roy, eight, slapped Janet, three, for picking his toy cowboys up out of line. Mother scolded, "What is the matter with you, Roy? Why can't you let her alone?" "Well, she's always bothering my things." "She's little, Roy. You don't have a right to hit her. Now go to your room." "You can't make me," Roy defied. "We'll see about that." And Mother dragged Roy to his room, shoved him in, and closed the door. He immediately opened it. Mother shoved him in again, closed the door, and held on to the knob. Roy fought from the other side to open the door. Finally Mother was worn out. She let go of the door, grabbed the hair brush, and whipped the boy. She left him screaming and kicking on his bed.

The next day Roy was playing with Janet. Mother walked into the room just in time to see Roy pulling a rope tightly around Janet's neck. "Roy!" she screamed as she dashed to them. She yanked Roy away and loosened the rope from Janet's neck. Janet had not complained. She did not utter a word, but watched solemnly as Mother whipped Roy.

Comment

This is a power struggle followed by revenge.

Mother cannot stop the various forms of retaliation. Every time she punishes Roy she makes him more determined to get even. Mother can mind her own business (23), stay out of the fight (21), let Janet take care of herself (19), and ignore each child's provocation. Naturally, she must remove the rope from Janet's neck! But do it quietly, without the drama that the boy had hoped for. He probably had no real intention to hurt his little sister; but he knew how to get Mother where she is vulnerable. Mother can do the unexpected (18): she can give Roy a hug or a kiss and a smile (Will *he* be nonplussed!). Then she must continue to work toward a correction of all relationships.

Example #33

Jay, four, was putting up a fight about getting into the car after the groceries had been put in. Mother dragged him by the arm. He stumbled, slid, fell, and yelled, as she continued to pull him. Finally Mother let go and Jay plopped himself on the asphalt beside the car. "All right, then, stay there," Mother angrily snorted. She got into the car and went through the motions of preparing to leave. Jay watched her out of the corner of his eye and continued to sulk. After a moment, embarrassed by the attention from bystanders, Mother jumped out of the car, grabbed Jay, hauled him into the car, and whacked him. Screaming and protesting, he jumped up and down on the back seat.

Comment

Mother said, "You will;" Jay said, "I won't." Mother used force and threatened an act she didn't intend to carry out.

Mother can take her sail out of Jay's wind. Upon leaving the store, she can go on to the car, assuming that Jay is with her. When Jay sees that Mother refuses to meet his demand for a fight to get him into the car, he will follow. If he refuses to get into the car, Mother can say, "Then I shall have to wait until you are ready to get in." She sits passively waiting—no anger, no fight. Jay will soon feel, "Oh, what's the use," and get into the car (11, 13, 14, 15). A second course open to

Mother is to realize that Jay must conform to order. If she considers this need rather than her desire to make Jay mind, she will not need anger. She can then quietly pick him up and put him into the car, completely cool and detached (6). He will sense her firmness, which requires a mental withdrawal in the face of Jay's continued storming.

Example #34

Louise, three, came to the table in a sulky mood. The youngest of four, she usually got what she wanted. After being served, she picked up her plate and threw it onto the floor, then started to kick and scream. Mother carried her out of the room and sat down with her. "What's the matter with you, Louise?" No answer. "What makes you do things like that? Shame on you." No comment. "Well, all right, then, sit here." Mother turned to leave. "I'm sorry, Mommie. I won't do it again." "All right. You may come back to the table again." Louise picked at her dinner. When dessert was served, she threw it on the floor. "Louise! You promised to behave yourself. For that, you get spanked."

Comment

The Little Princess proved her point. At first, Mother acted correctly by removing Louise; but then she "talked to her," accepted a promise, and finally, punished.

Louise can be excused with the fewest possible words. Her promise, which let her get by with misbehavior, should certainly be ignored. If Mother is very courageous, she can put Louise and all the others in the same boat. "You children don't know how to behave at the table. You may all leave" (27). No further comment, please (15).

Example #35

Greta, two and a half, pulled all her clothes out of the drawers in her room. When Mother discovered it, she scolded her, picked everything up, and put it back. As a final scold, Mother said, "For this, you can't have your ice cream this afternoon." When the ice cream wagon came, Greta ran out, calling to Mother to bring the money. "You can't have it today, Greta." The girl started to scream and stamp her foot. Mother picked her up and took her into the house.

Comment

Greta gets into mischief to keep Mother busy with her. Mother tries to train her daughter by scolding and depriving.

What has ice cream got to do with clothes pulled out of the drawer? Mother can ask, "Would you like me to help you put things back?" (11). If Greta indicates that Mother is to do it alone, Mother quietly withdraws (14).

Example #36

Willie, four, and Marlene, three, both had severe food allergies. Mother had seen the torments that Daddy suffered from hay fever, and now her children had allergies! She felt horribly sorry for them because they had to go through so much while so young and be denied foods that they wanted. She followed the doctor's orders strictly, preparing separate meals for each, since they had different allergies and could seldom eat the same foods. In spite of her care, they frequently broke out in hives, had spells of nausea, or didn't feel well. Whenever the children presented symptoms, she excused their misbehavior on the grounds that, "Poor kids. They don't feel well." Nor did she require any chores from them. It seemed that if she insisted that they do anything such as to pick up their toys before going to bed, it upset them and made them worse. So, she preferred to do everything herself and hoped that they would outgrow the allergies as the doctor said they might.

Comment

Those allergies are proving useful! The children prompt Mother to pity them and escape from the demands of the situation.

Mother must avoid the pitfalls of pity (24), help the children accept the problem of the allergies, and reduce the profits they realize through them. Order must still be maintained (6), and the children contribute their share. If they feel well enough to play, they feel well enough to pick up. If they are sick, they should be in bed and treated as ill children without the benefits of those who are up and well (3).

Example #37

Alec, four, was playing on the front steps. All at once he let out a piercing scream. "Mommie, Mommie." Mother dashed to him. Alec stood huddled against the screen door crying in terror. A dog was running and sniffing along the front walk. Mother opened the screen door and brought Alec in. "Honey, honey, come now. The dog won't hurt you." She took the boy into her arms and with many reassurances finally got him to quiet down. But Alec refused to go outside again as long as the dog was in sight.

Comment

Alec's fear of dogs impresses Mother very much and keeps her concerned.

Mother can stop falling for Alec's fears (22). She can give him encouragement with a casual, "You will find out the dog won't hurt you," and let it go at that (1).

INDEX